Arbitrage, Hedging, and Speculation

Arbitrage, Hedging, and Speculation

The Foreign Exchange Market

EPHRAIM CLARK AND
DILIP K. GHOSH

Westport, Connecticut
London

Library of Congress Cataloging-in-Publication Data

Clark, Ephraim
   Arbitrage, hedging, and speculation : the foreign exchange market /
Ephraim Clark and Dilip K. Ghosh.
      p.   cm.
   ISBN 1–56720–582–8 (academic)
   1. Arbitrage. 2. Hedging (Finance) 3. Speculation. 4. Foreign exchange
   market. I. Ghosh, Dilip K. (Dilip Kumar), 1942–. II. Title.
HG6024.A3G47   2004
332.4′5—dc22   2003026528

British Library Cataloguing in Publication Data is available.

Library of Congress Catalog Card Number: 2003026528
ISBN: 1–56720–582–8

First published in 2004

Praeger Publishers, 88 Post Road West, Westport, CT 06881
An imprint of Greenwood Publishing Group, Inc.
www.praeger.com

Printed in the United States of America

The paper used in this book complies with the
Permanent Paper Standard issued by the National
Information Standards Organization (Z39.48–1984).

10   9   8   7   6   5   4   3   2   1

Contents

Acknowledgments

The book is the end result of the collaborative efforts, commitments, and continuous revisions of several versions of the materials presented here. Many peers and colleagues have made us rethink various parts of these chapters, and their suggestions undoubtedly improved the quality and the style. The chapters have drawn on the research published in various journals by us, and we have also used the research of our co-thinkers and fellow researchers. We presented most of the chapters in the forms of papers in academic conferences, seminars, and workshops in various universities in Australia, Canada, England, France, Malaysia, Mexico, New Zealand, Singapore, Trinidad, Tunisia, the United States, and so on. We are grateful to many reviewers and participants at different workshops, seminars and conferences for their criticisms and constructive suggestions. Without making the list long, we would like to acknowledge our indebtedness to Lloyd Blenman, Janet Thatcher, Stephen Ferris, Arun Prakash, Edgar Ortiz, William T. Moore, Augustine Arize, Hillary Claggett, Nicole Cournoyer, the team at Impressions, and copy editors at Greenwood Press who have been wonderfully courteous and extremely helpful, and we express our note of thanks and appreciation for them for the final production of this book. Next, we acknowledge the financial and other support given to use by Kuala Lumpur Stock Exchange, Rutgers University, Universiti Ultara Malaysia, Middlesex University, and we express our sincere indebtedness to these institutions. Last, but not least, we must recognize our families whose love lifted us up all the time and inspired us to finish this task with pleasure.

Chapter 1

Arbitrage, Hedging, and Speculation: The Foreign Exchange Market

Arbitrage, hedging, and speculation are three distinct acts in market transactions in any items of trade—goods, securities, and currencies. In this book, we will discuss these three operational strategies in the foreign exchange market, but some of these strategies can be duplicated in other markets as well. On our chapter-by-chapter exposition and exploration throughout this book, we will delineate arbitrage, hedging, and speculation from the standpoint of a market participant—a trader, an individual, or an institution—with access to market data, economic judgment, and analytical skill.

ARBITRAGE

Arbitrage is the simultaneous purchase and sale of a commodity or asset in different markets with the sole intent to make profit from the difference in buying and selling prices. Here the asset is a currency. If, for example, the dollar price of a British pound sterling is $1.60 in Frankfurt but $1.50 in Paris, a trader can buy £1 in Paris, sell that pound in Frankfurt, and make a profit of $0.10 per pound, and if the trader buys 15 million pounds (£15,000,000), he makes $1,500,000 before any transaction costs, if they exist. Therefore, arbitrage is an exploitation of misalignment of market quotes. If the market is perfectly competitive, this sort of price differential cannot exist, thus, arbitrage profit cannot exist. In this sense, arbitrage profit is a possible outcome of market imperfection in which "buy cheap and sell dear" is a feasible act of a vigilant trader.

It should be pointed out that markets are mostly efficient, and hysteresis fades away pretty soon by the forces unleashed by the acts of buying low and selling high. In the scenario described above, if it persists, then the Paris market will feel a higher demand for the pound, and the Frankfurt market will experience a lower demand. The interactions of supply and demand will force the Paris price of the pound to rise and the Frankfurt price to fall, narrowing the differential continuously until it is reduced to zero. Arbitrage in this sense is a process of bringing the law of one price into reality, which can be called market equilibrium.

It should be noted that in the foreign exchange market, traders can buy and sell continuously—exchanging one currency for another and again for another currency, finally getting back to the original currency in the series of instantaneous transactions, and thus making profits by market quotes misalignment. This is a case of triangular arbitrage, and it is further discussed at the end of this chapter. But there is another arbitrage that involves other economic variable(s), such as interest rate(s), along with foreign currency, and currencies a trader can engage in profit making, finally bringing the market to equilibrium. In chapter 5, we will provide a better description of this type of arbitrage.

HEDGING

Hedging is a safety net—an insurance policy against any open position of a trader. It is an underlying cover. Consider an investor who converts his $15,000,000 at the cash market (where $1.50 = £1) for the British pound, and puts his £10,000,000 at the British bank for a year at 9.5 percent to get £10,950,000. But when he gets that British amount, if the exchange rate becomes $1 = £1, he is turning his $15,000,000 into $10,950,000, which is a total loss of $4,050,000 (27 percent).

To prevent such potential economic loss, many financial instruments have been created and are in existence for the investor. If at the time the investor exchanges his $15,000,000 and puts his converted amount into British pound, he has the option to sell his British amount at the rate $1.72 = £1 a year later, he can then turn his £10,950,000 into $18,834,000. This is a total gain of $3,834,000 (25.56 percent). Selling the future British amount at the available rate of $1.72 = £1 is an example of hedging. In the book, we bring out different instruments of hedging and explain how hedging works.

SPECULATION

Speculation is the polar opposite of hedging. It is the deliberate assumption of risk. This risk is a calculated risk assumed by the investor in anticipation of a bigger profit. Consider the example once again. Given the market quotes on the price of the British pound and the interest rate, he can, as we have noted, turn his $15,000,000 into £10,950,000 via currency conversion and deposit creation. If he decides not to sell that British amount at the available rate $1.72 = £1, but feels that the British pound will go up to, say, $1.80 = £1, he may not hedge and wait with his uncovered position. This is an act of speculation. By staying with his gut feeling (honestly, his assessment of the expected value of future British pound by probability calculation), he can make $19,710,000 if his expectation is realized, and thus end up with a total profit of $4,710,000 (31.4 percent). If, however, his expectation is mismatched, he may end up with a potentially lower profit or loss, depending on the actual price of the British pound a year later.

Many scenarios will be drawn up with different instruments with which an investor or a trader may speculate in the market.

MARKET

Now—what is a market? In the world of economics and finance, the term *market* means acts of transactions, buying and selling, the visible and invisible interactions of supply and demand. Market does not necessarily denote a place such as a mall or supermarket, where the business of buying and selling takes place. Foreign exchange market, in that spirit, is the market in which different national currencies are traded. It refers to the buying and selling of, for example, U.S. dollars for British pounds, German deutsche marks for Japanese yen, and so on. In our world, when one country's customers buy or sell goods and services from and to another country, the need to pay for those things in terms of the seller's monetary units (currency) is immediately created, and this leads to buying the seller's currency. However, the need for other countries' currencies does not arise only for merchandise trade alone; it may be due to buying financial assets—that is, for financial investments in different countries, for visiting other countries for touristic pleasure, for exploring overseas business possibilities, for stabilizing foreign exchange markets, and so on.

DEFINITION OF FOREIGN EXCHANGE

Foreign exchange means the price of one national currency in terms of another national currency. If two U.S. dollars can buy one British pound ($2 = £1), then the foreign exchange rate is: $^2/_1 = 2$.

Note that the price of one British pound is two U.S. dollars, and it is measured exactly the same way as the price of one gallon of milk. In the denominator, we have 1 unit—whether it is 1 British pound or 1 gallon of milk, and in the numerator, we put the units of U.S. dollars needed for it. It should be clear now that the currency or commodity should be measured at 1 (meaning one unit) in the denominator, and the price in terms of which it is expressed must be in the numerator. That is, $^2/_1$ the dollar price of 1 British pound. Similarly, if seven French francs can buy one U.S. dollar, then $^7/_1 (= 7)$ is the French franc price of one U.S. dollar. Each currency can thus be priced in terms of itself as well as in terms of each other's currency. When the price of a foreign currency is denominated, or expressed,

Table 1.1
Cross Rates

Cross Rates (*The Wall Street Journal*, February 26, 2002)				
Currency Sold		Currency	Purchased	
	U.S. ($)	U K (£)	France (FF)	Japan (¥)
U.S. ($)	1	0.7018	7.5471	133.86
U K (£)	1.4249	1	10.7539	190.74
France (FF)	0.1325	0.09299	1	17.737
Japan (¥)	0.00747	0.00524	0.05638	1

Source: The Wall Street Journal, February 26, 2002

in terms of the home currency (e.g., British pound in terms of U.S. dollars), the foreign exchange rate is said to be in *direct* quote. The direct quote is also known as an American quote, or a U.S. dollar equivalent quote. When the price of the home currency is denominated in foreign currency (e.g., U.S. dollars in terms of French francs), the foreign exchange rate is an *indirect* quote (or alternatively, European quote or foreign currency per U.S. dollar quote). Table 1.1 presents a matrix of direct and indirect quotations of foreign exchange rates among four currencies.

The first row in the table shows that one U.S. dollar can buy $1, £0.7018, 7.5471 FF, and ¥133.86. Similarly, the second row states that one U.K. pound can purchase $1.4249, £1, 10.7539 FF, ¥190.74. The second column, on the other hand, shows that one U.S. dollar can be sold to get $1, $1.4249 can be sold to obtain £1, $0.1325 U.S. dollar can be sold to get 1 FF, and $0.00747 is needed to purchase ¥1. Other entries in the matrix should be read in the same fashion. These rates are known as currency cross rates or exchange cross rates, regularly noted in *The Wall Street Journal* and in *Financial Times.*

SPOT RATE OF EXCHANGE AND FORWARD RATE OF EXCHANGE

In the foreign exchange market, there is one quote for most currencies, and there are two, or more, quotes of the rate of foreign exchange for some currencies. One quote is the *spot* rate of exchange and the second and other quotes are known as the *forward* rates of exchange. Spot rate means the exchange rate at which one currency is exchanged for another currency immediately. The term immediately, however, should be interpreted as follows: if the trading takes place in the continental America, the transactions must be completed within one business day; but if the parties to the transactions are on a further global scale, exchange may involve two consecutive business days. Forward rate of exchange means that the rate of exchange is agreed upon at that moment, but actual delivery (settlement of transactions) will take place at a future date. If 1.4225 is the 30-day forward rate of an exchange of a British pound for a U.S. dollar, it means that the parties agree that for £1, one must pay $1.4225, but the payer of $1.4225 receives £1 on the 30th day from the time of agreement. If, on the other hand, the spot rate of exchange of a Canadian dollar for a U.S. dollar is 0.6245, then the person holding the U.S. dollar pays $0.6245 and receives one Canadian dollar within a business day from the time of agreement. Forward rate is thus a rate of exchange with a delayed delivery. There are forward rates with different maturities such as a 30-day, 60-day, 90-day, 180-day, 52-week, and a few other maturities that can be customized according to the parties' needs and preferences. At this point, it may be instructive to take a look at *The Wall Street Journal* (or any other financial press, e.g., *Financial Times*). Look at Table 1.2.

Look at the four columns of quotes of different currencies in Table 1.2. The first two columns provide the *direct* (U.S. dollar equivalent) quotes of different currencies in two successive business days. The next two columns give the *indirect* (foreign currency per one U.S. dollar) quotes of the currencies concerned. Now, take a closer look at the table. One Argentine peso is worth $0.4751, one Australian dollar is worth $0.5140 at the end of the day on Monday in New York, February 25, 2002, and reported by *The Wall Street Journal* on Tuesday, February 26, 2002, and so on. When you move to the third column, you get the value of one U.S. dollar in terms of the other currencies. On Monday, 2.1050 Argentine pesos are worth one U.S. dollar; 1.9457 Australian dollars have been exchanged for one U.S. dollar, and so on. Next, look at the British pound. You see four quotes on each column. On Monday, 1.4249 is the spot rate of exchange—that is, £1 = $1.4249; next quote (one-month forward) is 1.4225. That means traders lock in this rate of exchange, but delivery of currencies for one another will take place one month from that Monday. In *The Wall Street Journal*, two other forward rates, three-month forward and six-month forward, are given. One can have almost any customized maturity, usually up to two years. Another notable point is that only a limited number of currencies—the British pound, the Canadian dollar, the French franc, the Japanese yen, the Swiss franc, the German deutsche mark, and the U.S. dollar have only forward quotes, and other currencies have only spot quotes.

Table 1.2
The Wall Street Journal Quotes

CURRENCY TRADING

Monday, February 25, 2002
EXCHANGE RATES

The New York foreign exchange mid-range rates below apply to trading among banks in amounts of $1 million and more, as quoted at 4 p.m. Eastern time by Reuters and other sources. Retail transactions provide fewer units of foreign currency per dollar. Rates for the 12 Euro currency countries are derived from the latest dollar-euro rate using the exchange ratios set 1/1/99

	U.S. $ Equivalent.		Currency Per U.S. $	
Country	Mon	Fri	Mon	Fri
Argentina(Peso)-y....	.4571	.4866	2.1050	2.0550
Australia(Dollar)....	.5140	.5125	1.9457	1.9514
Austria (Schilling)....	.06316	.06363	15.832	15.715
Bahrain (Dinar)....	2.6525	2.6525	.3770	.3770
Belgium (Franc)....	.0215	.0217	46.4130	46.0712
Brazil(Real)....	.4177	.4129	2.3940	2.4220
Britain(Pound)...	1.4249	1.4326	.7018	.6980
1-month forward..	1.4225	1.4302	.7030	.6992
3-months forward...	1.4175	1.4252	.7055	.7017
6-months forward...	1.4102	1.4180	.7091	.7052
Canada (Dollar)...	.6245	.6264	1.6012	1.5963
1-month forward..	.6244	.6263	1.6015	1.5966
3-months forward...	.6241	.6261	1.6022	1.5973
6-months forward...	.6238	.6257	1.6030	1.5982
Chile(Peso)....	.001480	.001480	673.65	675.45
China(Renminbi)....	.1208	.1208	8.2765	8.2765
Colombia(Peso)..	.0004323	.0004323	2313.50	2313.40
Czech.Rep(akoruna)....				
Commercial rate..	.02740	.02766	36.501	36.156
Denmark(Krone)....	.1169	.1178	8.5525	8.4875
Ecuador(US Dollar)-e...	1.0000	1.0000	1.0000	1.0000
Finland(Makka)....	.1462	.1473	6.8409	6.7905
France (Franc)....	.1325	.1335	7.5471	7.4915
Germany(Mark)....	.4444	.4477	2.2503	2.2337
Greece(Drachma)...	.002551	.002570	392.05	389.12
Hong Kong(Dollar)....	.1282	.1282	7.7993	7.7994
Hungary(Forint)....	.003568	.003593	280.28	278.32
India(Rupee)....	.02050	.02052	48.770	48.740
Indonesia(Rupiah)....	.0000983	.0000979	10178	10215
Ireland (Punt)....	1.1036	1.1117	.9061	.8995
Israel(Shekel)....	.2160	.2131	4.6300	4.6925
Italy(Lira)....	.0004489	.0004522	2227.77	2211.36
Japan(Yen)...	.007470	.007460	133.86	134.04
1-month forward....	.007481	.007471	133.67	133.85
3-months forward....	.007505	.007495	133.25	133.42
6-months forward....	.007544	.007534	132.56	132.73

Table 1.2
(Continued)

	1.4104	1.4104	.7090	.7090
Jordan(Dinar)....				
Kuwait(Dinar)....	3.2489	3.2510	.3078	.3076
Lebonan(Pound)....	.0006605	.0006605	1514.00	1514.00
Malaysia(Ringgit)-b....	.2632	.2632	3.8001	3.8000
Malta(Lira)....	2.1925	2.1993	.4561	.4547
Mexico(Peso)....				
Floating rate....	.1103	.1099	9.0655	9.0985
Netherlands(Guilder)....	.3944	.3973	2.5355	2.5168
New Zealand(Dollar)....	.4175	.4184	2.3952	2.3901
Norway(Krone)....	.1123	.1127	8.9035	8.8740
Pakistan(Rupee)....	.01665	.01665	60.050	60.050
Peru(New Sol)....	.2876	.2874	3.4768	3.4795
Phillipines(Peso)....	.01946	.01946	51.375	51.375
Poland(Zloty)-D....	.2388	.2398	4.1872	4.1695
Portugal(Escudo)....	.004335	.004367	230.66	228.97
Russia(Ruble)-a....	.03230	.03230	30.957	30.957
Saudi Arabia(Riyal)....	.2666	.2666	3.7506	3.7505
Singapore(Dollar)....	.5463	.5459	1.8306	1.8320
Slovak Rep.(Koruna)....	.02075	.02090	48.200	47.848
S.Afrika(Rand)....	.0872	.0877	11.4720	11.4020
S.Korea(Won)....	.0007582	.0007593	1318.90	1317.00
Spain(Peseta)....	.005224	.005262	191.44	190.03
Sweden(Krona)....	.0956	.0957	10.4577	10.4510
Switzerland(Franc)..	.5888	.5918	1.6983	1.6897
1-months forward..	.5889	.5919	1.6980	1.6895
3-months forward..	.5891	.5921	1.6975	1.6889
6-months forward	.5897	.5926	1.6959	1.6875
Taiwan(Dollar)....	.02854	.02853	35.040	35.050
Thailand(Baht)....	.02282	.02278	43.820	43.900
Turkey(Lira)-f....	.00000072	.00000072	1387000	1388000
United Arab(Dirham)....	.2722	.2722	3.6731	3.6731
Uruquay(Peso)....	.06780	.06757	14.750	14.800
Venezuela(Bolivar)....	.000914	.000900	1094.35	1110.60
SDR....	1.2466	1.2449	.8022	8033
Euro......	.8692	.8756	1.1505	1.1421

Special Drawing Rights (SDR) are based on exchange rates for the U.S., German, British, French, and Japanese Currencies, *Source:* International Monetary Fund. a-Russian Central Bank rate. b-Government rate. d-Floating Rate; trading band suspended on 4/11/00, e-Adopted U.S. dollar as of 9/11/00. f-floating rate, eff. Feb. 22, y-Floating rate.

Table 1.2
(Continued)

KEY CURRENCY CROSS RATES
Late New York Trading Monday, February 25, 2002

	Dollar	Euro	Pound	Sfranc	Guilder	Peso	Yen	Lira	D-Mark	Ffranc	CdnClr
Canada....	1.6012	1.3918	2.2815	0.9428	.63151	.17663	.01196	.00072	.71155	.21216	.....
France....	7.5471	6.5599	10.7539	4.4439	2.9766	.83251	.05638	.00339	3.3538	.....	4.7134
Germany....	2.2503	1.9560	3.2065	1.3250	.88752	.24823	.01681	.00101	.....	.29817	1.4054
Italy....	2227.8	1936.4	3174.3	1311.8	878.63	245.74	16.643	.....	989.99	295.18	1391.3
Japan....	133.86	116.35	190.74	78.820	52.794	14.766	.....	.06009	59.485	17.737	83.600
Mexico....	9.0655	7.8797	12.917	5.3380	3.5754	.....	.06772	.00407	4.0286	1.2012	5.6617
Netherlands....	2.5355	2.2039	3.6128	1.4930	.....	.27969	.01894	.00114	1.1267	.33596	1.5835
Switzerland	1.6983	1.4762	2.4199	.....	.66981	.18734	.01269	.00076	.75470	.22503	1.0606
U.K.....	.70180	.6100	.....	.4132	.27679	.07741	.00524	.00032	.31187	.09299	.43830
Euro....	1.15050	.....	1.6393	.67743	.45375	.12691	.00859	.00052	.51126	.15244	.71851
U.S.....	.....	.8692	1.4249	.58882	.39440	.11031	.00747	.00045	.44439	.13250	.62453

Source: The Wall Street Journal, February 26, 2002

Table 1.3
Financial Times Quotes

| | U.S. $ equivalent | | Foreign currency per U.S. $ | |
	bid	ask	bid	ask
British pound	1.4278	1.4280	0.700280	0.700378
French franc	0.132813	0.132874	7.5259	7.5294
Japanese yen	0.007469	0.007473	133.820	133.880

Source: Financial Times, February 26, 2002

These are quotes on bank drafts on wholesale spot rates and forward rates. Note also that these are the New York foreign exchange mid-rate rates that apply to trading among banks in amounts of 1 million dollars or more, as quoted at 4 P.M. Eastern time by Banker's Trust Company of New York. Retail transactions provide fewer units of foreign currency per U.S. dollar. The selling rates are called banks' (or foreign exchange dealers') *ask* or *offer* rate. When a bank buys a currency, the rate is called *bid* rate. If you walk into a bank or an office of any exchange dealer, you will find two different rates: the *ask* rate and the *bid* rate. In direct (U.S. dollar equivalent) quotes, the ask rate is usually higher than the bid rates. Table 1.3 shows these rates.

The difference between ask and bid quotes is called a *spread,* which usually is the measure of transaction costs, but for small amounts of conversion such as a few hundred dollars, a dealer may charge a fixed amount per every $100 or every $1,000 on top of the bid and ask quotes at the time. The banks or exchange dealers sell currency at a higher price than the price they pay to get the same currency, and thus make a profit. Note that if the quote is in foreign currency per U.S. dollar (indirect), the ask rate is lower than bid rate (see Table 1.3). In a direct quote, if the ask-and-bid prices of British pounds are $1.4278 and $1.4280, then the spread is $0.0002. In technical jargon, in this illustrative case, it is stated that the ask price is 2 points above the bid price. However, for currency such as the Japanese yen, the ask-bid quotes are in six decimal points (e.g., the ask quote is $0.007473 and the bid quote is $0.007469, and thus, the spread is $0.000004). Here also the spread is 4 points. The point refers to the difference in the last digits in the ask-bid quotes.

CONVENTIONS ON QUOTATIONS

Foreign exchange rates are quoted in two different ways. One style is to quote the rate in an *outright* form, and the other style is known as a *swap* quote. An example will illustrate these quotes in clear terms. If you call a bank for the spot forward quotes on, say, British pounds in terms of U.S. dollars, you may have the following quotations.

Rate of exchange	Bank's bid	Bank's ask
Spot	1.4278	1.4280
One-month forward	1.4281	1.4284
Three-month forward	1.4283	1.4287
Six-month forward	1.4268	1.4272

These quotations are straightforward. The bank's buying price and the selling price of the British pound in the spot cash market are $1.4278 and $1.4280, respectively. Similarly, the one-month forward rates for buying and selling the British pound are $1.4281 and $1.4284. These straight-forward quotes are known as *outright* quotes. There is, however, an alter-native way of quoting the rates—swap quotes. They are as follows:

Spot	One-month forward	Three-month forward	Six-month forward
1.4278/80	3/4	5/7	10/8

Here the spot quote 1.4278/80 means that the bank's bid rate and ask rate are 1.4278 and 1.4280. The one-monthly forward quote 3/4 here means that the one-month forward bid rate is 1.4281 (that is, 3 points are added to the last digit of 1.4278) and the ask rate is 1.4284 (4 points are added to the last digit to 1.4280). The three-month forward quote 5/7 means then that the three-month forward bid-and-ask rates are 1.4283 and 1.4287, respectively. Note here 3/4 and 5/7 are points in *ascending* order: 3 followed by the higher number 4, and 5 followed by 7. When you note this ascending order of points, these points must be *added* to the spot bid and spot ask rates. However, if the points are in *descending* order, as in the quote of six-month forward (10/8), the points must be *subtracted* from the spot bid-and-ask rates. That is, six-month forward bid-and-ask rates, in this instance, are 1.4268 and 1.4272. A caveat should be in order now. The points in ascending (descending) order with the slash (/) in between should be added (subtracted) if the spot rates (bid and ask) are in *direct* quotes. If the spot rates are in indirect quotation, the points in ascending (descending) order must be subtracted (added) to the spot quotes to determine the forward quotes in outright terms. Here is the summary of the conversion from swap quotes to outright quotes:

	Quotes	
Point Order	Direct	Indirect
Ascending	Add swap points to spot quotes	Subtract swap points from spot quotes
Descending	Subtract swap points from spot quotes	Add swap points to spot quotes

Let us summarize and review the exposition further in a diagrammatic framework as follows:

Spot Rates (S)
Means
Immediate exchange (not delayed) of currencies, for example, usually within one or two consecutive business days

Forward Rate (F)
Means
Delayed exchanges of currencies
One-month forward
Three-month forward
Six-month forward
One-year forward

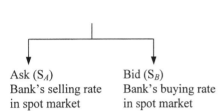

Ask (S_A)
Bank's selling rate
in spot market
1.4780

Bid (S_B)
Bank's buying rate
in spot market
1.4278

Ask (F_A)
Bank's telling rate
in forward market
1.4284

Bid (F_B)
Bank's buying rate
in forward market
1.4281

Once again, we re-express the quotation structure in the schematic form as follows.

Quotes

Direct	Indirect
or	or
American	European
or	or
U.S. Dollar Equivalent	Foreign Currency Equivalent
≡	≡
Price of one unit of foreign currency in terms of home currency	Price of one unit of home currency in terms of foreign currency
$1.4278 = £1 ($1.42782/£1)	£0.50 = $1 (£0.50/$1)
or $S^D = 1.4278$	or $S^I = 0.7004$

If in direct quote:

Ask price – Bid price = Spread
$S_A - S_B$ = Spot spread
$F_A - F_B$ = Forward spread
$\{(\text{Ask rate} - \text{Bid rate})/\text{Ask rate}\} \times 100$ = Percent spread
$\{(S_A - S_B)/S_A\} \times 100$ = % Spot spread, and
$\{(F_A - F_B)/F_A\} \times 100$ = % Forward spread.

Forward Premium and Discount:

The foreign currency (when quoted in direct, i.e., in U.S. dollar equivalent terms) is said to be in:

forward premium if: $\{(F - S)/S\} \cdot (1/n) > 0$;

forward par if: $\{(F - S)/S\} \cdot (1/n) = 0$;

forward discount if: $\{(F - S)/S\} \cdot (1/n) < 0$,

where n stands for forward contract maturity in terms of year. That means, 1 month = $1/12$ year, 2 months = $2/12 = 1/6$ year, and so on.

Examples:

$F = 2.15$ (1 month forward)

$S = 2.00$

Here: forward premium = $\{(2.15 - 2.00)/2.00\} \cdot \{1/(1/12)\} = 0.9$.

$F = 1.95$ (1 year forward)

$S = 2.00$

Here: forward discount = $\{(1.95 - 2.00)/2.00\} \cdot (1/1) = -0.025$.

TRIANGULAR ARBITRAGE

As pointed out earlier, arbitrage is the act of buying cheap and selling dear in order to make a profit. Consider a situation in which you know that Store A is selling VCRs for the price of $400, but in Store B, the same VCR is selling for $500. With this knowledge you will try to buy VCRs from Store A at $400 a piece and sell the same VCRs for around $490 a piece to the buyers who are about to enter Store B, thus making a nice profit of $90 per VCR. This will continue as long as the situation is unchanged. But most likely, perhaps within a short period, Store B, having no customers at all, will be forced to reduce the price of its VCR to, say, $470 a piece. On the other hand, Store A, faced with an increasing demand for VCRs, will jack up the VCR price to, say, $420 a piece. In this new situation, the man who is buying low and selling high (we call him *arbitrageur*), will continue to do exactly what he was doing before even though the profit margin is much reduced for him. The reasons for which Store B lowered its price and Store A raised its price still continue, and as a result, both the stores will continue revising their prices in the same fashion until the uniform price, somewhere between the original $400 and $500 (say, $454), is established because of arbitrage, and the arbitrageur is thrown out of business (of making profit). The force of competition finally wipes out the market imperfection and price alignment becomes perfect. In the currency market, foreign exchange rates are not fully aligned at every moment of business hours, and therefore, the scope for arbitrage exists exactly in the same way as in the case of Store A and Store B in our example. In fact, in a currency market, since there are different currencies and hence different rates of exchange, one can barter one currency for another, and then the second currency for a third currency, and so on, eventually getting back to the original currency the currency trader started with. This process is called *triangular arbitrage*. Triangular arbitrage is the buying and selling of one currency for another, ending with a return to the original currency for the purpose of making a profit.

Triangular arbitrage rests on the product of *cross rates*. The cross rate between dollar and DM (in the spot market) is defined as follows:

$$S(\$/DM) = S(\$/£) \cdot S(£/DM).$$

If the rate of exchange between the pound and the dollar is known and the rate of exchange between the deutsche mark (DM) and the pound is known, one can swiftly get the exchange rate between the dollar and DM by cross-multiplying those rates. Suppose you note the following rates between the dollar and the pound, and the pound and DM, respectively: $\$1.6420 = £1$ (that is, $S(\$/£) = 1.6420$), and $£0.4196 = DM1$ (i.e., $S(£/DM) = 0.4196$). The cross rate of exchange between the dollar and DM then is $S(\$/DM) = S(\$/£) \cdot S(£/DM) = (1.6420)(0.4196) = 0.6890$. This means you can buy one DM for $\$0.6890$ (or with one DM you can get $\$0.6890$ in exchange).

Now, consider the following scenarios: note the following quotes: $S(\$/£) = 1.6420$ (in New York), and $S(DM/\$) = 1.4645$ (in Tokyo), and $S(£/DM) = 0.4196$ (in London).

In this case, you have $S(\$/£) \cdot S(DM/\$) \cdot S(£/DM) = (1.6420) \cdot (1.4645) \cdot (0.4196) = 1.0009$. Note here that $S(\$/£) \cdot S(DM/\$)$ yields the cross rate between DM and the pound ($\equiv S(DM/£)$), and then when it is further cross-multiplied by $S(£/DM)$, it becomes a pure number, denominated in no currency unit. The signification can be concretely stated in the following way: you can exchange your £1 for dollar in New York and get $\$1.6420$; with this dollar amount, you get DM 2.4047 ($\equiv 1.6420$H 1.4645) in Tokyo, and finally, with that DM amount you can get £1.0090 ($\equiv 2.4047$H 0.4196) in London. This means exchanging your initial £1 into dollar, then dollar into DM, and then DM into pound to get £1.0090. It is a profitable situation for you, and it means that if you start off with £1,000,000 and go through these series of currency exchanges, you can make £9,000 without a doubt. Under the given scenario, you have just arbitraged and made a riskless profit out of a situation. This is the triangular arbitrage in currencies, and now you can see how triangular arbitrage rests on the product of cross rates. Diagrammatically, the process looks like the following:

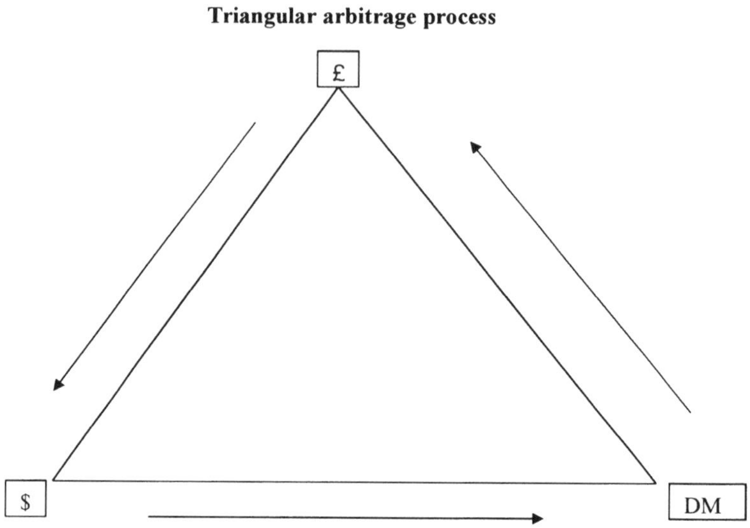

Triangular arbitrage process

Figure 1.1 Triangular arbitrage

Figure 1.1 exhibits through the arrows the directions of currency conversion, starting initially from pound into dollar, then into DM, and finally DM into pound back. One can start with another currency, converting that into some other currency, and through this process finally coming back to the original currency. One should note that triangular arbitrage is just a way to refer to multicurrency conversion process of buying low and selling high for the explicit purpose of making a profit.

Triangular Arbitrage Profits (in the absence of transaction costs)

Usually, each buying and/or selling of any asset, be it a stock, bond, or currency, involves a brokerage fee—more generally known as a transaction cost. In this section, we assume away that transaction cost of buying and selling any currency. Under this situation of zero transaction costs, the conditions for positive, zero, and negative triangular arbitrage profits are as follows:

when $S(DM/\$)S(£/DM) \cdot S(\$/£) > 1$, triangular arbitrage is profitable;
$S(DM/\$) \cdot S(£/DM) \cdot S(\$/£) = 1$, triangular arbitrage yields zero profit;
$S(DM/\$) \cdot S(£/DM) \cdot S(\$/£) < 1$, triangular arbitrage is unprofitable.

Consider a matrix of exchange rates to ascertain if there is any scope for profitable arbitrage (Table 1.4).

Table 1.4
Matrix of Exchange Rates

	Currency Purchased			
Currency Sold	$	£	DM	¥
$	1	1.8930	0.4530	0.00437
£	0.5260	1	0.2390	0.00231
DM	2.2050	4.41900	1	0.00966
¥	228.2000	433.5000	103.5000	1

A person who is holding one U.S. dollar can exchange his currency for DM 2.2050. With £0.2390/DM, this person can use DM 2.2050 to obtain £0.5270 (≡ 2.2050 × 0.2390). This amount of pound sterling can then be converted back into U.S. dollars at the rate of $1.8930/£, and he can receive $0.9976 (≡ 0.5270 × 1.8/2.2050 × 0.2390 × 1.8930).

In this case, this person starts off with $1 and ends up with $0.9976. Therefore, it is an unprofitable situation.

Triangular Arbitrage Profits (in the presence of transaction costs)

Thus far, we have assumed away transaction cost in the arbitrage activities. In reality, any financial transaction activity involves some transaction costs, and so it is instructive and practical to factor in transaction costs in the calculation to determine when triangular arbitrage is profitable and when it is not. Let us use the following notations for convenience:

$S_B(\$/£)$/the price (say, in dollar amount) that must be paid to a bank (or exchange dealer) to buy £1 (e.g., the price the bank is asking); $S_{B(\$/£)}$ the dollar amount received from a bank (or an exchange dealer) for the sale of one £1 (that is, for the bank's purchase of £1), and $T \equiv$ average one-way cost of transaction in the foreign exchange market.

That means:

$$S_A(\$/£) = (1 + T)\cdot S_M(\$/£), \quad (1.1)$$
$$S_B(\$/£) = (1 - T)\cdot S_M(\$/£), \quad (1.2)$$

where $S_{M(\$/\pounds)}$ is the middle rate—the midpoint between ask-and-bid rates. In numerical terms, if $S_A = 1.6230$, and $S_B = 1.6220$, then $S_M = 1.6225$.

From the equations 1.1 and 1.2 (that is, by subtracting equation 1.2 from 1.1), one can obtain:

$$S_A(\$/\pounds) - S_B(\$/\pounds) = 2T \cdot S_M(\$/\pounds), \text{ whence:}$$
$$T = (S_A(\$/\pounds) - S_B(\$/\pounds))/2S_M(\$/\pounds).$$

Again, if $S_A(\$/\pounds) = 1.6230$, $S_B(\$/\pounds) = 1.6220$, and hence $S_M(\$/\pounds) = 1.6225$, then $T = (1.6230 - 1.6220)/2H1.6225 = 0.0003$.

Now the question is: under transaction cost (T), how long is it profitable to engage in triangular arbitrage?

Starting with the dollars (\$) and arbitraging around the triangle, an arbitrageur can buy deutsche marks (DM), sell these DM for pounds (£), and sell these pounds for dollars. Arbitrage should continue until it is no more profitable. Arbitrageurs who start off with dollars should participate until no more than the original dollar amount can at least be recovered, that is, until:

$$[S_B(\pounds/DM) \cdot S_B(\$/\pounds)]/\{1/S_A(\$/DM) \leq 1 \tag{1.3}$$

Using the definitions of middle exchange rate and transaction cost, we can rewrite equation 1.3 as follows:

$$\{(1-T)^2/(1+T)\} \cdot S_M(\pounds/DM) \cdot S_M(\$/\pounds) \leq S_M(\$/DM) \tag{1.4}$$

With the reversal of directions, the arbitrageur may also make profit by buying pound with dollars, then exchanging these pounds for deutsche marks, and then finally selling these deutsche marks for dollars. This arbitrage process should continue, with transaction cost (T), the following conditions develop:

$$\{(1+T)^2/(1-T)\} \cdot S_M(\pounds/DM) \cdot S_M(\$/\pounds) \geq S_M(\$/DM) \tag{1.5}$$

The conditions, given by equations 1.4 and 1.5 together, define when triangular arbitrage with transaction cost (T) is unprofitable or profitable. Triangular arbitrage with transaction cost (T) is unprofitable if the following holds:

$$\{(1 + T)^2/(1 - T)\} \cdot S_M(\pounds/DM) \cdot S_M(\$/\pounds) \geq S_M(\$/DM) \geq \{(1 - T)^2/(1 + T)\} \cdot S_M(\pounds/DM) \cdot S(\$/\pounds). \tag{1.6}$$

This means that whenever the middle rate $S_M(\$/DM)$ lies outside the upper and lower limits established by relation of equation 1.6, the arbitrage is profitable. Figure 1.2 exhibits the conditions graphically.

Arbitrage with transaction cost (T):

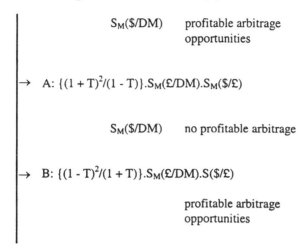

$S_M(\$/DM)$ profitable arbitrage opportunities

→ A: $\{(1 + T)^2/(1 - T)\}.S_M(£/DM).S_M(\$/£)$

$S_M(\$/DM)$ no profitable arbitrage

→ B: $\{(1 - T)^2/(1 + T)\}.S_M(£/DM).S(\$/£)$

profitable arbitrage opportunities

Figure 1.2   Zones of profitable and unprofitable arbitrage

Consider the following data: ask rate and bid rate for DM in terms of pound are as follows: $S_A(£/DM) = 0.4157$ and $S_B(£/DM) = 0.4152$; ask rate and bid rate pound in terms of dollar are: $S_A(\$/£) = 1.5530$ and $S_B(\$/£) = 1.5510$. Obviously then the middle rates are $S_M(£/DM) = 0.41545$, $S_M(\$/£) = 1.5520$, and the transaction cost is $T = 0.0006$. With all this information, the value of $\{(1+T)^2/(1-T)\}\cdot S_M(£/DM)\cdot S_M(\$/£) = 0.6459$, and $\{(1-T)^2/(1+T)\}\cdot S_M(£/DM)\cdot S(\$/£) = 0.6436$. If the middle rate of DM in terms of dollar $S_M(\$/DM)$ lies between 0.6436 and 0.6459, there is no scope for profitable triangular arbitrage with transaction cost of $T = 0.0006$. That means, under the given scenario, one will not be able to make profit of $S_M(\$/DM)$ equals, say, 0.6445. However, if the ask-and-bid rates move such that the middle rate of DM in terms of dollar equals either, say, 0.6438 or 0.6468, one can make a profit even with a transaction cost without taking any risk in the process since every bit of information for calculation is known with certainty.

FUTURES, SWAPS, AND OPTIONS

Like forward contracts, there are other instruments that a trader or an investor makes use of to stay and do well in the market—to arbitrage, to hedge, and to speculate—to gain and to manage risks. Currency futures are contracts similar to currency forwards, but there are important differences. A swap is basically a bilateral agreement to a sequence of exchange of one currency for another currency or a sequence of interest payment or a cocktail of the two. An option is the right offered to the holder of those derivative assets for a premium paid by the holder to the issuer in case of needed contingency claims. Many synthetic varieties with two basic types—a *call option* and a *put option*—can create a network of instruments that an investor can play with in the market. There are instruments such as options on futures, options on swaps (swaptions), and so on, to color the landscape of strategic instruments in the foreign exchange market. In the following chapters, we expound and explore these items in the arsenal of the market.

REFERENCES

Clark, E. (1998). *International Finance.* London: Thompson Publishing.

Ghosh, D. K. (1997). "Arbitrage with Hedging: Exploited and Exploitable Profits," *The European Journal of Finance* (November). Vol. 3, 349–361.

Ghosh, D. K., and E. Ortiz. (1994). *Changing Environment of International Financial Markets: Issues and Analysis.* London: Macmillan.

Ghosh, D. K., and E. Ortiz. (1997). *The Global Structure of Financial Markets.* London: Routledge.

Grabbe, J. O. (1991). *International Financial Markets,* 2nd ed. New York: Elsevier Science Publishing.

Levi, M. (1997). *International Finance.* New York: McGraw-Hill.

Neihans, J. (1984). *International Monetary Economics.* Baltimore: Johns Hopkins University Press.

Sercu, P., and R. Uppal. (1995). *International Financial Markets and the Firm.* Cincinnati, Ohio: South-Western College Publishing.

Chapter 2

Currency Futures, Swaps, and Hedging

Currency risk, or foreign exchange risk as it is often called, refers to the fluctuations in domestic currency value of assets, liabilities, income, or expenditure due to unanticipated changes in exchange rates. Many techniques are available to cover, or hedge, exposure to risk of this kind. The simplest and most common technique involves using a forward contract. However, forward contracts are relatively costly and lack a liquid secondary market where positions can be taken and undone cheaply and swiftly. Currency futures contracts traded on organized exchanges overcome these shortcomings but in so doing, they create problems of their own. Judging the relative merits of hedging with forwards or futures requires a firm grasp of the characteristics of each type of instrument. In chapter 1, we outlined the characteristics of the forward contract. In this chapter, we begin with a detailed presentation of the currency futures contract and its relation to the forward contract. We then establish the principles of hedging with the futures contract. In the last two sections, we look at currency hedging in more detail, including the role of discounts and premiums as well as long-term hedging with forwards and currency swaps.

MECHANICS OF CURRENCY FUTURES MARKETS

The Difference between Forwards and Futures

As discussed in chapter 1, a forward contract is an agreement to buy or sell an asset at a certain future time for a certain future price, whereas a spot contract is an agreement to buy or sell an asset on that day. Forward contracts are traded in the over-the-counter market and usually involve a financial institution on one side of the deal and either a client or another financial institution on the other side of the deal. One party to the deal takes a long position and agrees to purchase the asset. The other party takes the short position and agrees to sell the asset. The agreed price in the forward contract is called the delivery price, which is chosen so that the value of the contract to both sides is equal to zero. Consequently, it costs nothing to enter into a forward agreement.

A futures contract is very similar to a forward contract. It is an agreement between two parties to buy or sell an asset at a certain time for a certain price. Futures contracts are traded on organized exchanges. To facilitate trading, the exchange specifies certain standardized features of the contract, and trading takes place in such a way that the exchange is the ultimate counterparty to each transaction. Futures contracts differ from forward contracts in two other ways. First of all, payments are made over the life of the contract in what is called marking to market. Secondly, most futures contracts are closed out before maturity.

Thus, the organized futures markets have four important features: (1) the contracts are standardized, (2) trading is organized and centralized either in one physical location such as the trading pit or in a virtual location such as a computerized order book, (3) contracts are settled through the exchange's clearinghouse, (4) contracts are *marked to market* each day, which means that they are revalued according to their market value.

Standardized Contracts

The Chicago Mercantile Exchange (CME) is one of the world's largest commercial exchanges. It began as a commodities market and for many years only commodities were traded on it. On June 16, 1972, it opened the International Money Market to trade foreign exchange futures contracts on the pound sterling, the Canadian dollar, the German mark, the yen, the Mexican peso, the Swiss franc, and the Italian lira. Sometime later, it opened contracts on the French franc, the Dutch guilder, the Australian dollar, and the ECU. These contracts were patterned after the futures contracts for the commodities it had been trading for over a hundred years. The success of this format led to its widespread adoption by other exchanges. Hence, contrary to the workings of the interbank currency market, trading in currency futures conforms strictly to the exchange's internal rules. The traded currencies are limited in number. Maturities are based on a quarterly cycle of March, June, September, and December, and each contract has a precise delivery date, typically the third Wednesday of March, June, September, and December or the first business day following one of those Wednesdays. Trading stops two business days before the expiration date, and delivery takes place on the second business day after the expiration date.

Each contract also corresponds to a given amount of foreign exchange. For example, the CME's yen contract is for 12,500,000 yen and the euro

Table 2.1
A Sample of Currency Contracts

Contract	Exchange	Size
Japan yen	CME	JPY 12.5 million
German deutsche mark	CME	DEM 125,000
Canadian dollar	CME	CAD 100,000
British pound	CME	GBP 62,500
Swiss franc	CME	CHF1 25,000
Australian dollar	CME	AUD 100,000
Mexican peso	CME	MXN 500,000
Euro FX	CME	EUR 125,000

Source: Wall Street Journal Europe, October 6, 2000.

contract for 125,000 euros. Consequently, hedgers usually cannot get the exact maturities and amounts that they need and have to settle for the nearest date and the closest amount. Later in this chapter, we will look at these problems in detail. The maturity date is probably more of a problem than the amounts because maturity dates are relatively rare whereas the size of the contracts is small enough that most users' needs can be approximated quite well. Furthermore, the small size of the contract makes the futures market accessible to smaller investors. Finally, when contracts mature, the delivery procedure is effected according to the rules spelled out by the exchange. Table 2.1 gives some examples of the currency contracts traded on the CME.

Trading Procedures

Only commission houses registered as member firms are allowed to trade on the exchange. Anyone else who seeks access to the market must do so through a commission house by opening an account. All orders are then executed through the commission house. In the United States, for example, opening an account is subject to strict rules. Before opening an account, the client must read a number of documents and declare that he understands them. This is to ensure that the client understands the risks associated with the futures markets. Furthermore, opening an account is also subject to certain financial guarantees such as a deposit of cash or marketable securities.

When a client wants to trade, he transmits his order to the registered representative that manages his account for the clearinghouse. Different types of conditions can be attached to the order. The order can be limited to a certain period of time or to a certain price range or both. When the registered representative receives the order, he transmits it directly to the offices of the clearinghouse in the city where the futures market is located. From there, it is sent to the commission house's order desk or the trading floor. A messenger takes it to the commission house's trader. At each stage of the operation, the order is time-stamped so as to control the speed of execution and serve as proof in the case of a complaint.

Futures trading is organized around a centralized market that matches supply and demand. One method of matching supply and demand that is popular in continental Europe is centralizing limit orders in a computerized limit order book. In this system, brokers are linked through a computer network that makes it possible for them to electronically post and delete their own orders or fill orders posted by others on the screen. Another method of centralizing supply and demand is by *open outcry*. In this system, transactions take place either around a ring or inside a pit. The traders, either from different commission houses or independent speculators, take their places around the ring or on different steps of the pit based on the maturity date of the commodity getting traded. The messengers bring them the orders for execution and large electronic panels flash information that keeps them constantly informed of what is happening in the market. Trading is done by an auction system of open outcry where any trader can take the opposite side of a trade if he wants to. The voice is combined with a particular sign language to communicate prices, quantities and buys, or sells.

If, for example, a trader wants to buy 10 March pounds sterling (GBP) contracts at 1.4000 per pound, he signals this to the other traders. Any trader can answer, and if several do, the fastest to respond is the one who gets the deal. If no one responds, the trader knows that his price is off. He either has to wait to execute his order or he has to offer a better price. This system of continuous open outcry is transparent and competitive and ensures that the buy price is the same as the sell price. There is no bid-ask spread as there is in the interbank market. The broker makes his money by charging the client a commission, and in practice, commissions are quite small. A *round trip*, meaning one buy and one sell, can be as low as 0.05 percent of the value of the contract.

Exchange employees permanently monitor the activities of each pit or ring. After each order is executed, they enter the price in the computer system. In this way, all exchange members are kept informed of the market's evolution. Some exchanges link their computer systems to the outside for public distribution of the information.

Once an order has been executed, the floor broker uses a messenger to transmit the information to his desk. The desk then informs the client and transmits the information to the commission house's accounting services where the appropriate entries are recorded. Recording requirements do not end here, however. The clearinghouse, which is the ultimate counterparty to each trade, must also be informed. For this purpose, floor brokers are obliged to fill in a *trading card* for each transaction indicating the type of contract, its maturity, the number of contracts, the price, the commission houses' code numbers, and the floor broker's initials.

The Clearinghouse

The role of the clearinghouse is threefold. It records the existence of the contract; it manages settlement of day-to-day operations; and it guarantees delivery at the contract's maturity. Thus, there is no individual counterparty risk because all clients have the clearinghouse as the ultimate counterparty.

The modern system of clearing used today by almost all futures markets was developed in the United States about 1920. Most clearinghouses are specific to each exchange, although some clearing corporations, such as I.C.C.H. in London, act on behalf of several markets. Their role is always the same. They act as third-party guarantors to all futures contracts, and they manage the financial implications associated with their guarantee.

Once a trade has been completed, the commission houses on either side of the trade do not have an obligation to each other. They each have an obligation to the clearinghouse. The commission house on the buy side of the trade has an obligation to the clearinghouse to buy. The commission house on the sell side of the trade has an obligation to the clearinghouse to sell, and the clearinghouse has an obligation to sell to the buyer and an obligation to buy from the seller.

The role of the clearinghouse is essential for the smooth functioning of futures market. Clients do not have to worry about the solvability of the commission house nor do commission houses have to worry about the solvability of other exchange members. The only risk is the solvability of the clearinghouse itself. This risk is minimal since the clearinghouse is required to maintain an impregnable financial position.[1] All contracts are with the financially impregnable clearinghouse and, thus, for a given type are strictly equivalent. This facilitates trading and fosters liquidity. When a client wants to close out a position on a purchased futures contract, for example, he simply sells a contract to someone else. No one cares who makes the transaction because the ultimate counterparty is the clearinghouse. The clearinghouse keeps its accounts with each member and knows at all times the net position of each one.

Because of the clearinghouse's role as the ultimate counterparty, it is at risk from all the members with whom it does business. Consequently, it requires certain guarantees from each one. One of the most important guarantees of an exchange's financial system is the strict *clearing margin* imposed on members. A clearing margin is a deposit in the form of cash, government issued securities, stock in a clearing corporation, or letters of credit issued by an approved bank that clearing members leave with the clearinghouse. The size of the deposit is fixed by the clearinghouse based on the member's net position or on its long and short positions, and it can be revised upward or downward at any time depending on how the clearinghouse feels the market is going. Clearing margins are calculated every day in an exercise similar to the way that clients are marked to market. They must be large enough to cover maximum fluctuations in futures prices. Since prices vary day to day, initial margins may become inadequate if prices move strongly against one or more members. In this case, the clearinghouse can make a margin call against the deficient members. They then have one hour to effect a wire transfer of funds. These funds will be included in the end of day settlement procedures when all accounts are marked to market. It is clear that much care is taken to ensure the exchange's solvability and that the clearinghouse wields extensive power over its members.

Margin Calls and Marking to Market

As would be expected, member commission houses require the same type of guarantees from their clients that the clearinghouse requires of them. In fact, the margins that commission houses require from their clients are often higher than the margins required by the clearinghouse, although the deposits represent only a small proportion of the total contract and are virtually costless since interest-bearing treasury bonds can be used. Client accounts are marked to market at the end of each day, and clients are subject to margin calls if their position deteriorates. Margins and daily marking to market make client defaults a rare occasion and reinforce the overall financial soundness of the exchange.

Marking to market means that profits and losses are paid every day at the end of trading and is equivalent to closing out a contract each day, paying off losses or receiving gains, and writing a new contract. The procedure can best be illustrated by an example.

On Monday morning, an investor takes a long position in a euro futures contract at a price of $0.80. At the end of the day, the price has risen to $0.81. Since the amount of the contract is 125,000 euros, the investor's gain is:

$$(\$0.81 - \$0.80) \times 125{,}000 = \$1{,}250.$$

The investor receives his $1,250 and is the owner of a contract with a price that is now $0.81. On Tuesday evening, the price has fallen to $0.795. Therefore, he has to pay:

$$(\$0.81 - \$0.795) \times 125{,}000 = \$1{,}875;$$

and he now owns a contract with a price of $0.795.

In this context, the margin procedure is straightforward. An *initial margin* is deposited when a position is taken on a futures contract. This initial margin is usually set high enough so that the cost and inconvenience of frequent small payments can be avoided as the futures price is marked to market each day. Small losses are simply deducted from the initial margin until a predetermined lower bound, called the *maintenance margin,* is reached. At this point, the commission house issues a *margin call* requesting the client to deposit the funds necessary to bring the margin back to the initial level.

Futures Information

The financial press prints regular information on many of the currency futures traded on the different exchanges. Table 2.2, for example, shows the relevant data on the euro contracts traded on the Chicago Mercantile Exchange (CME) as reported in *The Wall Street Journal Europe* on Friday, October 6, 2000.

The heading on the line beginning with "EURO FX (CME)" tells us that the contracts concern the euro traded on the CME. Each contract is for EUR 125,000 and prices are given in U.S. dollars per euro. Column 1 gives the maturity month of each contract. Thus, the three active contracts were the contracts expiring in December 2000, March 2001, and September 2001, respectively. Column 2 (headed "Open") gives the price at the start of trading on Thursday, October 5, 2000; column 3 (headed "High") gives the highest transaction price during that day, and column 4 (headed "Low") gives the lowest transaction price during the same day. Column 5 (headed "Settle") shows the price representative of transactions near the market's close. It is this price that is used in the process of marking to market. For example, the settlement price for the March contract was $0.8757. Column 6 (headed "Change") shows the change in the settlement price between Wednesday and Thursday. For the March contract the settlement price change was $0.0057. Thus, on Thursday, October 5, 2000, the owner of this contract made a loss of $0.0057 × 125,000 = $712.50, and the seller made a gain of an equal amount. It is interesting to note that although the September contract did not trade on October 5, there is a reported settlement price of $0.8823 for a change of $0.0057. In fact, when a contract does not trade, the CME fixes the settlement price based on reported bid-ask quotes. Columns 7 and 8 (headed "Lifetime High" and "Lifetime Low") show the highest and lowest observed prices on each contract since its inception. As might be expected, the longer a contract has traded, the wider will be the high-low spread. Thus, the spread on the December contract is wider than the spread on the March contract, which is wider than the spread on the September contract. Column 9 (headed "Open Interest") reports the number of outstanding contracts. Again, the longer a contract

Table 2.2
Information on EUR Futures

						Lifetime		
	Open	High	Low	Settle	Change	High	Low	Open Interest
EURO FX (CME): Euro 125,000; U.S. Dollar per Euro								
Dec. '00	0.8770	0.8816	0.8709	0.8721	-0.0057	1.0572	0.8501	66,686
Mar. '01	0.8780	0.8845	0.8743	0.8757	-0.0057	0.9999	0.8554	784
Sept. '01	....	....	....	0.8823	-0.0057	0.8962	0.8616	165
Est. vol. 15,633; vol. Wed. 8,983; open int. 67,662, +66								

Source: Wall Street Journal Europe, October 6, 2000.

has been traded, the higher the number of outstanding contracts. Consequently, the December maturity has 66,686 contracts outstanding while the September contract has only 165. The last line in the table shows that the total number of contracts traded on Thursday was 15,633, that the total number of contracts traded on Wednesday was 8,983; and that the total number of contracts outstanding at the end of trading on Thursday was 67,662; an increase of 66 over Wednesday's close.

FUTURES CONTRACTS AND THE BASIS

Principles of Hedging with Futures Contracts

Exposure to foreign exchange risk can arise from a commercial transaction, a foreign investment, or a liability in foreign currency. A position is said to be long when foreign currency or a claim in foreign currency is owned. It is short when there is a liability in foreign currency. For example, an export billed in foreign currency creates a long position for the exporting firm in the form of a claim in foreign currency for the value of the merchandise. On the other hand, an import billed in foreign currency creates a short position for the importing firm in the form of a liability for the amount of the purchase.

A long position in foreign currency can be hedged by selling the foreign currency forward. When the domestic organized futures market is used to construct the hedge, a certain number of futures contracts are sold. Consider, for example, an American exporter who makes a sale for 1 million euros to be paid on December 15. To avoid a drop in the value of the euro, he goes to the CME and sells eight December euro contracts selling for 0.9100. Each contract is for EUR 125,000. In December, he receives the euros from his client and takes delivery on the futures contracts. He pays 8 × 125,000 = EUR 1,000,000 and receives 8 × 125,000 × 0.9100 = $910,000.

When a foreign futures exchange is used to construct the hedge, a certain number of currency futures are purchased. If, for example, a French exporter who has a USD 455,000 claim coming due in December uses the CME to hedge his foreign exchange risk, he will sell four December euro contracts at 0.9100. In December, he collects his USD 455,000 and takes delivery on the futures contracts. He pays 4 × 125,000 × 0.9100 = $455,000 and receives 4 × 125,000 = EUR 500,000.

Hedging a short position involves buying foreign exchange forward. When a domestic futures exchange is used to construct the hedge, a certain number of futures contracts are purchased. If a foreign futures exchange is used to construct the hedge, the futures contracts are sold.

The Basis

Although spot and futures prices converge at maturity, they can and do differ significantly before maturity. The difference between the futures price and the spot price is called the *basis*:[2]

$$\text{Basis} = F_{t,T} - S_t, \tag{2.1}$$

where $F_{t,T}$ is the futures price at time t for a contract maturing at time T and S_T is the spot exchange rate at time t. The basis and how it varies through time are important elements in hedging strategies that use the organized futures exchanges. Futures delivery dates, being relatively infrequent, will often not correspond perfectly with the maturity of the risk to be hedged. Consequently, the hedge might not eliminate all risk. This is because, although the futures price and spot (cash) price will converge at maturity, before maturity they can and do differ significantly.[3] Thus, the choice of a maturity date will affect the effectiveness of the hedge.

Determining the Basis

The evolution of the basis is crucial for the effectiveness of the hedge. Consequently, it is important to understand what determines the basis. The basis in currency futures is straightforward. Based on the principle of efficient markets and no arbitrage (see chapter 1), it generally depends on the difference between the interest rates on the domestic and foreign currencies. To see this, we start with the following notation and show the relationship between futures and spot prices:

T = Delivery date of the futures contract (years)

t = Current date (years)

$\tau = T - t$

$F_{t,T}$ = Price of a futures contract at time t for delivery at time T

S_t = Spot exchange rate at time t = amount of domestic currency for one unit of foreign currency

r = riskless rate of interest

r^* = the riskless rate on foreign currency.

The no-arbitrage (interest rate parity) relationship between F and S is:

$$F_{t,T} = S_t e^{(r-r^*)\tau}. \tag{2.2}$$

To see this, set up a portfolio by (1) selling a futures contract (cash flow = 0), (2) borrowing $F_{t,T}e^{-r\tau}$ (cash flow = $+ F_{t,T}e^{-r\tau}$), (3) buying $S_t e^{-r^*\tau}$ (cash flow = $-S_t e^{-r^*\tau}$) and lending. At maturity we will have:

$+S_T$,

$-F_{t,T}$ from paying off the loan, and

$+F_{t,T} - S_T$ from the futures contract.

This is equal to zero. The value of a portfolio with a certain zero outcome is equal to zero. Thus, $Fe^{-r\tau} - Se^{-r^*\tau} = 0$. Rearranging gives equation 2.2. Subtracting S_t from both sides of equation 2.2 gives:

$$Basis = S_t(e^{(r-r^*)\tau} - 1). \tag{2.3}$$

It is clear from equation 2.3 that, other things being equal, the interest rate differential determines the basis.

HEDGING CURRENCY RISK WITH FUTURES CONTRACTS

Hedging with futures is similar to hedging with forwards. To cover a short position, a futures contract can be bought. To cover a long position, a futures contract can be sold. Because the contracts are standardized and guaranteed by the clearinghouse, they are liquid and represent no counterparty risk. Hence, futures are generally cheaper than forwards and positions can be closed out or rolled over more easily and cheaply than they can with forwards. A short position in futures can be closed out by a purchase of the same contract. It can be rolled over by a simultaneous purchase of the same contract and the sale of a similar contract with a later maturity date. A long position in futures can be closed out by a sale of the same contract. It can be rolled over by a simultaneous sale of the same contract and purchase of a similar contract with a later maturity date.

The facility of opening and closing out positions makes it possible to manage relatively small levels of exposure on a continuous basis. This is especially attractive to commercial customers who have a fairly regular stream of payments and receipts. Furthermore, arbitrage ensures that pricing advantages between futures and forward markets should also be negligible. It is true, though, that because of marking to market, forward and futures prices can theoretically differ with the difference between the futures price minus the forward price depending on the correlation of the riskless interest rate with the futures price.[4] If the futures price falls when the riskless interest rate rises, and vice versa, the correlation is negative and the futures price will be below the forward price. If the futures price rises when the riskless interest rate rises, and vice versa, the correlation is positive and the futures price will be higher than the forward price. The reason is straightforward. Marking to market generates interim cash flows. A negative correlation between the futures price and the riskless rate means that for the buyer of a futures contract, on the average, financing costs of interim outflows when interest rates rise and futures prices fall will be higher than interest gains on interim inflows when interest rates fall and futures prices rise. For example, financing a $1,000 loss on a futures contract when the interest rate goes from 4 percent to 5 percent costs the annual equivalent of $50. A $1,000 gain on a futures contract when the interest rate goes from 5 percent to 4 percent only brings in an annual equivalent of $40. The expected return on the interim cash flows is negative. Consequently, to compensate for the expected losses on the interim cash flows, the buyer's price is lower than it would be for a forward contract that has no interim cash flows. For the seller of the futures contract, losses and gains are reversed and the seller is willing to accept a lower price than he would for a forward contract. If the correlation between the futures price and the riskless interest rate is positive, financing costs and gains are reversed and marking to market is an advantage for the buyer and a disadvantage to the seller, thereby causing the price of the futures contract to rise above that of the forward contract. In the case where the correlation is zero, futures and forward prices are the same. All this having been said, comparisons of futures and forward prices in the foreign exchange market have consistently revealed the absence of a significant difference between the two.[5] Consequently, for all practical purposes, the prices of futures contracts can be determined as if they were forward contracts.

Although futures contracts exhibit definite advantages with respect to forwards in transaction costs and ease of use because of standardization and liquidity, they also have some definite disadvantages.

- Futures contracts are only available for short maturities. The maximum maturity is one year and markets are usually thin for maturities exceeding six months. Hence, for long-term hedging, the futures markets are not a viable alternative to the forward and swap markets.
- The fixed contract size makes it difficult to make an exact match with the position to be hedged. As we mentioned, however, the size of the contracts is small enough that most users' needs can be approximated quite well.
- The infrequent maturity dates make it unlikely that the futures contract will correspond perfectly with the maturity of the cash flow to be hedged. In this case, hedging with futures requires setting up what is called a *minimum variance delta hedge*.
- The liquidity requirement on futures contracts limits them to a few, high turnover underlying assets. However, since many of the untraded, lower turnover assets are highly correlated with one of the high turnover assets that are traded, a traded asset can be used as a proxy to hedge a cash flow in an untraded asset. Using a futures contract in one asset to hedge a cash flow in another asset requires setting up what is called a *minimum variance cross hedge*.

The Minimum Variance Delta Hedge

As we saw in equation 2.3, it is the interest rate differential that determines the basis in currency markets.[6] Because the infrequent maturity dates on futures contracts make it unlikely that the maturity of the futures contract will correspond perfectly with the maturity of the cash flow to be hedged, basis risk must be taken into consideration when setting up a hedging strategy. To see how this can be done, consider the situation of a dollar-based agent expecting an inflow of £C at time 1. His hedge involves selling N futures contracts of size £Q that mature at time 2. Ignoring the interest rate risk associated with marking to market, at time 1 when the £C arrive, the agent will receive the dollar equivalent of £C converted at the spot exchange rate less N times the difference between the futures price at time 1 and the futures price contracted at time 0 multiplied by £Q, the size of the contract. The problem is to determine the optimum number of futures contracts to be sold. To answer this question, let:

S_1 = the spot exchange rate at time 1 (the number of dollars to purchase £1)

$F_{0,2}$ = the futures price of £1 at time 0 for delivery at time 2

$F_{1,2}$ = the futures price of £1 at time 1 for delivery at time 2.

Converting the pound into dollars at the maturity date's spot exchange rate gives:

$S_1 \times C$ dollars.

The difference between the futures prices gives:

$-N(F_{1,2} - F_{0,2}) \times Q$ dollars.

Thus the dollar value of the portfolio will be:

$$S_1 C - N(F_{1,2} - F_{0,2})Q. \tag{2.4}$$

Divide by C and define the hedge ratio as $\beta = NQ/C$ and equation 2.4 can be written as:

$$S_1 - \beta (F_{1,2} - F_{0,2}). \tag{2.5}$$

The idea is to choose β so that the variance of equation 2.5 is minimized. Since $F_{0,2}$ is known, the variance of equation 2.5 is:

$$\text{var}(S_1) - 2\beta\text{cov}(S_1, F_{1,2}) + \beta^2 \text{var}(F_{1,2}). \tag{2.6}$$

Taking the derivative of equation 2.6 with respect to β and setting it equal to zero gives:

$$-2\text{cov}(S_1, F_{1,2}) + 2\beta\text{var}(F_{1,2}) = 0,$$

which implies that

$$\beta = \frac{\text{cov} (S_1, F_{1,2})}{\text{var} (F_{1,2})}. \tag{2.7}$$

Thus, the optimal number of contracts is equal to

$$N = \beta \frac{C}{Q}. \tag{2.8}$$

EXAMPLE: THE MINIMUM VARIANCE DELTA HEDGE

Start with the following information:

$C = £3,125,000$ to be received in 1 month
$Q = £62,500$
Maturity date of the futures contract = 2 months.

We want to find N, the optimal number of futures contracts to be sold. The first step is to estimate β. Going back to equation 2.7, we can see that β is equal to the slope coefficient in the equation:

$$S_1 = \alpha + \beta F_{1,2} + \epsilon. \tag{2.9}$$

In theory, equation 2.9 should be estimated as a forecast. In practice, because the data necessary for making a reliable forecast is generally unavailable, equation 2.9 is usually estimated in a time series regression using historical data.[7] Using monthly historical data over a five-year period, we find $\beta = 0.895$. Hence, the number of contracts to be sold is:

$$N = 0.895 \frac{3,125,000}{62,500} = 44.75.$$

Rounded to the closest full contract, $N = 45$. If there were no basis risk, N would be equal to 50. Remember that basis risk is due to variations in the interest rate differential and that the effect of an interest rate differential increases with a contract's time to maturity. Thus, for currencies with historically large and volatile interest rate differentials, the optimal hedge N will be considerably different from the N for the perfect riskless hedge, and the difference will increase with the difference between the hedged cash-flow date and the date of the futures contract.

The Minimum Variance Cross Hedge

Since futures contracts are only available for a few high-turnover currencies, a cross hedge must be constructed to hedge cash flows in currencies with no futures contracts. The problem is similar to that of a maturity mismatch, except here the disparity arises because the spot price of the hedged currency and the futures price of the proxy currency are likely to differ at maturity. The problem is to minimize the difference between the two. The first and most obvious step is to choose a proxy currency with a close relationship to the currency to be hedged. The second step is to adjust the hedge for likely divergences.

To see how this can be done, consider the situation of a dollar-based agent expecting an inflow of C Danish krone (DKK) at time 1. Given the close relationship between the Danish and European economies, their exchange rates are highly correlated. In the absence of a futures contract on DKK, the futures contract on the euro will be his hedging vehicle. His hedge involves selling N futures contracts of size Q euros that mature at time 1, the same time as the krone inflow. Ignoring the interest rate risk associated with marking to market, at time 1 when the C krone arrive, the agent will receive the dollar equivalent of C krone converted at the spot exchange rate less N times the difference between the futures price of 1 euro on a contract maturing at time 1 and the futures price contracted at time 0 multiplied by Q euros, the size of the contract. The problem is to determine the optimum number of euro futures contracts to be sold. To answer this question start with the following notation:

S_1 (USD/DKK) = the spot exchange rate at time 1 (the number of dollars to purchase 1 DKK)

$F_{0,1}$ (USD/EUR) = the futures price of 1 EUR at time 0 for delivery at time 1

$F_{1,1}$ (USD/EUR) = the futures price of 1 EUR at time 1 delivery at time 1.

Converting the krone into dollars at the maturity date's spot exchange rate gives:

S_1(USD/DKK) $\times$ C dollars.

The difference between the futures prices gives:

$$-N[F_{1,1} \text{ (USD/EUR)} - F_{0,1} \text{ (USD/EUR)}] \times Q \text{ dollars.} \tag{2.10}$$

At maturity, the futures price converges to the spot price so that equation 2.10 becomes:

$$-N[S_1 \text{ (USD/EUR)} - F_{0,1} \text{ (USD/EUR)}] \times Q \text{ dollars.} \tag{2.11}$$

Thus, the dollar value of the portfolio will be:

$$S_1(\text{USD/DKK})C - N[S_1 \text{ (USD/EUR)} - F_{0,1}(\text{USD/EUR})]Q. \tag{2.12}$$

Divide by C and define the hedge ratio as $\beta = (NQ/C)$ and equation 2.12 can be written as:

$$S_1(\text{USD/DKK})C - \beta[S_1 \text{ (USD/EUR)} - F_{0,1}(\text{USD/EUR})]. \tag{2.13}$$

As with the delta hedge, the idea is to choose β so that the variance of equation 2.13 is minimized. Since $F_{0,1}$ is known, the variance of equation 2.13 is:

$$\text{var}(S_1(\text{USD/DKK})) - 2\beta \text{cov}(S_1 \text{ (USD/DKK)}), S_1(\text{USD/EUR}))$$
$$+ \beta^2 \text{var}(S_1(\text{USD/EUR})). \tag{2.14}$$

Taking the derivative with respect to β and setting it equal to zero gives:

$$\beta = \frac{\text{cov } [S_1(\text{USD}/\text{DKK}), S_1(\text{USD}/\text{EUR})]}{\text{var } (S_1(\text{USD}/\text{EUR}))}. \tag{2.15}$$

Thus, the optimal number of contracts is equal to:

$$N = \beta \frac{C}{Q}. \tag{2.16}$$

EXAMPLE: THE MINIMUM VARIANCE CROSS HEDGE

Start with the following information:

C = DKK 18,750,000 to be received in 1 month
Q = EUR 125,000.

We want to find N, the optimal number of futures contracts to be sold. As before, we start by estimating β, which, from equation 2.15, we can see is equal to the slope coefficient in the equation:

$$S_1(\text{USD}/\text{DKK}) = \alpha + \beta S_1(\text{USD}/\text{EUR}) + \epsilon. \tag{2.17}$$

Suppose that a time series regression using monthly data $\beta = 1.10$. The number of contracts to be sold is:

$$N = 1.10 \frac{18,750,000}{125,000} = 165.$$

In the absence of basis risk, $\beta = 1$ and the optimum hedge would be $N = 150$.

The Minimum Variance Delta Cross Hedge

Having solved the problems of the maturity and currency mismatches, it is easy to solve the problem when both mismatches occur simultaneously. If, for example, the date of the krone cash flow did not correspond to the maturity date of the futures contract in the foregoing example, the euro futures contract with the closest maturity date would be chosen as the hedging vehicle. We would proceed as before by minimizing the variance of the krone cash flow. In this case, β would depend on the covariance of the spot USD/DKK with the euro futures contract used for the hedge. For example, for a krone cash flow in period 1 hedged with a euro futures contract maturing at period two, β would be estimated as:

$$\beta = \frac{\text{cov}[S_1(\text{USD}/\text{DKK}), F_{1,2}(\text{USD}/\text{EUR})]}{\text{var }(F_{1,2}(\text{USD}/\text{EUR}))}.$$

Other Hedging Strategies

In the foregoing examples, the hedge ratio $\beta = NQ/C$ is found by minimizing the variance of the portfolio. This methodology is consistent with modern portfolio theory that seeks to maximize expected utility. Other objectives, however, are also possible.

The traditional strategy is to choose the hedge ratio equal to 1 so that the principal value of the futures contract is equal to the principal value of the spot position. Another popular strategy is to build a futures position so that its dollar market value is equal to the market value of the position in the underlying asset. In this strategy, the hedge ratio differs from 1 if the futures price is different from the spot price. In the chapters focusing on hedging the risks associated with specific assets we will come back to this issue.

MORE ON HEDGING WITH FUTURES AND FORWARDS

The principles of hedging with forwards and futures are the same. A long position in foreign currency is hedged by selling the currency for delivery at a future date. A short position is hedged by purchasing the foreign currency for delivery at a future date. The differences in the technical aspects of actually undertaking a hedging operation arise from the organization of the two markets.

Futures trading is centralized in a physical or virtual location, contracts are standardized in a limited number of currencies and maturities, and the clearinghouse is the unique counterparty, whereas forward contracts are made to order for virtually any currency and maturity in a diverse, over-the-counter market with many different counterparties. Futures contracts are relatively small (in thousands of units) and are marked to market each day. Trading costs are paid as commissions to the broker. Forward contracts are relatively large (in millions of units) and are settled in toto on the delivery date. Trading costs are paid in the form of a bid-ask spread.

Thus, futures contracts are generally cheaper and easier to use than forwards because of standardization and liquidity. However, these same features are the source of several disadvantages. Futures contracts are only available for short maturities of up to one year maximum, usually with thin trading in contracts above six months. Hence, for long-term hedging the futures markets are not a viable alternative to the forward and swap markets. Furthermore, standardization of futures contracts in a limited number of currencies makes it difficult to make an exact match with the position to be hedged, thereby requiring the construction of the hedging strategies discussed above.

In the following paragraphs, we will look at currency hedging in more detail, including long-term hedging and the role of discounts and premiums. Given the more general nature of the forward markets, we will use them in our examples while keeping in mind that the underlying principles apply to the futures markets as well.

Hedging a Long Position

Consider a French exporter with a long position of $1 million to be received in three months time, and examine the following information:

exchange rate in Paris = S_0(EUR/USD)bid = 1.1000
The Three-month forward rate = $F_{0,1/4}$(EUR/USD)bid = 1.1000.[8]

The French exporter can cover his long position by selling dollars forward at the three-month bid rate and receive EUR 1.10 × 1,000,000 = EUR 1,100,000.

Eliminating foreign exchange risk has disadvantages as well as advantages. The advantage is that if the value of the dollar falls, the company has no loss of income, which is guaranteed at 1.1 million euros. The disadvantage is that if the value of the dollar goes up, the company will not benefit from the appreciation. Furthermore, hedging the foreign exchange risk exposes the company to another kind of risk. If the exporter is not paid on time or if some of his merchandise is refused, he will not have enough dollars to honor his forward contract. In order to make up the difference he will either have to roll over the forward contract at a new rate or buy dollars at the going spot rate. Either rate might be different from the 1.1000 exchange rate of the forward contract. If the rollover rate is lower or the spot-ask rate is higher, the company will make an unanticipated loss. Hedging in the forward market is a two edged sword.

Hedging a Short Position

Hedging a short position involves buying foreign exchange forward. Consider a French importer with a short position of $1 million due in three-months time. The corresponding spot and forward rates in Paris are:

S_0(EUR/USD)ask = 1.1010
$F_{0,1/4}$(EUR/USD)ask = 1.1010.

The French exporter can cover his short position by purchasing dollars forward at the three-month ask rate and paying EUR 1.1010 × 1,000,000 = EUR 1,101,000. In three months, the French company will deliver 1.101 million euros and receive $1 million, no matter what the exchange rate is.

Here again, eliminating foreign exchange risk has disadvantages as well as advantages. The advantage is that if the value of the dollar rises, the company has no increase in expenditure, which is guaranteed at 1.101 million euros. The disadvantage is that if the value of the dollar goes down, the company will not benefit from the depreciation. Furthermore, as we saw in the preceding example, hedging the foreign exchange risk exposes the company to another kind of risk. If the delivery dates for the imported merchandise are not respected or if some of the merchandise is not up to standards and must be refused, expenditure for the merchandise will be lower than expected, which will leave the company with dollar balances once the forward contract is consummated. When the dollar balances are converted back into euros, the spot exchange rate might be higher or lower than the 1.1010 exchange rate of the forward contract. If it is higher, the company will make an unanticipated gain. If it is lower, it will make an unanticipated loss. This kind of risk would not be present in the absence of the forward contract.

Forward Discounts and Premiums: Long Positions

In the foregoing examples, we have assumed that the forward rate is the same as the current spot rate. While this is possible, we know from chapter 1 and equations 2.2 and 2.3 that it is more likely that the forward rate will be higher or lower than the current spot rate due to the interest rate differential. The existence of a forward premium or discount affects the economics of a hedging transaction.

Consider an American exporter with a long position in Swiss francs due in six months. The relevant currency rates in New York are:

$$S_0(\text{USD/CHF})\text{bid} = 0.6100$$
$$F_{0,1/2}(\text{USD/CHF})\text{bid} = 0.6000.$$

Because Swiss interest rates are higher than U.S. interest rates, there is a discount of 3.28 percent on the six-month forward franc. This means that if the American company hedges its position by selling its franc income forward, its dollar income will be 1.64 percent lower than it would be at the current spot rate (Premiums and discounts are quoted in yearly percentages; the yearly discount is 3.28 percent or 1.64 percent for six months). If the American company intends to hedge, the loss of income should be taken into consideration when establishing its price in francs.

The situation is different when the foreign currency to be received is at a premium. Consider a Mexican exporter with a long position in USD due in three months. The relevant information in Mexico City is:

$$S_0(\text{MXN/USD})\text{bid} = 9.3075$$
$$F_{0,1/2}(\text{MXN/USD})\text{bid} = 9.4266.$$

Because interest rates are higher on the peso than on the dollar, there is a premium of 5.12 percent (1.28 percent for three months) on the three-month dollar. The hedge can be effected by selling dollars forward at the bid rate. The gain resulting from the premium on the dollar should be considered when pricing the merchandise because this is the effective peso income generated by the transaction.

Forward Discounts and Premiums: Short Positions

Forward discounts and premiums also influence the economics of short positions. In the case of short positions, a discount is favorable to the hedger because it enables him to obtain foreign exchange at a rate lower than the current spot rate. On the other hand, a premium is unfavorable because it makes forward foreign currency more costly.

Take, for example, the case of a Korean importer of petroleum products who must pay 10 million dollars in three months. He is faced with the following situation:

S_0(KPW/USD)ask = 1313
$F_{0,1/4}$(KPW/USD)ask = 1329.

The dollar is at a premium. At the current spot exchange rate, the importer's cost in won would be 13.13 billion won. At the forward exchange rate, it would be 13.29 billion won, considerably higher than the 13.13 billion at the current spot rate. Buying forward effectively eliminates the exchange risk but at a price higher than the current exchange rate. Thus, if the Korean importer hedges, the price he charges his customers should be calculated on the forward rate and not the current spot rate. If he does not hedge he, of course, would not know what his cost is until he actually pays for the merchandise.

Hedging Positions Longer than One Year

Hedging positions longer than one year can be derived directly from equation 2.2, reproduced here:

$$F_{t,T} = S_t e^{(r-r^*)\tau},$$ (2.2)

where r and r^* represent the continuous time interest rates on zero coupon domestic and foreign loans, respectively.

EXAMPLE:

Consider a bank contemplating a two-year forward contract to buy Swiss francs. The relevant information is given as follows:[9]

τ = Two years
The spot USD/CHF exchange rate S_0(USD/CHF) = 0.6005 − 0.6015
r = Continuous time interest rate on two-year zero coupon dollar loans = $4^1/_2 − 4^3/_4$
r^* = Continuous time interest rate on two-year zero coupon franc loans = $9^3/_4 − 10$.

According to equation 2.2, the bank could hedge a two-year forward contract to buy francs by borrowing francs for two years, selling the francs spot for dollars and lending the dollars for two years. The forward rate that the bank would have to charge its customer would be somewhere below:

$$F_{0,2}(\text{USD}/\text{CHF})_{bid} = 0.6005e^{(0.045-0.10)^2} = 0.5379.$$

In practice there are not many zero coupon loans available. Consequently, an exact hedge calculation must take into consideration the cash flows resulting from interest payments at the end of the year.

Rolling Over and Closing Out Forward Contracts

As we mentioned above, expected inflows or outflows of foreign currency are not always realized. When this happens, it is often useful to change the hedge. When a futures contract is used as the hedging instrument, the operation is straightforward and involves closing out the old position on the market and taking up a new one. Although more costly, the same result can be achieved on the forward market by either rolling the forward contract over or making a partial settlement and rolling over the difference. The procedure is straightforward and is equivalent to closing out the old forward contract and making a new one.

EXAMPLE:

Take the case of an Israeli company that bought $1 million, three-months forward at the end of June at 5.0860 shekels (ILS) for one USD. At the end of September, the merchandise that it ordered still has not been shipped, so the treasurer calls his bank and asks to roll the forward contract over for two months. On the day he calls, the spot ask rate is 5.1500 and the two-month forward premium on the dollar is 765 (see chapter 1 for foreign exchange quotations). The new forward rate is thus 5.1500 + 0.0765 = 5.2265. However, the company has made a profit on the difference between the current spot rate and the old forward rate equal to:

5.1500 − 5.0860 = 0.064.

The effective rate that the company will pay for the dollars after the forward contract is rolled over is equal to the new forward rate less the profit on the old forward contract:

5.2265 − 0.064 = 5.1625.

It is higher than the 5.0860 that it would have paid had the merchandise been shipped on time but it is lower than the 5.2265 that it would have had to pay if there had been no forward cover at all.

A company can also terminate a forward contract before maturity. Suppose that for some reason foreign currency that was expected in three months is actually paid at the end of two months. The company can terminate the forward contract by buying foreign currency one month forward to offset the ongoing forward three-month contract. It then sells the currency it has received on the spot market.

EXAMPLE:

Consider the following information.

- An ongoing forward contract that matures in one month to sell 1 million dollars at 5.0100 shekels per dollar
- Spot exchange rate = 4.9950 − 5.0050
- One month forward rate = 5.0100 − 5.0231

The company can terminate the ongoing forward contract by buying $1 million, one month forward at the ask rate of 5.0231. It loses the difference between what it receives for the dollars it sells in the ongoing contract and what it pays for the dollars in the new one-month forward contract:

$$(5.0100 - 5.0231) \times \$1,000,000 = -13,100 \text{ shekels.}$$

It then sells its dollars at the spot bid rate and receives:

$$4.9950 \times \$1,000,000 = 4,995,000 \text{ shekels.}$$

Thus, ignoring discounting on the 13,100 shekels it loses on the difference between the two forward contracts, it nets only 4,981,900 or 4.9819 shekels per dollar. Part of the difference is that the dollar is selling at a premium and part is due to the bid-ask spreads on the supplementary forward and spot transactions. If the dollar were at a discount, there would be a gain if the ongoing forward contract were terminated prematurely. However, part of the gain on the offsetting forward transaction would be neutralized by the cost implicit in the bid-ask spreads.

CURRENCY SWAPS

A swap is an agreement between two institutions to exchange cash flows in the future. The agreement specifies the dates when the cash flows are to be paid and the way that they are to be calculated. A currency swap involves the exchange of a loan in one currency for a loan in another currency where both principal and interest payments are exchanged. Thus, a forward contract is a simple example of a currency swap. The exchange of the notional amount takes place at the beginning and at the termination of a currency swap. When the notional amount is exchanged at the beginning and at the end, neither party is exposed to foreign exchange risk, which make them useful instruments for hedging currency risk associated with long-term assets and liabilities.

The interest rates on the loans in the currency swap can both be fixed. In this case we speak of a *fixed-to-fixed* currency swap. If both are variable we speak of a *floating-to-floating* currency swap. If one is fixed and the other is floating, we speak of a *fixed-to-floating* currency swap.

Currency swaps are larger are often backed by a Eurobond issue, which traditionally varies between amounts of $100 million and $1 billion or more. They also usually pass through the U.S. dollar no matter what currencies are involved. For example, a fixed-to-fixed currency swap of euros for yen would be constructed of a swap of fixed euros for dollar LIBOR and dollar LIBOR for fixed yen. Any fixed rate currency swap against floating U.S. dollar LIBOR payments is called a *circus swap*. In other words, currency swaps are composed of two circus swaps. The reason for this is that dollar LIBOR serves as a common denominator between fixed euros and fixed yen. It is extremely doubtful that counterparties in euros and yen could be found with exactly the same maturities and amounts. However, since virtually all banks and most multinationals that participate in the swap market have access to interbank LIBOR funds, it is highly probable that one party could be found for the swap of euros for LIBOR and another party for the swap of LIBOR for yen.

HISTORICAL BACKGROUND

The precursor to today's currency swap was the *parallel loan* developed in the United Kingdom in the 1970s as a means of avoiding the premium on investments outside the United Kingdom. At the time, exchange controls required that all purchases of foreign currency for the purpose of foreign investment be made at a premium over the spot rate. To circumvent this regulation, the U.K. company would make a sterling loan to the U.K. subsidiary of a foreign-based company. In return, the foreign company would lend the equivalent amount in another currency to the foreign subsidiary of the U.K. company. These parallel loans had three disadvantages.

1. It was difficult to find a partner to do the deal with.
2. The credit risk was with the subsidiary and not the mother company.
3. Both groups' outstanding liabilities were increased.

The first currency swap in 1976 organized by two U.S. banks, Continental Illinois and Goldman Sachs, was between the Dutch firm Bos Kallis and the British firm ICI Finance. Since then, the market has grown by leaps and bounds, fueled by the banks' inventiveness and the development of the bond market. Currency swaps, for example, grew from almost nothing at the end of the 1970s to over $500 billion of total notional principal value outstanding at the end of 1990. Since then the growth has been nothing short of phenomenal. The International Swaps and Derivatives Association (ISDA) reports that measured in notional principal outstanding amounts, market growth in interest rate swaps, currency swaps and interest rate options, as reported by member organizations for the six months ending June 30, 2000, totaled $60.366 trillion, compared with $58.265 trillion at the end of 1999.[10]

Technical Background

On the bond market, fixed interest payments are made either annually or every six months. Sterling, U.S. dollar, and yen fixed interest payments are made every six months, for example. Several important dates figure in the swap agreement. First of all, there is the *trade date* that corresponds to the date when the parties make the swap deal. Secondly, there is the *effective date* that corresponds to the precise moment that interest starts to be calculated. It normally begins two working days after the trade date but can be chosen in any way agreeable to the two parties. It can even be applied retroactively. The *termination date* specifies the date that the swap agreement ends.

When payment dates fall on nonworking days, one of three conventions is usually adopted:

- Following day: interest is paid on the first working day following the payment date.
- Preceding day: interest is paid on the last working day preceding the payment date.
- Modified following business day: interest is paid according to the following day format if it falls in the same month as the payment date, otherwise, interest is paid according to the preceding day format.

The amount of interest to be paid by each party is calculated according to the following formula:

Interest payment = (notional amount) × (interest rate) × (day count fraction).

There are several ways to calculate the day count fraction:

- the actual number of days from the beginning of the calculation period to the end divided by 360 (Actual/360); the actual number of days in a year is usually 365 except in leap year when it is 366;
- the actual number of days from the beginning of the calculation period to the end divided by 365 (Actual/365);
- the actual number of days from the beginning of the calculation period to the end divided by the actual number of days in the year (Actual/Actual);
- the number of 30-day months from the beginning of the calculation period to the end divided by 360 ($30n/360$).

Thus, a calculation period that begins on January 10 and ends on April 15 of a leap year will have the following day count fractions according to the different bases:

- Actual/360 = 96/360
- Actual/365 = 96/365
- Actual/Actual = 96/366
- $30n/360$ = 95/360.

Hedging with Currency Swaps

Although using swaps as vehicles for hedging and funding primary operations is a relatively new phenomenon, foreign exchange traders have been employing the principle for years. Remember from chapter 1 that when a foreign exchange dealer receives an order to sell foreign exchange forward, he covers himself by borrowing in domestic currency, purchasing foreign currency spot, and lending the foreign currency. In this operation, he effectively swaps a liability in foreign currency for a liability in domestic currency. The current swap market is an extension of the foreign exchange trader's basic technique to a wide range of financial instruments.

EXAMPLE:

In the case of a fixed rate currency swap, a company seeks to exchange a loan in one currency for a loan in another. Three stages are involved: First, the principal is exchanged at the spot rate. Second, on each coupon date, interest payments are exchanged. Third, at the swap's maturity, the principal is re-exchanged, usually at the original exchange rate.

Suppose, for example, that a German company wants to invest in Mexico. If it finances its investment by borrowing euros, it will be exposed to exchange risk. The problem is that it is not known by Mexican banks and cannot borrow pesos directly on favorable terms. It decides to borrow

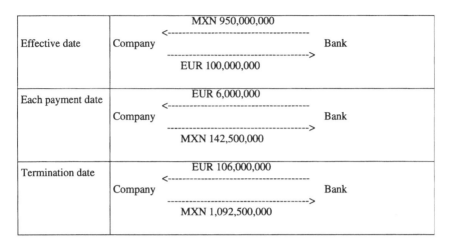

Figure 2.1   Cash flows from the currency swap

100,000,000 euros at 6 percent for five years with the principal to be repaid at maturity. To eliminate the foreign exchange risk, it wants to exchange its euro debt for peso debt and use the peso cash flows generated by the investment to service the peso debt. It goes to its bank and arranges a swap with the following terms:

- 6 percent on the euro loan
- 15 percent on the peso loan
- Spot exchange rate: 9.5 MXN = 1 EUR.

The outcome of the operation is summarized in Figure 2.1. On day 1 the company gives the bank 100,000,000 euros and receives 950,000,000 pesos. Each year on the coupon date, the bank gives the company 6,000,000 euros and receives 142,500,000 pesos from the company. On the termination date the bank gives the company 100,000,000 euros plus the last interest payment and the company gives the bank 950,000,000 pesos plus the last interest payment.

The swap gave the company access to credit in pesos on favorable terms. By exchanging its loan in euros, it was able to use 950,000,000 pesos for five years. There was no exchange risk on the principal because it was exchanged at the same, fixed rate. There was no exchange risk on the interest payments because the 6,000,000 euros paid by the bank covered the 6,000,000 euros that the company was obliged to pay on its loan. A currency swap, then, is like a series of forward foreign exchange contracts. The forward rate for each year that only involves interest payments is the ratio of the two cash flows:

MXN 142,500,000/EUR 6,000,000 = 23.75.

On the last year of the swap, both interest and principle are exchanged. The cash flow in pesos is:

950,000,000 + 142,500,000 = MXN 1,092,500,000.

The cash flow in euros is:

100,000,000 + 6,000,000 = EUR 106,000,000.

The forward rate for the termination date is the ratio of these two cash flows:

MXN 1,092,500,000/EUR 106,000,000 = 10.3066.

Pricing Currency Swaps

In a currency swap, each leg of the initial swap is denominated in a different currency. Finding the value of a currency swap requires estimating the present values of each leg based on the interest rate structure in each currency. The repayment of the swap amount at maturity creates no complication. It is treated as just another cash flow. Once the present values of both legs have been found, one of the two present values is converted into the other currency at the prevailing spot exchange rate. The value of the swap is the difference between this converted value and the present value of the other leg.

EXAMPLE:

Going back to the example above, suppose that at the end of the first year, the German company wants to undo the swap. The problem for the bank is to price the swap undertaken one year ago. The exchange rate is MXN 10 = EUR 1. Table 2.3 gives the market information on interest rates in both countries. We need to know the actuarial interest rates reflected in the rates given in Table 2.3.

Step 1: Calculate the interest rates based on a 365-day year. For example, the one-year euro rate can be adjusted to 365 days as follows:

$$7.00 \times \frac{365}{360} = 7.0972\%.$$

This rate is the annual rate proportional to a one-year loan based on a 365-day year. There is no adjustment for the peso rates because they are quoted on an actual/actual basis.

Table 2.3
Market Information

Maturity	Euro Yield to maturity% Actual/360	Peso Yield to maturity% Actual/Actual
1 year	7.00	15.00
2 years	7.20	15.00
3 years	7.30	15.00
4 years	7.40	15.00

Step 1: Applying all the euro interest rates gives the effective yields to maturity presented in Table 2.4.

Step 2: Calculate the term structure of interest rates (correct valuation of future cash flows involves discounting them at the spot interest rate on a zero coupon basis).

Step 3: Convert the interest rates from a coupon basis to a zero coupon basis. A simple method can be applied. Assume that each interest rate is associated with a straight bullet bond issued at par and trading at par. Then, line up the cash flows for the one-year bond and solve for r_1, the yield on a bond with only one cash flow. The cash flow is equal to the interest payment of 7.0972 plus the principal payment of 100:

$$100 = \frac{7.0972 + 100}{1 + r_1}$$

$$r_1 = 0.070972.$$

For the two-year interest rate, the cash flows are the interest payment of 7.30 the first year, and the interest payment of 7.30 the second year plus the principal repayment. Since the zero coupon interest rate for one year is known, only r_2 is unknown. We solve for r_2:

$$100 = \frac{7.30}{1.070972} + \frac{7.30 + 100}{(1 + r_2)^2}$$

$$r_2 = 0.073074.$$

For the three-year bond we do the same thing. The interest payments are 7.4014 for each year plus the principal repayment at the end of the third year. With r_1 and r_2 known we solve for r_3:

$$100 = \frac{7.4014}{1.070972} + \frac{7.4014}{(1.073074)^2} + \frac{7.4014 + 100}{(1 + r_3)^3}$$

$$r_3 = 0.074141.$$

Table 2.4
Adjusted Euro Rates *Yield to Maturity*

Maturity	Yield %
1 Y	7.0972
2 Y	7.3000
3 Y	7.4014
4 Y	7.5028

Table 2.5
Spot Interest Rates on a Zero Coupon Basis

Maturity	Zero coupon rate %
1 Y	7.0972
2 Y	7.3074
3 Y	7.4141
4 Y	7.5245

The same process applied to calculate r_4 gives 0.075245. The set of zero coupon interest rates is given in Table 2.5.

The value of the swap can be found by discounting the cash flows (CF) of the two bonds at the appropriate zero coupon spot rate, translate the peso leg into euros and subtract one from the other. Because of the flat term structure and the fact that the yields are given in actual/actual, there are no calculations required to calculate the zero coupon interest rates in pesos. They are all equal to 15 percent. Thus, the value of the Mexican bond is given as:

$$\text{Value of the peso leg} = \sum_{t=1}^{4} CF_t (1+r_t)^{-t} = \text{MXN } 950,000,000.$$

Value of the peso leg in euros = 95,000,000/10 = EUR 95,000,000.

The value of the euro leg is calculated as:

$$\frac{6m}{1.070972} + \frac{6m}{(1.073074)^2} + \frac{6m}{(1.074141)^3} + \frac{106m}{(1.075245)^4} = \text{EUR } 94,954,936.$$

The value of the swap is EUR 95,000,000 − EUR 94,954,936 = EUR 45,064. Thus, since the company is paying in pesos, it will have to pay the bank 45,064 euros to undo the swap.

Currency Swap Default Risk

The value of the euro leg of the foregoing fell from EUR $100m$ to EUR $94.955m$ because of changes in the term structure of interest rates. Besides risk arising from fluctuations in the interest rate, currency swaps are exposed to risk resulting from variations in the exchange rate as well. In the example above, the peso leg of the swap fell from EUR $100m$ to EUR $95m$ because the exchange rate went from 9.50 to 10. The magnitude of the exposure depends on the type of instruments that are swapped. Fixed to fixed swaps are exposed to interest rate changes in both currencies as well as to changes in the exchange rate. Fixed to floating currency swaps are exposed to interest rate changes in the fixed rate currency and to changes in the exchange rate. There is little or no exposure to changes in the floating rate. Floating to floating currency swaps are exposed only in terms of changes in the exchange rate. Fixed to fixed currency swaps, then, generate maximum exposure.

This brings up the problem of default risk. Consider a fixed to fixed currency swap on a notional amount of 50 million dollars where the bank pays fixed dollar amount of 10 percent to A and receives fixed Swiss francs of 5 percent from A. From B the bank receives fixed dollars at 10 percent and pays fixed francs at 5 percent. If A defaults, the bank will have to borrow 50 million dollars at the prevailing interest rate, buy francs at the current spot rate, and invest the proceeds in fixed francs for the remaining life of the swap. If the prevailing dollar interest rate is lower than the contract dollar rate of 10 percent, the bank gains. In the opposite case, the bank loses. If the dollar has appreciated since the contract's effective date, the bank will gain. If it has depreciated, the bank will lose. If the prevailing franc interest rate is higher than the contract rate of 5 percent, the bank gains. If it is lower, the bank loses. If B defaults, the bank will borrow francs, buy dollars spot with the proceeds, and lend dollars for the remaining life of the swap. The bank gains if the franc rate is lower than 5 percent and loses if it is higher. The bank gains if the dollar has depreciated and loses if it has appreciated. The bank gains if the dollar rate is higher than 10 percent and loses if it is lower.

The magnitude of gain or loss thus depends on which party defaults, when the default occurs, the levels of dollar and franc interest rates, and the prevailing exchange rate.

NOTES

1. Impregnable might be a slight exaggeration. In the late 1980s, the French MATIF went bankrupt and had to be bailed out by the government.

2. The alternative definition is Basis = $S_t - F_{t,T}$. We use the definition in equation 2.1.

3. Samuelson (1968) showed that futures prices will become more volatile as they approach maturity. Rutledge found empirical support for this law. Other studies supporting Samuelson's Law are Anderson (1985) and Milonas (1986). This means that the volatility of the basis for a particular contract may tend to increase as the contract approaches maturity.

4. See Cox, Ingersoll, Jr., and Ross (1981).

5. See Cornell and Reinganum (1981); Park and Chen (1985); Chang and Chang (1990).

6. In this section, we follow Clark, Marois, and Cernès (2001, pp. 256–261).

7. For technical reasons due to problems of stationarity, it might be necessary to estimate β-based on changes in the spot and futures rates rather than on the actual rates themselves. Stationarity and related topics such as co-integration are routinely explained in standard econometrics texts. See, for example, Gujarati (1995, pp. 709–733).

8. From equations 2.2 and 2.3, this means that the interest rates on both currencies are equal and the basis is equal to 0.

9. As convention has it, the first rate is the bid rate and the second is the ask rate.

10. www.isda.org (August 8, 2001).

REFERENCES

Anderson, R. (1985). "Some Determinants of the Volatility of Futures Prices," *Journal of Futures Markets,* 5 (Fall), 331–348.

Chang, C. W., and J. S. K. Chang. (1990). "Forward and Futures Prices: Evidence from the Foreign Exchange Markets," *Journal of Finance,* 45, 297–306.

Clark, E., B. Marois, and J. Cernès. (2001). *Le Management des Risques Internationaux.* Paris: Economica.

Cornell, B., and M. Reinganum. (1981). "Forward and Futures Prices: Evidence from the Foreign Exchange Markets," *Journal of Finance,* 36, 1035–1045.

Cox, J., J. Ingersoll, Jr., and S. Ross. (1981). "The Relation between Forward Prices and Futures Prices," *Journal of Financial Economics,* 9, 321–346.

Gujarati, D. N. (1995). *Basic Econometrics* (3rd ed.). New York: McGraw-Hill.

Milonas, N. (1986). "Price Variability and the Maturity Effect in Futures Markets," *Journal of Futures Markets,* 6 (Spring), 443–460.

Park, H. Y., and A. H. Chen. (1985). "Difference between Futures and Forward Prices: A Further Investigation of Marking to Market Effects," *Journal of Futures Markets,* 5, 77–88.

Rutledge, D. (1976). "A Note on the Variability of Futures Prices," *Review of Economics and Statistics,* 58, 118–120.

Samuelson, P. A. (1968). "Proof That Properly Anticipated Prices Fluctuate Randomly," *Industrial Management Review,* 6, 41–49.

Appendix 2.1

Interest Rate Swaps

The most common type of swap is the interest rate swap. It involves the exchange of fixed rate interest payments on a given principal amount for floating rate interest payments on the same principal amount for a given number of years. The notional amount itself is not exchanged and serves only to calculate the interest payments.

Interest rate swaps are quoted in relation to the fixed interest rate applicable to the *fixed leg* of the swap. The fixed leg refers to the series of fixed interest rate payments. The *variable leg* of the swap refers to the series of variable interest rate payments and is usually determined by six month LIBOR. For certain currencies, however, the reference for the variable leg will not be LIBOR. On the Canadian dollar, for example, they are given against bankers' acceptances because LIBOR on the Canadian dollar does not exist. When setting up the swap, traders express their position in relation to whether they pay or receive the fixed interest.

In a USD interest rate swap, for example, fixed rates are equal to the rates on the U.S. Treasury yield curve for the corresponding maturity plus a spread expressed in basis points as a bid/ask quote. Thus, if the yield on a 10-year treasury bond is 8 percent, the swap dealer's quote on a 10-year swap could be: UST + 75 – 78 bp. This means he is willing to write a 10-year swap where he pays a fixed rate of 75 basis points over the yield of a 10 year U.S. Treasury bond, in this case 8.75 percent, and receive six month LIBOR. Alternatively, he is willing to receive a fixed rate of 78 basis points over the yield on a U.S. Treasury bond, in this case 8.78 percent, and pay six month LIBOR. The convention of quoting the fixed leg as U.S. Treasury yield plus a spread gives stability to the quotes because the spreads change infrequently whereas the U.S. Treasury yield changes continuously over time as the market prices for bonds change.

The procedure for pricing interest rate swaps is the same as for pricing currency swaps. The value of each leg is estimated separately. The difference between the two gives the value of the swap.

Chapter 3

Currency Options

In chapters 1 and 2, we have noted what hedging is and how forward and futures contracts can be used to set up a fixed hedge. The advantage of a fixed hedge is that it enables the company treasurer to avoid a loss when the exchange rate moves against him. The disadvantage is that it also eliminates the possibility of making a gain if it moves in his favor. A fixed hedge strategy should be used when the treasurer assigns a strong probability to a move against him and a weak probability for a move in his favor. Another way to look at foreign exchange hedging, however, is to consider the case in which a treasurer feels that there is an equally strong chance for favorable and unfavorable moves. In this situation, a fixed hedge might not be the best solution because the advantage of avoiding the loss is offset by the disadvantage of missing out on the gain. The fixed hedge is still useful but its usefulness is considerably diminished. Another type of coverage in the form of a currency option might therefore be preferable. Currency options make it possible to take advantage of potential gains while limiting downside risk. Using currency options properly requires a clear understanding of what an option is and the elements that determine its price. This is the object of this chapter.

CURRENCY OPTIONS: FEATURES AND MARKETS

The Features of Currency Options

A currency option is a contract that gives its owner the right for a given period of time to buy or sell a given amount of one currency for another currency at a fixed price, called the *exercise price* or the *strike price*. If the right can be exercised at any time during the life of the option, it is called an *American option*. If the right can be exercised only at the option's expiration date, it is called a *European option*. The right to buy is called a *call*. The right to sell is called a *put*. The buyer of the option pays the seller, or the *writer*, a certain sum, called the *premium*, for the right to buy or sell at the prescribed price. The characteristic elements of an option contract can be summed up as follows:

- the nature of the transaction: call or put,
- the underlying currency,
- the quotation currency,
- the amount of the underlying currency,
- the strike price,
- the expiration date,
- the premium.

Consider a European call option on USD 1,000,000 for DKK with a maturity of three months and a strike price of 6.19. It gives the buyer the right to buy USD 1,000,000 for DKK at the rate of 6.19 krone per dollar in three months. The underlying currency is the U.S. dollar and the quotation currency is the Danish krone. If the premium is 2.83 percent, this means that the buyer has to pay the writer USD 28,300 ($1,000,000 × 2.83%) at the outset. The premium can also be expressed in DKK. In this case, the spot exchange rate is used to make the conversion. If, for example, the spot bid rate is 6.2000, the premium is DKK 175,460 ($28,300 × 6.2000).

A European put option on GBP 500,000, a strike price of USD 1.40, and a maturity of six months gives the buyer the right to sell GBP 500,000 at the rate of 1.40 dollars per pound in six months. If the premium is 1.32 percent, the buyer has to pay the writer GBP 6,600 (£500,000 × 1.32%) at the outset. The premium can also be expressed in dollars by using the spot exchange rate. If, for example, the spot bid rate is 1.45, the premium will be USD 9,570 (£6,600 × 1.45).

Option contracts are listed according to the underlying currency, the expiration date, and the strike price. The two types of option are *calls* and *puts*. All options of the same type in the same currencies constitute an *option class*. All options in the same class with the same expiration date and the same strike price constitute an *option series*.

Over-the-Counter Markets

In an over-the-counter (OTC) market, options are written and traded by financial institutions. This market has features similar to those of the forward foreign currency market described in chapter 1. Although maturities of three or six months are customary, like forward contracts, OTC options can be made to order with the expiration date, contract size, and strike price determined to suit the buyer's particular needs. However, where trading in forward contracts is very rare, OTC options are relatively liquid since the institutions that write these contracts quote regular bid-ask prices and stand ready to buy them back at any moment. This liquidity has a cost in that the bid-ask spreads are relatively high.

It is customary in the OTC market to write options with the strike price equal to the current spot exchange rate and to quote the premium to clients as a percentage of the underlying value. The norm for quoting strike prices is two decimal places. Among themselves, traders do not usually quote a price. Instead, they quote volatility from which the price can be inferred. Later in this chapter we will see why this is so.

Organized Exchanges

Organized options exchanges share many features of the futures markets described in the preceding chapter. Contracts are standardized. On the Philadelphia Stock Exchange, for example, all options are American style and expire on the third Wednesday of March, June, September, or December. Early exercise is possible until the last Saturday of the option's life. Each currency has a standard contract size: GBP 31,250, JPY 6,250,000, and so on, with strike prices conforming to prearranged formulas depending on the currency: multiples of 1 U.S. cent for the GBP, 2 U.S. cents for the EUR, and so on. Premiums are quoted in U.S. cents per unit of foreign currency. Table 3.1 gives an example of the information for options on the pound sterling traded on the Philadelphia Exchange as reported in the *Financial Times* on September 29, 2000.

Table 3.1
Currency Options on the Pound Sterling in Philadelphia

Pound sterling: £31.250; U. S. cents per pound

	Calls			Puts		
Strike Price	Oct. *Col. 2*	Nov. *Col. 3*	Dec. *Col. 4*	Oct. *Col. 5*	Nov. *Col. 6*	Dec. *Col. 7*
1.450	2.11	2.80	3.44	0.75	1.45	2.05
1.460	1.50	2.29	2.89	1.14	1.88	2.51
1.470	1.02	1.79	2.45	1.67	2.40	2.95

Previous day's volume: calls 0, puts 0
Previous day's open interest: calls 915, puts 258
Source: Financial Times, September 29, 2000

The first line of the table tells us that the options are on a contract of GBP 31,250. Line 2 shows that the table is divided into information on calls and puts. Column 1 gives the strike price. Columns 2, 3, and 4 give the prices for calls expiring in October, November, and December. Columns 5, 6, and 7 give the prices for puts expiring in October, November, and December. For example, the last traded price of a call with a strike price of USD 1.45 expiring in October was 2.11 U.S. cents. The last two lines give the trading volume and the open interest. Open interest means the number of options outstanding.

Organized options exchanges are organized around a *clearinghouse*, which records the transactions concluded by each one of its members. Each member is also required to keep records of its clients' accounts. Just as in the futures markets, the role of the clearinghouse is crucial. It guarantees the execution of all contracts negotiated on the exchange and effectively becomes the counterparty to both sides of the transaction. The role of the clearinghouse and contract standardization facilitate trading and make the market more liquid as the exchanges continually write new options as well as closing out ongoing positions. An investor who has written an option can close out his position by buying an equivalent option, whereas an investor who has bought an option can close out his position by selling an equivalent option. Since the contracts are standardized and the clearinghouse is the counterparty to both sides of the contract, all options in the same series are equivalent, no matter who the end buyers and sellers are.

Currency options are not limited to a spot exchange rate. They can also be written on a futures rate quoted on the futures markets. Some exchanges, such as the Chicago Mercantile Exchange (CME), offer options on futures contracts. In this case, the buyer of a call has the right to buy a given futures contract on the CME at a price equal to the option's strike price. The buyer of the put has the right to sell a given futures contract at a price equal to the option's strike price. In practice, these options are used in a manner similar to the options linked directly to the spot rate. Their usefulness lies in the fact that it is often cheaper and more convenient to deliver and take delivery of a futures contract than it is to deliver the foreign exchange itself. Thus, exercise of a futures option does not normally lead to delivery of the underlying currency because, as mentioned in chapter 2, most futures contracts are closed out before delivery. We will revisit this question later on.

Information on traded futures options is published daily in the financial press. Table 3.2 shows an example of the information on currency futures options from the *Wall Street Journal Europe* on October 6, 2000.

The information in Table 3.2 is similar to that of Table 3.1. The first line of the table tells us that the options are on a futures contract of GBP 62,500 quoted in U.S. cents per pound. Line 2 shows that the table is divided into

Table 3.2
Information on GBP Futures Options

British Pound (CME): 62,500 pounds; U.S. cents per pound						
	Calls-Settle			Puts-Settle		
Strike	Oct.	Nov.	Dec.	Oct.	Nov.	Dec.
Price	*Col. 2*	*Col. 3*	*Col. 4*	*Col. 5*	*Col. 6*	*Col. 7*
1.450	0.36	1.50	2.16	0.54	1.68	2.34
1.460	0.16	1.06	1.72	1.34	2.24	2.90
1.470	0.04	0.76	1.40	2.22	2.94	....
Est. vol. 1,182 Wed.: 242 calls, 126 puts						
Open int. Wed.: 12,091 calls, 10,108 puts						

Est. vol. 1,182 Wed.: 242 calls, 126 puts
Open int. Wed.: 12,091 calls, 10,108 puts
Source: Wall Street Journal Europe, Friday–Saturday, October 6 and 7, 2000

Table 3.3
Sample of the Currency Futures Options Traded on the CME

Futures Options	Size
Currencies	
Japan yen	JPY 12.5 million
Canadian dollar	CAD 100,000
British pound	GBP 62,500
Swiss franc	CHF 125,000
Mexican peso	MXN 500,000

information on calls and puts. Column 1 gives the strike price. Columns 2, 3, and 4 give the prices for calls expiring in October, November, and December. Columns 5, 6, and 7 show the prices for puts expiring in October, November, and December. For example, the last traded price of a put with a strike price of USD 1.460 expiring in December was 2.90 U.S. cents. The last two lines give the trading volume and the number of options outstanding. The estimated volume for Thursday was 1,182 contracts. The preceding days volume (Wednesday) was 242 calls and 126 puts. The preceding days open interest (Wednesday) was 12,091 calls and 10,108 puts.

Table 3.3 gives a sample of the currency futures options traded on the CME.

Currency Option Pricing

Options pricing theory is one of the most important contributions to the theory and practice of finance over the last 50 years. Much of the credit goes to F. Black, M. Scholes and R. Merton for the development of a workable option pricing formula (Black and Scholes, 1973). Garman and Kohlhagen (1983) extended the Black-Scholes option-pricing model to the domain of currency options. Before presenting the Garman and Kohlhagen option-pricing model, a model that can effectively be used in foreign exchange risk management, we will first present the economic logic behind the pricing of currency options.

The Elements of Currency Option Value

First of all, the value of a currency option depends on the underlying exchange rate, or, more precisely, on the level of the exchange rate and on the exchange rate's volatility. Second, it depends on the specific features of the contract itself with respect to the strike price and the expiration date. Third, it depends on the level of the short-term interest rates on the two currencies involved.

The Premium and the Spot Exchange Rate: European Options

The premium on a currency call option is higher when the exchange rate on the underlying currency is higher. This is easy to understand. If the spot exchange rate on the dollar is DKK 5.30, an investor will be willing to pay more for the right to buy the dollars at DKK 5.00 than if the spot rate were at DKK 5.15. On the other hand, the premium on a put will be higher when the spot exchange rate on the underlying currency is lower. An investor will be willing to pay more for the right to sell dollars at DKK 5.00 if the spot rate is DKK 4.85 than if it is DKK 5.15.

No matter what the level of the exchange rate is, the premium on a call or a put will always be positive, although it can be very small. The reason is that as long as there is still some time before expiry, there is always at least a remote possibility that something will happen to make the option profitable. Even if the spot rate is DKK 5.00 and the strike price on a call with a week to expiration is DKK 7.50, an event like a natural catastrophe, a presidential assassination, a war, or a revolution could possibly take place before the option expires, which would push the exchange rate above DKK 7.50. If it does not take place, the option expires worthless but would only costs the investor the premium that he had originally paid for. The right to a possible gain with no chance of a loss is clearly worth something.

For an option on the spot rate, when the spot rate is very high compared to the strike price, the probability that the call option will be exercised is also very high. Since exercise uncertainty decreases with the rise in the spot rate, the value of a European call will tend to approach the value of the spot exchange rate minus the strike price (multiplied by the nominal amount of the contract). In this situation, the option starts to resemble a fixed forward contract where the strike price is the forward rate. Similarly, when the spot exchange rate is very low compared to the strike price, the probability that a European put option will be exercised becomes very high. Its value approaches the difference between the strike price and the spot exchange rate. Again, because of the high probability of exercise, the option begins to resemble a fixed forward contract, where the strike price plays the role of the forward rate. If the option is on a futures contract, the same arguments hold except that the futures rate replaces the spot rate in the formulation.

Figures 3.1 and 3.2 summarize the relationship between the value of European currency calls and puts, respectively, and the spot exchange rate. The solid line in Figure 3.1 represents the difference between the spot rate and the strike price. The broken line represents the value of the call. At very high levels of the spot rate, the value of the call comes close to this line. At very low levels of the spot rate, the value of the option approaches zero. When the spot rate is lower than the strike price, the value of the option is totally due to its *time value,* that is, the possibility that the spot rate will climb above the strike price before expiry. When the spot rate is above the strike price, the option's value comes partially from time value and partially from the fact that the spot price is already above the strike price. In this case, the difference between the spot rate and the strike price is called the *intrinsic value.*

In Figure 3.2, the solid line represents the difference between the strike price and the spot exchange rate for a put. At very low levels of the spot

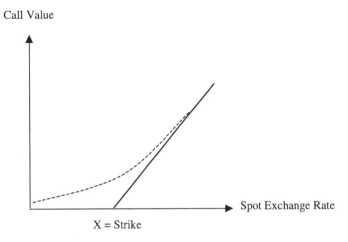

Figure 3.1   European Call Value and the Spot Exchange Rate

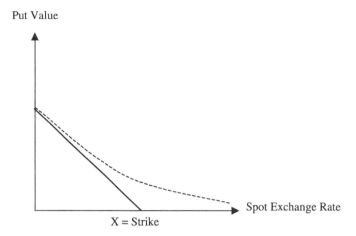

Figure 3.2   European Spot Value and the Spot Exchange Rate

rate, the value of the put option comes very close to this line. At very high levels of the forward rate, it approaches zero.

The Premium and the Spot Exchange Rate: American Options

American options are more complicated than European options because American options can be exercised at any time during their life. When the spot exchange rate is very high compared to the strike price, it will sometimes be advantageous for the call buyer to exercise before the expiration date, if the forward exchange rate is at a discount. This is because the spot rate is higher than the forward rate. Just when it is advantageous to exercise will be discussed below. For now, the fact that early exercise is a possibility and that it will sometimes be advantageous to exercise early when the forward rate is at a discount means that the value of an American call option will be higher than the value of an otherwise equivalent European option.

The same type of reasoning can be applied to an American put. It will sometimes be advantageous for the put buyer to exercise early when the forward rate is at a premium. When the forward rate is at a discount, early exercise will never be advantageous because the spot rate is higher than the forward rate.

The Premium and the Strike Price

A higher strike price gives a lower call value and a higher put value. On the other hand, a lower strike price gives a higher call value and a lower put value. The reason is straightforward. Since a call is the right to buy at a given strike price, the lower the price, the more chance there is that the market price of the underlying currency will surpass it for a profit. Conversely, since a put is the right to sell a given strike price, the higher the price, the more chance there is that the market price of the underlying currency will fall below it for a profit. At a lower strike price, the results are reversed.

When the strike price is higher than the spot exchange rate, the value of a call is due entirely to its time value, that is, the possibility that the spot price will rise above the strike price before the option expires. The call is then said to be *out-of-the-money*. On the other hand, if the strike price is lower than the spot rate, there is an immediate gain, called the *intrinsic value*, which is equal to the difference between the spot rate and the strike price. The option is said to be *in-the-money*. Besides the intrinsic value, though, the possibility that the rate could go higher before the option expires still exists. Hence, the value of an in-the-money option is equal to its intrinsic value plus its time value. When the spot rate and the strike price are equal, the option is said to be *at-the-money*.

The same expressions are used to qualify puts. If the strike price is higher than the spot rate, there is an immediate gain for the buyer insofar as the writer contracts to pay a higher price than the current market price. The put is in-the-money. Conversely, if the strike price is lower than the spot rate, the put has only time value and is said to be out-of-the-money. When the spot rate and the strike price are equal, the put is at-the-money.

The Premium and Exchange Rate Volatility

The volatility of the exchange rate is the most important factor in determining the time value of an option. In fact, in markets, traders tend to quote options in terms of volatility rather than in terms of prices. The higher the volatility of the exchange rate, the higher the probability that a strong rise or fall will occur. As we have seen, this is exactly what the buyer of the option is hoping for. A sharp rise in the exchange rate will be extremely profitable for the owner of a call. On the other hand, if a sharp fall occurs, he loses nothing but the premium he paid for the option. The outcome is similar for a put whose owner is hoping for a fall in the underlying rate. The larger the fall, the greater is his gain. On the other hand, if there is no fall or even a sharp rise, the option expires worthless and he only loses the premium he paid when he bought it. The value of a put increases with the volatility of the underlying rate.

The Premium and the Expiration Date

When the time to expiration is longer, the chances for fluctuations in the exchange rate are increased, thereby increasing volatility.[1] An option that expires in six months is worth more than an option that expires in three months.

For the paragraphs on option pricing that follow, it is important to remember that an option's time value is not proportional to its time to expiration. In fact, as far back as 1900, Bachelier showed that it is the square root of the time to expiration that influences an option's time value. Exactly why this is so will become clear as we proceed with option pricing.

BINOMIAL APPROACH TO OPTION PRICING

The pricing of currency options requires incorporating all the complex interrelationships among the foregoing variables as well as all the factors that could possibly affect participants' judgments in a free market. Professional traders and arbitragers, who have very low transaction costs, have developed pricing rules based on the arbitrage arguments of Black and Scholes, which they use in their day-to-day operations. Theorists have summarized their experiences in a number of pricing models that are useful tools for effective risk management. The binomial model emphasizes the main elements of these models and is also the simplest and easiest to understand.

The One-Period Currency Call Option

The binomial option-pricing model is a simple and straightforward application of the basic principles of option pricing. The binomial model assumes that, given the current level of the exchange rate, there are only two values for next period's exchange rate—an upward move or a downward move. Hedging is then combined with borrowing and lending to determine the option's value. The following numerical examples illustrate the basic features of options pricing techniques.

We start with the following notation.

C_t = the value of the call on one unit of the underlying asset after t moves

u = an upward move equal to 1 plus a percentage gain

d = a downward move equal to 1 minus a percentage loss

r = the riskless interest rate in domestic currency

$R = 1 + r$

r^* = the riskless interest rate in foreign currency

$R^* = 1 + r^*$

X = exercise price

Δ = delta: the number of units of the underlying asset to be held per option shorted to create a riskless hedge

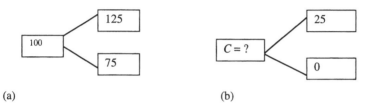

Figure 3.3   (a) Exchange rate in a one-step binomial tree; (b) Call price

For simplicity, we assume that u, d, and the foreign and domestic interest rates are constant over time. In order to rule out risk-free arbitrage profits, we also have the constraint that

$$d < \frac{1+r}{1+r*} < u.$$

Valuing a One-Period Call

Now consider the following information.

$S = 100$
$u = 1.25$
$d = 0.75$
$r = 0.10$
$r* = 0.03$
$R = 1 + r = 1.07$
$R* = 1.03$
$X = 100$

Figure 3.3a shows the exchange rate movements with probability $q = 0.5$ of an upward move and probability $1 - q = 0.5$ of a downward move. Figure 3.3b shows the value of the option if the exchange rate moves up or down. Notice that the probabilities q and $1 - q$ are absent from Figure 3.3b. This is because the procedure for option valuation eliminates the need to make assumptions about the probability distribution of the price of the underlying asset.

Using the foregoing information, our problem is to determine the value of a call option with one period until expiration during which the exchange rate can either move up to 125 or down to 75. We proceed in four steps.

1: First, build a portfolio by selling a call on one unit of the foreign currency and simultaneously purchasing Δ units of the same currency.

2. Second, make the portfolio risk free. To do this, we choose Δ so that the outcome will be the same whether the exchange rate moves up or down.

3. Third, we expand the portfolio by borrowing an amount that will yield a net cash flow of zero in period 1.

4. Fourth, we find the value of the call by applying the well-known fact that the value of an investment with zero net cash flows equals zero.

In Step 1 our cash flows are equal to $C_0 - \Delta S$. When we sell the call, we receive C_0 and we pay ΔS when we purchase the foreign currency. At the end of the period, if the asset price moves up to uS, the call will be worth 25, the difference between the exchange rate and the exercise price. Since we sold the call, we have to pay this amount. From our long position in foreign currency we receive ΔuS, the value of our investment in foreign currency, plus $r^*\Delta uS$, the interest on the investment in foreign currency. Thus, we receive $\Delta 125 + 0.03 \times \Delta 125 - 25 = \Delta 128.75 - 25$. If the asset price moves to dS, the call expires worthless and we receive $\Delta 75$, the value of the investment in foreign currency, plus the interest from the investment in foreign currency, $0.03 \times \Delta 75$.

In Step 2 we choose Δ so that the outcomes are the same:

$$\Delta 128.75 - 25 = \Delta 77.25,$$

so that

$$\Delta = 0.4854.$$

In Step 3, we borrow an amount equal to $(0.4854 \times 77.25)/(1.07)$ or $(0.4854 \times 128.75 - 25)/(1.07)$, since they are equal. In Table 3.4 we see that this will give a net cash flow of zero in period 1. Thus, in Step 4 we apply the principle that a portfolio with zero net cash flows has a value equal to zero:

$$+C_0 - 48.54 + 37.5/1.07 = 0$$
$$C_0 = 13.50.$$

Table 3.4 summarizes the operations.

The One-Period Binomial Formula

Using the same methodology as above, we can derive a simple formula for one-period binomial pricing of a currency option.

First, we sell C_0 and purchase ΔS. The net cash flow is equal to $C_0 - \Delta S$. In period 1 our cash flows will either be $-C_u + \Delta uS(1 + r^*)$ or $-C_d + \Delta dS(1 + r^*)$. To find the value of Δ that makes both outcomes independent of the

Table 3.4
One-Period Cash Flows

	Flows at period 0	Flows at period 1	
		$uS = 125$	$dS = 75$
Write a call	$+C_0$	$-C_u = -25$	$C_d = 0$
Purchase Δ units of foreign currency	$-\Delta S =$ $0.4854 \times 100 = 48.54$	$0.4854 \times 128.75 = 62.5$	$0.4854 \times 77.25 = 37.5$
Borrow	$(0.4854 \times 77.25)/(1.07)$ $= 37.5 \big/ 1.07$	-37.5	-37.5
Total	$+C_0 - 48.54 + 37.5\big/1.07$	0	0

move in the exchange rate, set the two possible period 1 outcomes equal and solve. This gives:

$$-C_u + \Delta uS(1+r^*) = -C_d + \Delta dS(1+r^*)$$

$$\Delta = \frac{C_u - C_d}{S(u-d)(1+r^*)}. \tag{3.1}$$

We then borrow $\dfrac{-C_d + \Delta dS(1+r^*)}{R}$ so that the net outcomes in period 1 are zero. Since the investment generates zero net cash flows, its value is zero as well. Thus,

$$C_0 - \Delta S + \frac{-C_d + \Delta dS(1+r^*)}{R} = 0. \tag{3.2}$$

Substituting the value of Δ from 3.1 and rearranging gives:

$$C_0 = \frac{C_u \left[\dfrac{\dfrac{R}{R^*} - d}{u - d}\right] + C_d \left[1 - \dfrac{\dfrac{R}{R^*} - d}{u - d}\right]}{R}. \tag{3.3}$$

This seemingly complicated formula can be simplified. Define $P = \{[(R/R^u) - d]/u - d\}$ and substitute this definition into equation 3.3. This gives:

$$C_0 = \frac{C_u P + C_d [1 - P]}{R}. \tag{3.4}$$

To check that this formula does indeed give the correct option price, we substitute the information from the numerical example,

$$C_0 = \frac{20\left[\dfrac{\dfrac{1.07}{1.03}-0.75}{1.25-0.75}\right]+0\left[1-\dfrac{\dfrac{1.07}{1.03}-0.75}{1.25-0.75}\right]}{1.07},$$

and find that C_0 does indeed equal 13.50.

Delta and Risk-Neutral Valuation

We defined delta as the number of units of the underlying asset to be held (shorted) per option shorted (held) to create a riskless hedge. The creation of a riskless hedge then made it possible to derive equation 3.4. Going back to Figure 3.3a, it is important to notice that the original probabilities of upward and downward moves are absent from this equation. In fact, the option was priced without making any assumptions about the probabilities of up and down moves in the exchange rate. However, we can interpret P as the probability of an upward move in a world without risk and $1 - P$ as the probability of a downward move in a world without risk.[2] The reason for this is that risk was eliminated when we chose Δ, so that the outcome of the portfolio was the same whether there was an up move or a down move in the underlying asset. The absence of risk makes it possible to discount and compound the expected cash flows at the riskless rate.

This result is an example of what is called *risk-neutral valuation*. It means that an option can be priced by using the risk-neutral probabilities, pretending that investors are neutral to risk. This is an application of what is known as the *Girsanov Theorem*. The new probabilities change the mean but leave the volatility structure intact. The answers obtained in this way are valid in all worlds, not only in the risk-neutral world.[3]

In practice, the construction of a binomial tree involves defining the volatility of the price of the underlying security σ so that $\sigma\sqrt{dt}$ is the standard deviation of the return on the security over a short period of time. We then choose the parameters u and d to match the volatility of the asset price. The values for u and d suggested by Cox, Ross, and Rubenstein (1979) are:

$$u = e^{\sigma\sqrt{dt}}$$

and

$$d = e^{-\sigma\sqrt{dt}}.$$

Valuing European Puts

The same recursive methodology used to value European calls can be used to value European puts. We build a riskless portfolio composed of the put and Δ units of the foreign currency, borrow the appropriate amount and end up with the equivalent of equation 3.4 where p represents the value of the put:

$$p_0 = \frac{p_u P + p_d [1-P]}{R}.$$ (3.5)

As an example, start with the information above and consider a one period European put with a strike price of 100. If the spot price moves up to 125, the put expires worthless. If the spot price falls to 75, the put will be worth $100 - 75 = 25$. Thus $p_u = 0$, $p_d = 25$ and

$$P = \frac{\frac{1.07}{1.03} - 0.75}{1.25 - 0.75} = 0.5777$$

$$p_0 = \frac{(0 \times 0.5777) + (25 \times 0.4223)}{1.07}$$

$$p_0 = 9.87.$$

Valuing European Calls and Puts on Currency Futures Contracts

For the binomial form of a currency futures option, remember that when a futures position is taken, there is no cash outlay and therefore its value is zero. An asset with a value of zero has an expected return equal to zero. If this were not true, there would be arbitrage possibilities. Going through the same steps as before gives equations 3.4 and 3.5 where P' replaces P. Since there is no yield and no return on a *futures contract* in a risk neutral world, P', the risk neutral probability of an up move is given as

$$P' = \frac{\frac{1+0}{1+0} - d}{u-d} = \frac{1-d}{u-d}.$$

The Multi-Period Model

Valuing a Two-Period Call

Valuing a call with more than one period to expiration involves the same procedure as before, although the calculations are more complicated. We start at the option's value on the expiration date and work backward to the present. Figure 3.4a shows the different possible values of the asset price in a two-period binomial tree, and Figure 3.4b shows the corresponding value of the option at each period. There are three steps to the valuation procedure.

Step 1: Use C_{u^2} and C_{ud} to calculate C_u, the value of the option if the asset price makes one upward move. C_{u^2} is the terminal value of the option if the

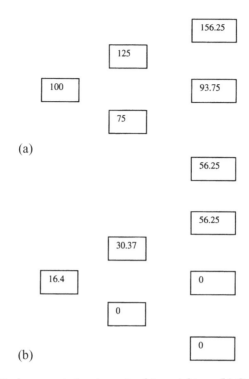

Figure 3.4   (a) Exchange rate in a two-step binomial tree; (b) Call price

asset price makes two upward moves and C_{ud} is the terminal value of the option if it makes one upward and one downward move.

Step 2: Use C_{ud} and C_{d^2} to calculate C_d, the value of the option if the asset price makes one downward move. C_{d^2} is the terminal value of the option if the asset price makes two downward moves.

Step 3: Use the calculated values of C_u and C_d to calculate the value of C_0.

In Step 1, we proceed as we did for a one-period option. Table 3.5 consolidates the information from Figures 3.4a and 3.4b necessary to calculate the value of C_u. First, we find Δ by equating the cash flows for the two possible outcomes and solving:

$$-56.25 + \Delta 160.94 = \Delta 96.56$$
$$\Delta = 0.8738.$$

Next, we borrow $\dfrac{0.8738 \times 96.56}{1.07} = 78.85$ so that net cash flows are equal to zero in period 2. Since the net cash flows are zero, the value of the investment is also zero. Thus,

Table 3.5
Two-Period Cash Flows

	Flows at period 1	Flows at period 2	
		$u^2S = 156.25$	$udS = 56.25$
Write a call	$+C_u$	$-C_{u^2} = -56.25$	$-C_{ud} = 0$
Purchase Δ units of foreign currency	$-\Delta uS = 0.8743 \times 125$	$+\Delta u^2 S(1+r^*) = 0.8738 \times 160.94 \quad = 140.7$	$+\Delta udS(1+r^*) = 0.8738 \times 96.56 = 84.37$
Borrow	$\dfrac{(-C_{ud} + \Delta udS(1+r^*))}{R}$ $= 0 - 0.8738 \times 96.56$	$C_{u^2} - \Delta u^2 S(1+r^*) = -84.37$	$C_{ud} - \Delta udS(1+\delta) = 0 - 0.8738 \times 96.56 = -84.37$
Total	$+C_u$ -109.23 + 78.86	0	0

$$+C_u - \Delta uS + \frac{-C_{ud} + \Delta udS(1+r^*)}{R} = 0$$

$$C_u = 0.8738 \times 125 - 78.85$$
$$C_u = 30.37.$$

In Step 2, $C_d = 0$ because both C_{ud} and C_{d2} are equal to zero. Since we know C_u and C_d, Step 3 boils down to calculating the value of a one-period option. First, we find Δ using 3.1

$$\Delta = \frac{30.37 - 0}{100 \times (1.03) \times (1.25 - 0.75)}$$
$$\Delta = 0.5897.$$

Next, we borrow $\dfrac{0.5897 \times 75 \times 1.03}{1.07} = 42.57$, so that net cash flows will equal zero. Finally, we set the investment in period 0 equal to zero and find that

$$C_0 = 0.5897 \times 100 - 42.57$$
$$C_0 = 16.4.$$

Valuing American Style Currency Options

The difference between European and American style options is that American style options can be exercised at anytime over the option's life, whereas European style options can only be exercised at expiration. This added flexibility makes the American style option more valuable than the European style option. Unfortunately, it also makes it more complicated to compute the price. In fact, an extra step must be added in the computation of the price of an American style option:

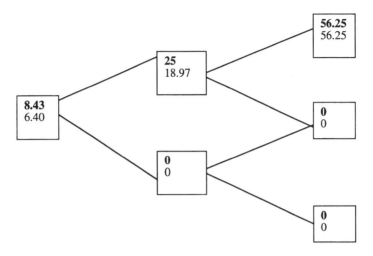

Figure 3.5   American call price **(in bold)** and European call price

Step 1: Start from the right-hand side as before and compute the expiration values
   of the option.

Step 2: Work toward the left using the expiration values and the risk-neutral probabilities to compute the option value if it is not exercised.

Step 3: Compute the option's value if it is exercised.

Step 4: Compare the two values and choose the higher of the two.

Step 5: Return to Step 2 and repeat this process until the initial period is reached.

Consider the following information, which is the same as before except
that $r^* = 15\%$ instead of 3%. Notice that $r^* > r$ means that the foreign currency is selling at a discount. As we mentioned above, when the foreign
currency is selling at a discount, there is a possibility that early exercise
might be profitable.

$S = 100$
$u = 1.25$
$d = 0.75$
$r^* = 0.15$
$r = 0.07$
$X = 100$

Figure 3.5 shows the value of the American style option (in bold) and
the value of the European style option. In the upper-middle node, we
can see that the option is worth 18.97 alive. It is worth 25 if it is exercised.

Since the value of the option is higher if it is exercised, it will be exercised. Thus, to compute the value of the American style option at the initial period, the value of the option in the first period after an upward move will be 25 rather than 18.97. The value of the American style option is considerably higher than the equivalent European style option (8.43 versus 6.40).

THE CONTINUOUS TIME MODEL

The Garman-Kohlhagen Model

The Garman-Kohlhagen currency option-pricing model is a general form of the preceding multi-period binomial model. The difference between the two is that the binomial model refers to a limited number of discrete time periods, whereas the Garman-Kohlhagen model was developed in the context of a multitude of infinitely small periods, known as continuous time.

Suppose that the change of the logarithm of the exchange rate in the time interval dt follows the normal law with an expected return of μdt and variance $\sigma^2 dt$. We can write the hypothesis like this:

$$\ln(S_{t+dt}) - \ln(S_t) \approx N(\mu dt, \sigma^2 dt), \tag{3.6}$$

where S refers to the spot exchange rate, ln refers to the natural logarithm and N refers to the normal law. This hypothesis can have the following interpretation. The change in the exchange rate has two determinants. The first, μdt, is deterministic and corresponds to the deterministic influence of well-known, continuous economic phenomena. The second, $\sigma^2 dt$, is generated by a random or stochastic element and reflects the influence of shocks whose intensity increases as σ increases.[4]

Suppose further that foreign exchange and options transactions can take place on a continuous or nearly continuous basis. In reality, it is true that all currencies are not traded 24 hours a day, seven days a week. Nevertheless, the major currencies are traded around the clock and transactions are frequent enough that the continuous time hypothesis is acceptable. In this case, we can say that the spot exchange rate follows a continuous stochastic process.

The Garman-Kohlhagen model refers to a European option traded on a continuous market. As in the binomial model above an investor builds a portfolio by selling a call and purchasing $\Delta e^{-r^*(T-t)}$ in foreign currency. At the date t, the value of this portfolio, denoted as $V(t)$, in domestic currency will be equal to:

$$V(t) = \Delta S(t)e^{-r^*(T-t)} + C(S,t), \tag{3.7}$$

where:

$S(t)$ = the spot exchange rate defined as the number of units of domestic currency for each unit of foreign currency

$e^{-r^*(T-t)}$ = the present value discount factor (the present value in foreign currency of a loan that pays 1 on the maturity date, T

$C(S,t)$ = the value in domestic currency of a European call on one unit of the foreign currency.

The term $\Delta S(t)e^{-r^*(T-t)}$ represents the domestic currency cost of an asset that will yield Δ units of foreign currency at maturity, T. The discount factor $e^{-r^*(T-t)}$ reflects the fact that money borrowed and lent earns interest. $V(t)$ is the value of the overall position, composed of a call on one unit of foreign currency plus the domestic currency value of $\Delta e^{-r^*(T-t)}$ units of foreign currency. Consequently, $C(S,t)$ gives the value of the option in units of domestic currency as is the custom on the organized exchanges. The over-the-counter markets prefer to give the premium as a percentage of the amount of foreign currency.

By taking the total differential of V, we can write the change in the overall position as:

$$dV = \Delta e^{-r^*(T-t)}dS + \Delta S r^* e^{-r^*(T-t)}dt + dC, \tag{3.8}$$

where the arguments have been dropped for ease of notation.

The strike price is a parameter that defines the option and remains constant over its life. Assuming that the interest rates (r^* and r) and the volatility of the exchange rate (σ) also remain constant, the premium on the call is a function only of time and the spot exchange rate:

$$C = C(S, t).$$

Since we have assumed that the exchange rate follows a continuous Wiener process, we can write that the variation in the premium[5]

$$dC = C_s dS + C_t dt + \frac{1}{2}C_{ss}\sigma^2 S^2 dt, \tag{3.9}$$

where the subscripts refer to first and second partial derivatives.

If we substitute equation 3.9 into equation 3.8 and rearrange, we get the following expression:

$$dV = (\Delta e^{-r^*(T-t)} + C_s)dS + (\Delta S r^* e^{-r^*(T-t)} + C_t + \frac{1}{2}\sigma^2 S^2 C_{ss})dt. \tag{3.10}$$

As we did in the binomial model, we want to choose Δ so that the portfolio is riskless. In equation 3.10, the only random variable is dS. Hence, if we choose Δ so that $\Delta e^{-r^*(T-t)} + C_s = 0$, the variation in V, the overall position, will be known with certainty and will consequently be riskless. For this to be the case: $\Delta = -C_s e^{r^*(T-t)}$. This ratio represents the *hedge ratio*, that is, the amount of foreign currency that must be purchased to cover the risk on a short position in a call on one unit of foreign currency. The ratio has to be revised constantly because neither $e^{r^*(T-t)}$ nor C_s are constant over time. Remember that in the two-period numerical example, there was a different Δ for each period. The same phenomenon is at work here where, in order to remain perfectly hedged, the position must be adjusted continually.

Choosing the appropriate hedge ratio and substituting $\Delta = -C_s e^{r^*(T-t)}$

$$dV = (-C_s Sr^* + C_t + \frac{1}{2}\sigma^2 S^2 C_{ss})dt. \tag{3.11}$$

In this way we have eliminated the risk associated with $V(S,t)$. Since it is riskless, it yields the domestic riskless interest rate, r. Hence, the change in V per unit of time will be $rVdt$. Substituting the hedge ratio for Δ and equation 3.7 for V, we can write equation 3.11 as:

$$r(C - C_s S)dt = (-C_s Sr^* + C_t + \frac{1}{2}\sigma^2 S^2 C_{ss})dt. \tag{3.12}$$

Rearranging gives the partial differential equation for the call

$$\frac{1}{2}\sigma^2 S^2 C_{ss} + (r - r^*)SC_s - rC + C_t = 0. \tag{3.13}$$

Because of the characteristics of the call option we know that on the expiration date its value will be equal to the difference between the spot exchange rate and the strike price, X, if the spot rate is greater than the strike price. Otherwise, it will expire worthless. Thus, the first two boundary conditions are:

$$C(S,T) = S_T - X, \text{ if } S > X \tag{3.14}$$
$$C(S,T) = 0 \text{ if, } S_T \leqslant X. \tag{3.15}$$

Finally, if the exchange rate goes to zero, it stays at zero and the option is worthless:

$$C(0,t) = 0. \tag{3.16}$$

Using the foregoing boundary conditions for C, the PDE yields an exact analytical solution. In Appendix 3.2 we show how the solution can be obtained by calculating the true expectation:

$$C(S,t) = S(t)e^{-r^*(T-t)}N(d_1) - Xe^{-r^*(T-t)}N(d_2), \tag{3.17}$$

where

$N(d)$ = the value of the cumulative normal distribution evaluated at d.

$$d_1 = \frac{\ln(S/X) + (r - r^* + \sigma^2/2)(T-t)}{\sigma\sqrt{T-t}}$$

$$d_2 = \frac{\ln(S/X) + (r - r^* - \sigma^2/2)(T-t)}{\sigma\sqrt{T-t}}$$

Currency Option Put

Using the same methodology with boundary conditions 3.14 and 3.15 replaced by

$$C(S,T) = 0, \text{ if } S_T > X \tag{3.18}$$

$$C(S,T) = X - S_T, \text{ if } S_T < X, \tag{3.19}$$

gives the formula for currency option put:

$$p = Xe^{-r^*(T-t)} N(-d_2) - S_t e^{-r^*(T-t)} N(-d_1). \tag{3.20}$$

The main difference between this formula and the original Black-Scholes formula stems from the fact that the opportunity cost to the investor is not the domestic riskless rate, as it would be for an ordinary asset. In fact, the opportunity cost is the difference between the domestic and foreign riskless rates. When setting up the riskless hedge, we borrow domestic currency and invest in foreign currency. The cost of the hedge is the difference between the cost of borrowing at the domestic rate less the return on the investment at the foreign rate.

Black's Model for Pricing Options on Currency Futures Contracts

As we mentioned above, many options are written on currency futures contracts (see Black, 1976). To price an option on a currency futures contract, remember that no payouts are made when a futures contract is purchased. Since there is no investment, there is no return and equation 3.6 becomes

$$\ln(F_{t+dt,T}) - \ln(F_{t,T}) \approx N(0,\sigma^2 dt). \tag{3.21}$$

With this in mind, we use the methodology in Appendix 3.2 to solve the equation

$$C = e^{-r(T-t)} E[\max(F_{T,T} - X, 0)] \qquad (3.22a)$$

for a call, and

$$p = e^{-r(T-t)} E[\max(X - F_{T,T}, 0)] \qquad (3.23a)$$

for a put. This gives:

$$C = e^{-r(T-t)} E[F_{T,T} N(d_{F1}) - XN(d_{F2})] \qquad (3.22b)$$

and

$$p = e^{-r(T-t)} [XN(-d_{F2}) - F_{T,T} N(-d_{F1})] \qquad (3.23b)$$

where

$N(d)$ = the value of the cumulative normal distribution evaluated at d.

$$d_{F1} = \frac{\ln(F_{t,T}/X) + \sigma^2/2(T-t)}{\sigma\sqrt{T-t}}$$

$$d_{F2} = \frac{\ln(F_{t,T}/X) - \sigma^2/2(T-t)}{\sigma\sqrt{T-t}} = d_1 - \sigma\sqrt{T-t}.$$

USING THE CONTINUOUS TIME MODEL

Calculating the Premium

In spite of the apparent complexity of the formula, using the model to derive the theoretical value of a currency option is quite simple. All that is necessary is a table giving the values for $N(d)$ and a hand calculator. Consider the following information:

S(USD/CHF) = 1.50
r_s = 4%
r_f = 9%
$T - t$ = 6 months = 0.5 years
σ = 10%
X = 1.55

Substituting this information into the formulas for d_1 and d_2, the calculation is straightforward:

$$d_1 = \frac{\ln(1.50/1.55) + (0.09 - 0.04 + 0.01)0.5}{0.1\sqrt{0.5}} = -0.0748$$

$$d_2 = \frac{\ln(1.50/1.55) + (0.09 - 0.04 + 0.01)0.5}{0.1\sqrt{0.5}} = -0.1455.$$

By looking up these values in the cumulative normal curve tables we find:

$N(d_1) = N(-0.0748) = 0.4702$
$N(d_2) = N(-0.1455) = 0.4584.$

Substituting this information into equation 3.17 yields

$$C = 1.50e^{-0.04(0.5)}0.4702 - 1.55e^{-0.09(0.5)}0.4584 \cong 0.0121.$$

Thus, the investor must pay 0.0121 CHF per dollar. If he wants to calculate the premium in dollars rather than francs, all he has to do is divide by the spot rate. In this case $0.0121/1.50 = 0.81\%$.

Estimating Volatility

Although the Garman-Kohlhagen model is easy to use, it has a number of shortcomings. First of all, it can only be used for European options. Because of the possibility of early exercise, American options are worth more than European options. Money managers should be careful about this.

Another practical difficulty resides in the choice of the volatility parameter, σ. One possible solution is to estimate volatility using past values of the exchange rate. Unfortunately, experience has shown that volatility is not stable and tends to fluctuate considerably over time. The volatility estimate necessary for the Garman-Kohlhagen model is not past volatility but the volatility expected over the life of the option. This variable is not directly observable, of course, because it depends on the anticipations of all the participants in the foreign exchange market. Consequently, investors have developed another use for the Garman-Kohlhagen model. Rather than using it to determine the theoretical price of an option, they take the price observed on the market and use the model to determine the volatility that the market price implies. In fact, professional options traders do not quote a price for an option. Instead, they quote a level of volatility from which the price can be deduced.

Take, for example, a call on dollars for Swiss francs that expires in six months with a strike price of 1.50 and quoted at 0.0694 francs per dollar. The investor can substitute the value 0.0694 into equation 3.17:

$$0.0694 = 1.50e^{-0.04(0.5)}N(d_1) - 1.55e^{-0.09(0.5)}N(d_2)$$

and solve for σ. The only unknown in the equation is σ in the formulas for $N(d_1)$ and $N(d_2)$. There is no explicit solution to the equation but an iterative trial and error method can get the job done quickly. In fact, 12 percent is the solution to this problem, which means that 12 percent is the value of σ that makes it possible to find the market price of 0.0694. This is called *implied volatility*.

Because there are numerous calls with different strike prices and expiration dates quoted on the same currency, implied volatility can be used in several ways. First of all, it can be used as a gauge of the relative expensiveness of the different calls. Those with the highest volatility are the most expensive and to be avoided by buyers. Secondly, if we make the assumption that market anticipations only evolve slowly, the best estimation of anticipated risk is the weighted average of all the different implicit volatilities. In fact, this use seems to give the best results.

CURRENCY OPTION MANAGEMENT TOOLS

The usefulness of the Garman-Kohlhagen model, as well as the original Black-Scholes model, goes beyond the limited scope of pricing European call options. The model expresses in a relatively simple manner the relationships between the price of the option and the principle variables: the spot exchange rate, volatility, time, and the domestic and foreign interest rates. It allows investors to anticipate the effects of a change in one of these variables on the value of the overall position. There are five basic tools to be derived from the model: the delta (Δ), the gamma (Γ), the theta (Θ), the vega, and the sensitivity to the two interest rates.

The Delta

We have seen that when the spot exchange rate is higher, the option premium is also higher. Mathematically, we can say that the option premium is an increasing function of the spot exchange rate. The Garman-Kohlhagen model makes it possible to state the relationship precisely. In fact, we can use the first partial derivative of the option premium with respect to the spot exchange to calculate what is called the *delta*. For a call it is equal to

$$\Delta = \frac{\partial C}{\partial S} = e^{-r^*(T-t)} N(d_1). \tag{3.24}$$

For a put it is

$$\Delta = \frac{\partial p}{\partial S} = e^{-r^*(T-t)} [N(d_1) - 1]. \tag{3.25}$$

A call's delta is always positive and measures the sensitivity of the premium to a small change in the spot exchange rate. For the writer of a call wanting to hedge his exposure, it represents the number of foreign currency units to be bought spot and invested at the foreign riskless rate. For the owner of a call wanting to hedge his exposure, it represents number of foreign currency units to be sold. For a put, the delta is always negative and represents the number of foreign currency units to be shorted.

When an investor has accumulated a position composed of calls with different strike prices and expiration dates, he would like to know how sensitive his overall position is to changes in the exchange rate. Individual call deltas can be used for this purpose. His overall position can be defined as the weighted sum of the value of the premiums of all the calls he has bought or written. Let H be the overall position. Then:

$$H = \sum_{1}^{n} x_i C_i, \tag{3.26}$$

where x_i is the number of calls in series i that have been bought if $x > 0$ and the number of calls that have been written if $x < 0$. The sensitivity of his overall portfolio to a change in the spot exchange rate, Δ_H will then be the weighted average of the sensitivities of the different calls:

$$\Delta_H = \sum_{1}^{n} x_1 \Delta_1. \tag{3.27}$$

The investor can evaluate how well he is covered by comparing the delta of his overall position in calls with his foreign exchange exposure. This technique is frequently used by professional investors.

The Gamma

Delta only measures the sensitivity of the premium to changes in the exchange rate in the neighborhood of the actual exchange rate. If the exchange rate undergoes a large change, the delta will change considerably. Hence, if options are used to hedge foreign exchange risk, the level of exposure would automatically change if there is a large move in the exchange rate. The slope of the curve showing the relationship between the call premium and the spot exchange rate changes much more when the call is at-the-money than when it is way in or out-of-the-money. The rate at which it changes, then, is an important factor in the riskiness of the investor's position. *Gamma,* which is the second partial derivative of C with respect to S, measures the rate of change in delta. For a European call or put gamma is given as[6]

$$\Gamma = \frac{\partial \Delta}{\partial S} = C_{ss} e^{-r^*(T-t)} \frac{1}{\sigma S \sqrt{2\pi(T-T)}} e^{\frac{(d_1)^2}{2}}. \tag{3.28}$$

As with delta, the gamma of the overall position can be calculated by taking a weighted average of all the calls:

$$\Gamma_H \sum x_i \Gamma_i. \tag{3.29}$$

Since the x_i can be negative (calls sold), the gamma of a portfolio can be negative as well. Negative gammas can be dangerous in the case of a wide swing in the exchange rate. A negative gamma will make hedging a short position in foreign exchange with sold puts less and less effective in the case of a rise in the exchange rate because delta will fall as the exchange rate rises. Covering a long position in foreign exchange with sold calls is also less and less effective when the exchange rate falls because delta will decrease as the exchange rate falls. Furthermore, in the case of opposite moves, the position will immediately show a tendency to be over hedged, which is costly. Some professional investors speak of *negative gamma hell.*

Theta

The value of a call is indisputably a function of the time to expiration. The Garman-Kohlhagen model makes it possible to specify the exact role that time plays. The first partial derivative of the value of the call with respect to time is called *theta.* For a call it is equal to

$$\Theta = \frac{\partial C}{\partial t} = r^* S(t) e^{-r^*(T-t)} N(d_1) - rX e^{-r(T-t)} N(d_2) - \frac{S\sigma e^{-r^*(T-t)} N'(d_1)}{2\sqrt{T-t}}, \qquad (3.30)$$

and for a put,

$$\Theta = \frac{\partial p}{\partial t} = -r^* S(t) e^{-r^*(T-t)} N(-d_1) - rX e^{-r(T-t)} N(-d_2) - \frac{S\sigma e^{-r^*(T-t)} N'(d_1)}{2\sqrt{T-t}}. \qquad (3.31)$$

Normally, the value of a call diminishes as time passes and it usually diminishes faster as the call approaches its expiration date. Therefore, theta is usually negative. Here, however, theta can sometimes be positive. It depends on the values of the other parameters. If the call is way in-the-money and if the foreign interest rate is higher than the domestic rate ($r^* > r$ means that the forward exchange rate is at a discount), theta can be positive. This signifies that the option gains time value as it gets closer to its expiration date. In this case, if it is an American option, it is better to exercise immediately. This situation reminds us that the Garman-Kohlhagen model is not directly applicable to American options.

Vega

The value of a call or a put is a direct function of the volatility of the spot exchange rate. Higher volatility raises the value of the call. On the organized exchanges, most options positions are closed out before expiration. Consequently, the price of the option comes into play twice, once when it is bought and once when it is sold. It is thus important for an investor to have an idea of what the effect of an anticipated change in the volatility of an option will have on its premium. For example, a fall in volatility will cause a fall in the option's premium.

The relationship between the option's premium and volatility can be expressed with the help of the Garman-Kohlhagen model by taking the first partial derivative of C or p with respect to σ:[7]

$$\frac{\partial C}{\partial \sigma} = \frac{\partial p}{\partial \sigma} = S\sqrt{T-t}\, e^{-r^*(T-t)} \frac{1}{\sqrt{2\pi}} e^{\frac{(d_1)^2}{2}}. \tag{3.32}$$

This derivative is called *vega*. It measures the increase in the premium for a small change in volatility. As with the other parameters, vegas can be added to calculate a global position consisting of different calls.

Rho: Interest Rate Sensitivity

Both the foreign and domestic interest rates figure in the currency option formula. To show the sensitivity of the options premium to the small changes in the two interest rates, we can do as we have done for the other parameters and take the first partial derivative of C and p with respect to each rate.

$$\frac{\partial C}{\partial r} = (T-t)Xe^{-r(T-t)}N(d_2) \tag{3.33}$$

$$\frac{\partial P}{\partial r} = (T-t)Xe^{-r(T-t)}N(-d_2) \tag{3.34}$$

$$\frac{\partial C}{\partial r^*} = -(T-t)Se^{-r^*(T-t)}N(d_1) \tag{3.35}$$

$$\frac{\partial p}{\partial r^*} = (T-t)Se^{-r^*(T-t)}N(-d_1) \tag{3.36}$$

For calls, the result shows that a higher domestic interest rate has a positive effect on the premium. A higher domestic rate lowers the present value of the strike price $[e^{-r(T-t)}X]$ and increases the difference with the present value of the exchange rate, thereby increasing the premium. On the other hand, a higher foreign interest rate lowers the present value of the exchange rate $[e^{-r^*(T-t)}S]$ and decreases the difference with the present value of the strike price, thereby lowering the premium. For puts, the effects are reversed.

Table 3.6
Put-Call Parity: Cash Flows

Operation	Cash flow at time 0	Outcome if $S > X$	Outcome if $S < X$	Outcome if $S = X$
Buy call	$-C$	$-X + CHF\ 1$	0	0
Sell put	$+p$	0	$-X + CHF\ 1$	0
Sell forward	0	$+F - CHF\ 1$	$+F - CHF\ 1$	$+F - CHF\ 1$
Buy spot	—	—	—	$-S + CHF\ 1$
Result	$p - C$	$F - X$	$F - X$	$F - S = F - X$

Put-Call Parity

There is an important relationship between puts and calls called *put-call parity*. On the futures and options markets, a distinction is usually made between hedging, speculation, and arbitrage. Arbitrage operations are undertaken by professionals and involve establishing a riskless position that generates a net profit. Positions like this are hard to come by insofar as the markets are extremely competitive. They require low transaction costs and constant vigilance on the part of the arbitragers in the markets. The put-call parity relation is a well-known example. It is interesting to study because it illustrates the relationships between calls and puts and all the other positions that incorporate calls and puts.

Consider the following operations undertaken at time 0:

- buy a call on CHF 1,
- sell a put on CHF 1,
- sell CHF 1 forward.

The cash flows generated by these operations and their outcomes at time 1 is summarized in Table 3.6.

We can see that the cash flows generated by the portfolio are the same for all possible outcomes of S. Since the outcome of the portfolio is certain, the investment should earn the riskless rate in domestic currency. The investment is equal to $C - p$ and the investment return is $F - X$. Thus, when t is the time to expiration:

$$(C - p)e^{r(T-t)} = F - X. \tag{3.37}$$

This means that the compounded value of the put premium less the compounded value of the call premium is equal to the difference between the forward rate and the strike price.

From interest rate parity, we know that:

$$F = S\frac{e^{r(T-t)}}{e^{r^*(T-t)}}. \tag{3.38}$$

Substituting this value for F in equation 3.37 and dividing by $e^{r(T-t)}$ gives the put-call parity equation

$$p - C = -Se^{-r^*(T-t)} + Xe^{-r(T-t)}. \tag{3.39}$$

NOTES

1. As we will see in the following sections, volatility is equal to $\sqrt{t} \times \sigma$, where t is the time to maturity and σ is the instantaneous standard deviation of the percentage change in the underlying rate.

2. We can verify that $E(S_1)$ is equal to $S_0\{R/(1+r^*)\} = PuS_0 + [1-P]dS_0$ by substituting the value of P.

3. For a more detailed discussion, see Hull (2003) and Neftci (1996).

4. The hypothesis of the normal law is one of the weaknesses of the Garman-Kohlhagen model because the normal law does not accommodate large, sudden jumps, sometimes called rare events, in the variables; movements of this kind, however, are not uncommon in the foreign exchange markets. Rare events can easily be incorporated into the analysis. See Merton (1990).

5. See Appendix 3.1 for the definition and characteristics of a general Weiner process.

6. The value of gamma can be worked out as follows:

$$C_{ss} = e^{-r^*(T-t)}\frac{\partial N(d_1)}{\partial d_1}\frac{\partial d_1}{\partial S},$$

where from the normal distribution:

$$\frac{\partial N(d_1)}{\partial d_1} = \frac{1}{\sqrt{2\pi}}e^{-\frac{(d_1)^2}{2}}$$

$$\frac{\partial d_1}{\partial S} = \frac{1}{\sigma S\sqrt{(T-t)}}.$$

Putting these together yields the derivative in the text.
7. The other member of the derivative disappears because:

$$S(t)e^{-r^*(T-t)} N'(d_1) - Xe^{-r(T-t)}N'(d_2) = 0.$$

REFERENCES

Black, F. (1976). "The Pricing of Commodity Contracts," *Journal of Financial Economics*, 3, 167–179.

Black, F., and M. Scholes. (1973). "The Pricing of Options and Corporate Liabilities," *Journal of Political Economy*, 81, 637–659.

Cox, J., S. Ross, and M. Rubenstein. (1979). "Option Pricing: A Simplified Approach," *Journal of Financial Economics*, 7, 229–264.

Garman, M., and S. Kohlhagen. (1983). "Foreign Currency Options Values," *Journal of International Money and Finance*, 2, 231–237.

Hull, J.C. (2003). *Options, Futures, and Other Derivations*, 5th ed. Upper Saddle River, NJ: Pearson Education.

Merton, R.C. (1990). "On the Mathematics and Economic Assumptions of Continuous Time Models," In Robert C. Merton, *Continuous Time Finance* (pp. 57–93). New York: Basil Blackwell.

Neftci, S.N. (1996). *An Introduction to the Mathematics of Financial Derivatives.* San Diego, CA: Academic Press.

Appendix 3.1

Ito's Lemma

In this appendix, we present Ito's lemma.

A WEINER PROCESS

Suppose that the percentage change of the price of the underlying asset in the time interval dt follows a continuous stochastic process of the type

$$dS(t) = \mu S(t)dt + \sigma S(t)dz(t), \tag{A.1}$$

where S refers to the price of the asset, μ is the expected percentage change in the asset price, called the drift, σ is the volatility and $dz(t)$ is a standard Weiner process sometimes referred to as Brownian motion. A Weiner process is a particular type of stochastic process, called a Markov process, where only the present value of the variable is relevant for predicting its future evolution. The major properties of a standard Weiner process are as follows:

1. $dz = \epsilon\sqrt{dt}$ where ϵ is a standardized random variable following the normal law with a mean of 0 and variance of $1 : N(0,1)$.
2. The values of dz for any two different short time intervals are independent.
3. $E(dz) = 0$
4. $E(dzt) = 0$
5. $E(dz^2) = dt$
6. The variance of $dz^2 = 0$.
7. $E[(dzdt)^2] = 0$
8. The variance of $dzdt = 0$.

ITO'S LEMMA

Equation A.1 is a generalized Weiner process known as geometric Brownian motion with drift equal to μ and volatility equal to σ. It is also called an Ito process after the mathematician who discovered an important result on stochastic processes. The result is called *Ito's lemma*. Ito's lemma shows that a function of an Ito process is itself an Ito process.

Let $C(S,t)$ represent the value of a call on one unit of the underlying asset. To apply Ito's lemma expand C in a Taylor series:

$$dC = \frac{\partial C}{\partial S}dS + \frac{\partial C}{\partial t}dt + \frac{1}{2}\frac{\partial^{2C}}{\partial S^2}dS^2. \qquad (A.2)$$

In stochastic calculus, the term dS^2 does not disappear as it would in ordinary calculus even though higher order terms do vanish. This is because dS is a normally-distributed random variable whose variance is proportional to dt. To see this, compute

$$dS^2 = \mu^2 S^2 dt^2 + 2\mu\sigma S^2 dzdt + \sigma^2 S^2 dz^2. \qquad (A.3)$$

The first term on the right-hand side vanishes because $dt^2 = 0$. From properties 4 and 8, $dzdt = 0$, and the second term also vanishes. From properties 5 and 6, $dz^2 = dt$ so that equation A.3 reduces to:

$$dS^2 = \sigma^2 S^2 dt. \qquad (A.4)$$

Substituting equations A.1 and A.4 into equation A.2 gives:

$$dC = \left[\frac{\partial C}{\partial S}\mu S + \frac{\partial C}{\partial t} + \frac{1}{2}\frac{\partial^2 C}{\partial S^2}\sigma^2 S^2\right]dt + \frac{\partial C}{\partial S}\sigma S dz. \qquad (A.5)$$

This is clearly another Ito process with a drift rate of

$$\frac{\partial C}{\partial S}\mu S + \frac{\partial C}{\partial t} + \frac{1}{2}\frac{\partial^2 C}{\partial S^2}\sigma^2 S^2$$

and variance of $\left(\frac{\partial C}{\partial S}\right)^2 S^2\sigma^2$.

Appendix 3.2

Derivation of the Value of the Currency Call Option

In this appendix we derive the expected expiration value of the call option on an asset with a continuous yield. This involves solving the equation

$$C = e^{-r(T-t)}E[\max(S_T - X, 0)]. \tag{B.1}$$

Going through the steps of setting up a riskless portfolio as in chapter 3, we know that the return on S is r. Interest on the foreign currency is equal to r^* so that the risk neutral growth rate of S is equal to $r - r^*$. Thus the risk neutral process of the price of S is:

$$dS = (r - r^*)Sdt + \sigma Sdz. \tag{B.2}$$

We know that S is lognormally distributed. Applying the lognormal distribution to equation B.1 gives

$$C = e^{-r(T-t)} \int_{\ln X}^{\infty} \frac{1}{\sqrt{2\pi\sigma^2(T-t)}} \frac{1}{S_T} e^{-(\ln S_T - m)^2/2\sigma^2(T-t)} [S_T - X)]dS_T$$

$$= e^{-r(T-t)} \left[\frac{1}{\sqrt{2\pi\sigma^2(T-t)}} \int_{\ln X}^{\infty} e^{-(\ln S_T - m)^2/2\sigma^2(T-t)} dS_T - X \frac{1}{\sqrt{2\pi\sigma^2(T-t)}} \int_{\ln X}^{\infty} \frac{1}{S_T} e^{-(\ln S_T - m)^2/2\sigma^2(T-t)} dS_T \right], \tag{B.3}$$

where m is the mean of S_T.

First we evaluate the second interval on the RHS of B.3. Let $\epsilon = \{(\ln S_T - m)/\sigma\sqrt{T-t}\}$ and make the change of variable, knowing that $\{(d\epsilon/dS_T) = (1/S_T/\sigma\sqrt{T-t})\}$ This gives

$$-X\frac{1}{\sqrt{2\pi}}\int\limits_{\frac{\ln X-m}{\sigma\sqrt{T-t}}}^{\infty}e^{-\varepsilon^2/2}\,d\varepsilon.\qquad\text{(B.4)}$$

Equation B.4 is X multiplied by the probability that $S_T > X$. This probability can be visualized as the area under the standard normal curve to the right of the cut-off point. As we know, the convention in option pricing is to use areas to the left of the cut-off point. Thus, since the standard normal curve is symmetrical around zero, the probability that $\varepsilon > \{(\ln\ X-m)/\sigma\sqrt{T-t}\}$ is the same as the probability that $\varepsilon<-\{(\ln\ X-m)/\sigma\sqrt{T-t}\}$. Making this transformation gives

$$-X\frac{1}{\sqrt{2\pi}}\int\limits_{\infty}^{\frac{m-\ln X}{\sigma\sqrt{T-t}}}\varepsilon^{-\varepsilon^2/2}\,d\varepsilon.\qquad\text{(B.5)}$$

To find the parameters for S_T, let

$$y = \ln S_T.\qquad\text{(B.6)}$$

Apply Ito's lemma to B.6 and substitute from equation B.2:

$$dy = \frac{1}{S_T}dS_T - \frac{1}{2S_T^2}dS_T^2$$

$$dy = \frac{1}{S_T}[(r-r^*)S_T dt + S_T\sigma dz] - \frac{1}{2S_T^2}\sigma^2 S_T^2 dt$$

$$dy = (r-r^*-\frac{\sigma^2}{2})dt + \sigma dz.\qquad\text{(B.7)}$$

Integrate B.7:

$$y_T = y_t + (r-r^*-\frac{\sigma^2}{2})(T-t) + \sigma\varepsilon\sqrt{T-t}.\qquad\text{(B.8)}$$

Since $E(dz) = 0$, the mean of $\ln S_T$ is $y_t + (r - r^* - \sigma^2/2)(T-t)$ and the variance is $\sigma^2(T - t)$. Substituting the mean as $\ln S_t + (r - r^* - \sigma^2/2)(T-t)$ for m in equation B.5 means that B.5 is evaluated at:

$$d_2 = \frac{\ln \frac{S_t}{X} + (r - r^* - \frac{\sigma^2}{2})(T - t)}{\sigma\sqrt{T - t}},$$

(B.9)

which gives

$$-XN(d_2).$$

(B.10)

To evaluate the first integral on the RHS of equation B.3 we proceed as before. Let $\epsilon = \{(\ln S_t - m)/\sigma\sqrt{T} - t\}$ and make the change of variable, knowing that $d\epsilon/dS_T = \{1/S_T\sigma\sqrt{T} - t\}$. This gives:

$$\frac{1}{\sqrt{2\pi}} \int_{\ln\frac{X-m}{\sigma\sqrt{T-t}}}^{\infty} S_T e^{-\epsilon^2/2} d\epsilon.$$

(B.11)

Substituting from equation B.8 for S_T in the first integral on the RHS of equation B.3 gives:

$$\frac{1}{\sqrt{2\pi}} S_t e^{(r-r^*-\frac{\sigma^2}{2})(T-t)} \int_{\ln\frac{X-m}{\sigma\sqrt{T-t}}}^{\infty} e^{\sigma\epsilon\sqrt{T-t}} e^{-\epsilon^2/2} d\epsilon.$$

(B.12)

Add $\{\sigma^2(T - t)/2\} - \{\sigma^2(T - t)/2\}$ to the exponents in the integral to complete the square. This gives:

$$\frac{1}{\sqrt{2\pi}} S_t e^{(r-r^*-\frac{\sigma^2}{2})(T-t)+\frac{\sigma^2}{2}(T-t)} \int_{\ln\frac{X-m}{\sigma\sqrt{T-t}}}^{\infty} e^{-\frac{1}{2}(\epsilon^2 - 2\sigma\epsilon\sqrt{T-t} + \sigma^2(T-t))^2} d\epsilon.$$

(B.13)

Make the change of variables $\omega = \epsilon - \sigma\sqrt{T - t}$,

$$\frac{1}{\sqrt{2\pi}} S_t e^{(r-r^*)(T-t)} \int_{\ln\frac{X-m}{\sigma\sqrt{T-t}} - \sigma\sqrt{T-t}}^{\infty} e^{-\frac{\omega^2}{2}} d\omega.$$

(B.14)

Substituting the value for m and translating from the right of the cut-off point to the left gives:

$$\frac{1}{\sqrt{2\pi}} S_t e^{(r-r^*)(T-t)} \int_{-\infty}^{d_1} e^{\frac{-\omega^2}{2}} d\omega, \tag{B.15}$$

where

$$d_1 - \frac{\ln\frac{S_t}{X} + (r - r^* + \frac{\sigma^2}{2})(T-t)}{\sigma\sqrt{T-t}}. \tag{B.16}$$

Thus, the first integral on the RHS of equation B.3 is equal to:

$$S_t e^{(r-r^*)(T-t)} N(d_1). \tag{B.17}$$

Putting equations B.10 and B.17 together gives:

$$C = S_t e^{-r^*(T-t)} N(d_1) - X e^{-r(T-t)} N(d_2). \tag{B.18}$$

Chapter 4

Hedging and Trading Strategies: Simple Options and Exotics

Currency options are a valuable tool for managing exchange risk, and their scope is really quite broad since they make it possible to eliminate much of the risk that treasurers deem excessive. They are also effective at ensuring wealth protection while avoiding many costly and useless transactions. Although options markets are essentially different from the traditional futures and forwards markets, they are, at least, auxiliary to them.

Besides hedging risk, currency options are useful as highly levered investment vehicles for those who anticipate short-term currency movements better than the average. In this sense, the options markets attract a clientele of speculators whose activity allows hedgers to offset their risk. Nevertheless, hedging should not be confused with speculation, although they are both often present in a single transaction. In what follows, we will present the different intervention strategies of hedging and speculation, conscious of the fact that for a given level of risk, some strategies will interest hedgers and other speculators, but that in any single transaction, both can be present.

HEDGING WITH OPTIONS

Imports, exports, foreign investments, and loans raised in other currencies are some of the most common transactions that require currency hedging. The positions can be long or short and the options to hedge them can be traded on either a domestic market or a foreign market. Finally, the hedge can be constructed by buying an option, by selling an option, or by a combination of both. In this section, we will consider the basic strategies. More sophisticated strategies will be treated in the next section.

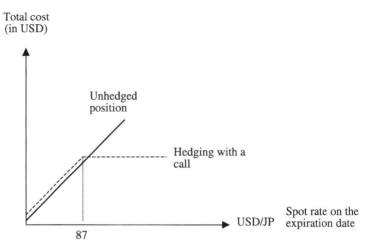

Figure 4.1   Hedging a short position with a call

Hedging with an Option Purchase

A long position refers to a claim in foreign currency such as a receipt from exports, while a short position refers to a liability such as a payment for imports. The appropriate hedging strategies are symmetrical. To hedge a long position in foreign currency on the domestic market (where the exchange rate is quoted as the number of units of domestic currency to buy one unit of foreign currency [S(domestic/foreign)]), puts should be purchased. To hedge a short position, calls should be purchased. If hedging is done on a foreign market, the operations would be reversed.

Hedging a Short Position

Suppose that an American importer has to pay a bill for 50 million yen in two months time. The spot rate in New York, S(USD/JPY) is $0.8696 per 100 yen. To hedge against an appreciation of the yen, the importer purchases a call.

As an example, suppose that the importer purchases a call with a strike price of 87 for a contract expiring in two months at a price of $1.18. In other words, he can buy the right to buy 50 million yen in two months for $0.87 per 100 yen for $0.0118 per 100 yen. Figure 4.1 illustrates the possible outcomes to be obtained in two months according to how the exchange rate behaves.

If in two months the exchange rate is a higher than $0.87, the calls will be exercised and he will pay $435,000 for the 50 million yen. The total cost

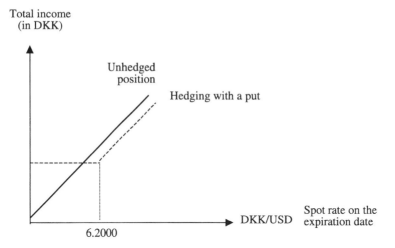

Figure 4.2   Hedging a long position with a put

of the operation will be $440,900 ($435,000 for the yen plus $5,900 for the premium) and the effective exchange rate will be $0.8818 [$440,900/ (50,000,000/100)]. If the exchange rate is lower than $0.87, at $0.82, for example, the calls will expire worthless. In this case, the effective exchange rate will be $0.8318 ($0.82 plus the premium of $0.0118 paid for each 100 yen). Thus, although he would pay more for the yen than the current exchange rate because of the premium, he still would benefit considerably from the yen's fall. If the hedging had been done on the Japanese market, it would have involved purchasing a put.

Hedging a Long Position

Consider a Danish company that has just signed a contract for $1 million worth of exports that will be paid in three months. The spot rate is DKK 6.2000 for 1 USD. To hedge on the Danish market against a fall in the dollar, a put should be purchased.

As an example, suppose that the company purchases an at the money put with a strike price of 6.2000, an expiration date that coincides with his expected dollar income in three months and a premium of 2 percent. This put on $1 million will cover him if the dollar falls sharply. If, for example, it falls to 5.8000, the treasurer will exercise the put and receive an effective rate of DKK 6.0760 (6.2000 − 0.02 × 6.2000). If the dollar rises above 6.2000, the put will expire worthless and the treasurer will sell his dollars at the spot rate. His effective rate will be equal to the spot rate less the premium of DKK 0.124. Figure 4.2 shows the payoff schedule.

Advantages and Disadvantages of Hedging with Currency Options

The obvious advantage of hedging with options is that losses are limited to the cost of purchasing the option if the exchange rate moves unfavorably while gains are unlimited if the rate moves favorably. The main disadvantage is that options are costly. When the maximum cost of foreign currency hedged with an option (the strike price plus the premium for a call; strike price minus the premium for a put) is compared with the cost of a forward contract, option hedging is always more costly.

We should also point out that the option hedge has another advantage when the commercial cash flow is not entirely certain. The order could be canceled, for example. With a classic hedge of dollars sold forward, the exporter would find himself in a purely speculative position. On the maturity date he would have to come up with the dollars. If the value of the dollar falls, he would make money but if it rises, he would lose money. The potential loss is theoretically unlimited. As we saw in chapter 2, it is always possible to close out the position, but that would generate another transaction cost, and the treasurer would still have to pay the difference in the two forward prices if the rate has moved against him. In the case of a put, he is still in a speculative position but his exposure is limited to the amount of the premium. In the case of a potential unwanted speculative position generated by foreign currency hedging, the option hedge is clearly preferable.

With this in mind, the question is: When should a call be used to hedge foreign exchange risk? To answer this question we must distinguish between three situations:

(a) when a rise (fall) in the exchange rate is expected and the probability of this outcome is very high,

(b) when a fall (rise) in the exchange rate is expected and the probability of this outcome is very high,

(c) when there is an expected movement one way or the other but there is also a strong possibility of a move in the opposite direction.

In case (a), when a rise (fall) in the exchange rate is very probable, a classic forward hedge is the best strategy because it is the least costly. In case (b), when a fall (rise) in the exchange rate is very probable, the best strategy is not to cover and avoid all costs while benefiting fully from the lower (higher) rate. In case (c), where there is considerable uncertainty, the option might be the best strategy. If there is a sharp rise (fall) in the exchange rate, total costs are limited. If there is a sharp fall (rise), some of the benefits are captured. Only in the zone of relative stability between the forward rate and the forward rate plus the option premium is an option hedge clearly the inferior strategy. This is because it is the costliest strategy and no benefits accrue to the option holder if the exchange rate does not move outside this range. In conclusion, we can say that hedging with options is the most advantageous when uncertainty is the greatest and big moves in both directions are a strong possibility. Remember that the purchase of an option gives the holder the rights to gains from a positive gamma. This right has a cost that can only be recovered through a strong price movement.

Covering an Export from Europe on the American Futures Market

As we mentioned, the Chicago Mercantile Exchange (CME) trades puts and calls on currency futures rather than on the currency itself. The buyer of a call on a futures contract buys the right to buy a futures contract on the underlying currency on a given expiration date. The futures position is recorded with respect to the corresponding futures contract traded on the CME. The use of these options is very close to the use of straightforward currency options. An example will illustrate how they can be used.

Suppose that a Swiss exporter expects a payment of 344,000 USD four months in the future from a South American client. The exchange rate in Zurich is CHF 1.8200 for USD 1. To hedge against a fall in the value of the dollar, he decides to purchase a call on the CME's Swiss franc futures contract. An American broker quotes him a price of 0.98 for a call on a Swiss franc futures contract with a strike price of 55 and expiration time of three months. This means that by paying $0.0098 per franc he has the right in three months time to buy a futures contract worth 125,000 francs for a price of $0.55 per franc. When the three months are up, he will have to decide whether or not to exercise his option to buy a futures contract on francs. If he exercises, he will own a futures contract on francs but not the francs themselves. In fact, if he exercises, he will receive the difference between the previous day's settlement price and the option's strike price as well as the futures contract. The option, in this case, will have been transformed into a firm futures position. The important point to remember is that the exchange rate pertinent to the option contract is the futures rate and not the spot rate.

Since he is expecting $344,000 and each contract is worth CHF 125,000, he will need about 625,000 francs or five calls. If in three months the one-month futures rate on francs is higher than $0.55 (USD: 1.8182 CHF), he will exercise his call. If it is lower, he will let it expire.

For example, if the futures rate goes to $0.60 (USD: 1.6667 CHF), the Swiss exporter will exercise his option and acquire five one-month futures contracts for a total amount of 625,000 francs. Abstracting from the intricacies of the marking-to-market operations on futures contracts, he will end up paying $343,750 (0.55 × 625,000) for 625,000 francs. The calls cost him $6,125 (0.0098 × 625,000) or 11,147.50 CHF converted at the spot rate of 1.8200 CHF when he bought the calls. His net income in francs, then, was 613,852.50 CHF (625,000 – 11,147.50) and he paid $343,750 for an effective exchange rate of 1.7858, better than the futures rate of 1.6667 on the call's expiration date.

If the dollar does not appreciate, it is obvious that the Swiss exporter will not exercise the calls. Suppose that on the expiration date the futures exchange rate is $0.50 (2.0000 CHF). They will not be exercised because it is lower than the strike price of $0.55. This brings up another problem. Because the exporter will not receive his dollars for another month, he has to decide whether or not to hedge his exposure for the remaining month. He could hedge by purchasing five futures contracts at $0.50. In this case, he will have paid $312,500 for which he receives 625,000 francs. This leaves him with $31,500 left over, which cannot be covered on the organized exchange because the mark value is lower than the standardized contract for 125,000 francs. His effective exchange rate for the full $344,000 depends on the rate he gets for the $31,500 balance. One choice is to take the exchange risk and leave the balance unhedged. Another choice is to cover it with a forward contract.

Hedging by Selling Options

As we mentioned above, the main disadvantage of using options to hedge foreign exchange risk is the cost, that is, the premium that they must pay. An option purchase is only advantageous if wide swings of the exchange rate in both directions are probable (high volatility). If the forecast is for relative stability (low volatility), it might be better to sell options. In this section we will consider two examples: covering a short position by selling puts and covering a long position by selling calls.

Covering a Short Position by Selling Puts

A liability in foreign exchange is exposed to the risk that the foreign exchange will become more costly before the bill is due. To reduce or eliminate this risk, he can buy calls on the foreign currency if he uses his domestic market or buy puts on the domestic currency if he uses a foreign market. We characterized this position as having a positive delta, meaning that if the foreign currency gains in value our position also gains in value. Another way of generating a positive delta is to sell a put on the foreign currency because a put's delta is negative. Shorting a negative delta generates a positive delta. As usual, the best way to illustrate this point is with an example.

Imagine the case of a Korean importer of petroleum products who has a bill of $10 million to pay in three months time. The current spot exchange rate in Seoul is USD: 1780 KPW and the three-month forward rate is 1814. A three-month dollar put with a strike price of 1780 is selling over the counter at 3.37 percent, or about 60 won per dollar. If the dollar appreciates to 1820 won in three months, the put will expire worthless and the importer will keep the premium. The cost of his dollars will then be 1820 won paid spot less the 60 won received for the premium for a total of 1760 won per dollar. This rate is far better than the spot rate of 1820 or the 1814 he could have paid to cover himself with a forward contract. If the value of the dollar falls to 1740, the put will be exercised and the importer will pay 1780 for the dollars. His all-in cost will be the 1780 paid less the 60 received for the premium for a total of 1720, a much better price than the market rate of 1740 or the forward rate of 1814.

Hedging by selling puts is the best strategy as long as the exchange rate stays between 1720 (1780 − 60) and 1874 (1814 + 60). One of the reasons that the band is so wide is that the forward dollar is at a premium. If it had been at a discount, the band would have been narrower. In any case, selling puts can be a profitable hedging strategy if the exchange rate is expected to remain relatively stable. Otherwise, it is not the best strategy. If the dollar falls to 1700, for example, the put will be exercised and the cost to the importer will still be 1720, far higher than the spot rate. By the same token, if the dollar rises to 1900, the put will expire and the cost of the dollar will be 1840, the spot rate less the premium. This rate is higher than the 1814, which could have been obtained with a forward contract and, thus, the hedge was inadequate.

Covering a Long Position by Selling Calls

Claims in foreign currency are exposed to the risk that the value of the currency will fall. If wide swings in the value of the currency are expected, currency puts can be purchased to eliminate or reduce this risk. We characterized this position as having a negative delta, meaning that if the foreign currency loses value, our position gains in value. Another way of generating a negative delta is to sell a call on the foreign currency because a call's delta is positive. Shorting a positive delta generates a negative delta. As usual, the best way to illustrate this point is with an example.

Imagine a Russian exporter with a claim in dollars, and he wants to protect himself against a fall in the value of the dollar. In Moscow, the spot exchange rate is USD: 25.0000 RUR and 25.2500 three-month forward. He sells a three-month call on U.S. dollars with a strike price of 25 to his bank for 2.7 percent, or 0.675 rubles, for each dollar. If the value of the dollar falls below 25.00 to 24.60, for example, the call will not be exercised. He will sell his dollars for the spot rate of 24.70 and pocket the premium of 0.675 on the call. His effective exchange rate will be 25.375, better than the spot rate or the forward rate of 25.25 he could have contracted for.

Suppose that the dollar appreciates to 25.30. The call will be exercised and he will receive 25 rubles for each dollar. His effective rate will be the

25-ruble strike price plus the 0.675 ruble premium for a total of 25.675, a rate better than the spot rate of 25.30 and the forward rate of 25.25.

The risk from selling the call comes if the dollar falls sharply in value, to 24, for example. The call is not exercised and the exporter receives the spot rate plus the premium for each franc, a rate of 24.675, far lower than the forward rate.

Hedging by selling calls is the best strategy as long as the exchange rate stays in the band between 24.5750 (25.2500 – 0.675) and 25.6750 (25.0000 + 0.675). Selling puts can be a profitable hedging strategy if the exchange rate is expected to remain relatively stable.

Tunnels: Hedging with Sales and Purchases of Options

Hedging by purchasing options is costly because of the premium and effective only in times of high volatility. Hedging by selling options can be advantageous in times of low volatility. The two strategies are complementary and lead to strategies that combine both of them.

The Tunnel for Short Positions

Covering exchange risk on a short position in foreign currency can be achieved on the domestic (foreign) market by buying (selling) calls or by selling (buying) puts. To reduce the cost of an option hedge, the treasurer may want to combine both of them. Selling the put reduces the cost of purchasing the call. The cost is completely eliminated if the premium on the sale of the put covers the premium on the call purchase.

Consider a Swiss manufacturer with a three-month dollar liability, and suppose that the spot exchange rate is USD: 1.8200 CHF and the three-month forward rate is 1.8382. The price of a three-month, out-of-the-money call with a strike price of 1.9000 is 0.4 percent. The call is not expensive because the strike price is high. He can also sell a three-month put with a strike price of 1.7600 for 0.4 percent. The two premiums offset each other and the cost is zero.

Figure 4.3 illustrates the outcome profile of this strategy. If the dollar appreciates sharply, the call will be exercised at 1.9000 for a cost of 1.9000 francs per dollar. On the other hand, if the dollar depreciates sharply, the put will be exercised and the cost will be 1.7600 marks per dollar. The band between these two limit rates is called a *tunnel*. Inside the tunnel, the importer will receive whatever the spot rate happens to be, but he can never pay more than 1.9000 and never less than 1.7600. The disadvantage of this position resides in the fact that if the rate goes below 1.7600, he will not benefit from the lower rate. The advantage of a tunnel is that the cost of the premium is reduced, risk is limited, and gains from favorable moves in the exchange rate can be realized.

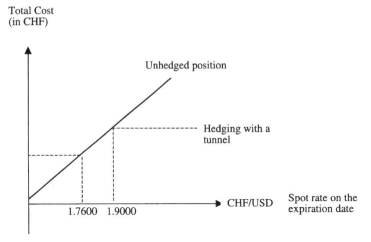

Figure 4.3   Hedging a short position with a tunnel

The Tunnel for Long Positions in Foreign Currency

The tunnel for long positions is symmetrical to the tunnel for short positions. On the domestic (foreign) market, the hedger simultaneously purchases (sells) a put and sells (purchases) a call. Both instruments are chosen out-of-the-money. Thus, if the value of the foreign currency falls sharply, the put guarantees a minimum price. If it rises sharply, the call will be exercised but will have benefited from the rise up to the strike price. Costs are reduced because the premium received from the sale of the call goes to offset the purchase of the put. The two premiums might not be equal so the net cost will be the difference between the two premiums. Figure 4.4 shows the outcome profile when the tunnel is generated on the domestic market.

SPECULATIVE USES OF OPTIONS

On-the-spot market profits can be made when the price rises if one buys before the rise. If a fall is anticipated, profits can be made by selling short. On-the-futures market profits can be made with a rise or a fall. Selling (buying) forward before a fall (rise) and buying (selling) back after it yields a profit. If the price does not move, however, profits cannot be made even on the futures markets. With options markets, the possibilities are even broader. Profits can be made if the price rises, if it falls, and even if it remains unchanged.

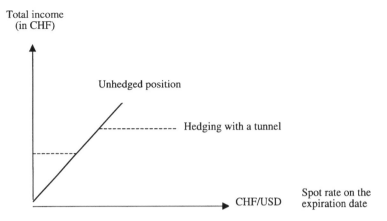

Figure 4.4   Hedging a long position with a tunnel

Speculating on a Price Rise: Buying Calls

Figure 4.5 illustrates what happens on a call's expiration date. If the spot exchange rate is higher than the strike price plus the premium paid for the call, there is a profit for the buyer. If the exchange rate is equal to or lower than the strike price, he loses the full value of the premium. If it is between the strike price plus the premium, he loses part of the premium. Calls, then, have a very risky side to them. Take the case of the most popular calls, those that are close-to-the-money. If the exchange rate stays stable over the life of the option, the outcome for those having an uncovered position in foreign exchange is neutral. They neither gain nor lose. For the option holder the result is different. He loses the entire amount of the premium if the exchange rate stays stable over the life of the option even if it soars in the days following the expiration date. The call option is risky, then, for two reasons: First, because it is a bet on the evolution of the exchange rate. Second, because the expected evolution must take place in a limited period of time.

Take an out-of-the-money, three-month call on the euro with a strike price of 0.90 quoted at 2 percent and a spot rate of 0.88 on the purchase date. In U.S. dollars the premium is worth $0.02 \times 0.88 = 0.018$ USD. On the expiration date, if the spot rate has moved to 0.90, the call buyer will have lost the whole premium, whereas someone who had been long in dollars would have made nearly 2.3 percent $(0.09/0.88 - 1)$. If the rate has moved to 0.918, the option buyer still would not make a profit while the long position in foreign exchange would show a return of more than 4 percent. Above the rate of 0.918, the option holder begins to make a profit where

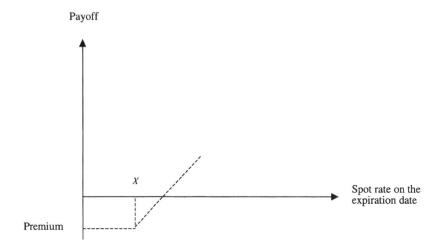

Figure 4.5 Payoff on a purchased call

small increases yield high returns. At a rate of only 0.92, he would have a return of more than 11 percent [(0.92 − 0.918)/0.018]. The long position would only yield slightly more than 4.5 percent. If the rate goes to 0.95, the long position will yield about 8 percent while the call buyer's return will be more than 177 percent. Calls have a very high degree of leverage.

Buying a currency call means betting on a relatively sharp move in the exchange rate in a limited period of time. The time frame is limited to the life of the call, leverage is considerable and losses are limited to the amount of the premium paid. Furthermore, for a given currency, an investor has several different calls to choose from. The performance of the individual calls can be quite different, depending on their strike price and expiration date.

Calls deeply in- and out-of-the-money have low gammas. At-the-money calls have the highest gammas and these are the ones that truly represent unique properties compared to other types of financial instruments. In practice, it is at this level that transaction volume is highest and the market is the most liquid.

Speculating on a Price Fall: Buying Puts

The purchase of a put is especially recommended if a fall in the exchange rate is anticipated. Although the principle of a put is similar to that of a call, a put is not perfectly symmetrical with a call. As we will see in the next section where we deal with combinations of calls and puts, it

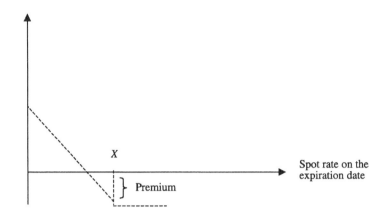

Figure 4.6   Payoff on a purchaser put

would be a costly error to think that the simultaneous purchase of a call and a put constitutes a position with no risk.

Figure 4.6 illustrates the profit and loss implications of a long position in puts on the expiration date. If the spot exchange rate is lower than the strike price minus the premium paid for the put (the break even point), the transaction will be profitable. If the exchange rate is equal to or greater than the strike price, the whole amount of the premium will be lost. As with a call, a put is a bet on future movements in the exchange rate within a fixed time period.

Puts on the same currency but with different strike prices are widely available. A put with a high strike price (deep in-the-money) is likely to be exercised and resembles a futures contract in the zone with the most likely outcomes for the exchange rate. A put with a very low strike price (deep out-of-the-money) resembles a lottery ticket in that it is a long shot and the price paid for it will probably be lost. Once again, it is at-the-money puts that have the highest gammas and represent truly unique properties compared to other types of financial instruments. It is also at this level that transaction volume is highest and the market is the most liquid.

Speculating on Price Stability: Selling Puts and Calls

Selling a naked call or put involves writing an option without taking an offsetting position on-the-spot or forward market. This is a very risky strategy because gains are limited to the amount of the premium whereas losses are virtually unlimited. However, if it is well understood and correctly employed, this strategy can offer solid opportunities for profit making when the exchange rate is stable.

On organized exchanges, it is always possible for the speculator to close out his position before the expiration date. This contract liquidity enables speculators to limit their losses. In this sense, writing a naked call does not expose its author to unlimited risk, although it is always a speculative operation. In the absence of sharp moves in the exchange rate and variations in volatility, writing a naked call is profitable. The simple passage of time guarantees a profit. This strategy is only optimal when the exchange rate is stable. For example, if the exchange rate falls sharply, the speculator would have done better to buy a put. If it rises sharply, he loses his shirt. The delta of writing a naked call is negative since the call is sold. The gamma is also negative. The theta is positive and reflects the favorable effect of the passage of time.

Writing a naked put completes the picture. It also is a risky strategy. In exchange for a small, limited profit (the premium) the speculator is exposed to substantial though not unlimited losses. The risk is not unlimited because the exchange rate cannot be negative. As in the case of the naked call, the existence of organized exchanges makes it possible to limit the risks and make the strategy accessible to competent speculators.

ADVANCED TRADING STRATEGIES

In the previous section we focused on trading strategies involving first a single option and then the simultaneous purchase and sale of a call (put) and a put (call). In this section, we will look at other combinations of simple options and how they can be used. The operations often seem complex and the language that describes them is colorful but we can basically distinguish between two types of combinations. The first type, called *spreads*, combines options of different series but of the same class, where some options are bought and others are written. The second type, like *straddles* and *strangles*, combines different types (calls and puts) of options.

Strategies Based on Call Combinations

The simplest strategies combine the purchase and sale of calls with the same expiration date but with different strike prices or with the same strike price but different expiration dates. When the expiration date is the same and the strike price is different, they are called *vertical spreads*. When the expiration date is different and the strike price is the same, they are called *horizontal* or *calendar spreads*.

Purchased (Bullish) Vertical Spreads

Three types of purchased vertical spreads can be distinguished: out-of-the-money, at-the-money, and in-the-money. Purchased vertical spreads are also called bullish spreads because upward moves in the exchange rate make them profitable.

1. An out-of-the-money purchased (bullish) vertical spread involves buying a call with a strike price above the spot exchange rate and selling a call with the same expiration date at an even higher strike price. Both calls are out-of-the-money. In this type of spread, the investor is looking for a rise in the exchange rate. His maximum loss is equal to the cost of the spread, which is the difference between the premiums of the two options. His maximum gain is equal to the difference in their strike prices minus the cost of the spread.

EXAMPLE:

Table 4.1 shows the quotes on the Philadelphia Stock Exchange for premiums on Swiss franc calls at various strike prices and expiration dates.

With the spot exchange rate at 55.11 an out-of-the-money bullish spread involves purchasing a CHF 55 1/2 JUL and selling a CHF 56 JUL. The cost of the spread is 0.35 – 0.18 = 0.17. For the investor to make money the exchange rate must go above 55.67. If it rises to 56, the investor's gain will be 0.50 – 0.17 = 0.33, the difference in the strike prices minus the cost of the spread.

2. At-the-money purchased vertical spreads involve the purchase of an in-the-money call and the sale of an out-of-the-money-call with the same expiration date. For example, in Table 4.1, the purchase of a CHF 55 AUG and the sale of a CHF 55 1/2 AUG would be an at-the-money purchased vertical spread. In spreads of this type, the investor is looking for a rise in the exchange rate, but the exchange rate has to rise less than an out-of-the-money spread to give a profit. Again, his maximum loss

Table 4.1
Quotes on Swiss Franc Calls

Currency	Strike	July	August	September
CHF	53 1/2	1.61	1.66	—
CHF	54	1.12	1.26	1.42
CHF	54 1/2	0.75	1.14	—
CHF	55	0.54	0.85	1.08
CHF	55 1/2	0.35	0.63	—
CHF	56	0.18	0.45	—

Spot Rate = 55.11

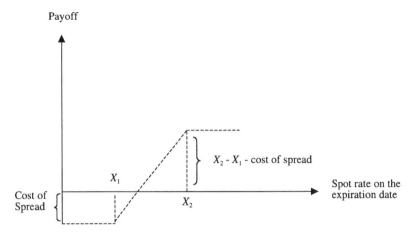

Figure 4.7   Payoff profile of a purchased vertical call spread

is equal to the cost of the spread, which, because the spread is at the money, will be higher than the out-of-the-money spread. The investor's maximum gain is equal to the difference in their strike prices minus the cost of the spread.

3. In-the-money purchased vertical spreads involve the purchase of an in-the-money call and the sale of another in-the-money call, but with a strike price higher than the call that is purchased: a CHF 54 JUL purchased and a CHF 54 1/2 JUL sold. An investor in this position is not hoping for a rise in the exchange rate. He is hoping that the exchange rate stays at its current level or that at least, it does not go below the strike price of the written call.

Figure 4.7 shows the payoff for purchased vertical spreads.

Written (Bearish) Vertical Spreads

Written vertical spreads generate a net cash inflow at the outset. They are also called bearish spreads because a favorable outcome depends on a fall in the exchange rate. As with the purchased vertical spreads, written vertical spreads can be grouped into three categories: out-of-the-money, at-the-money, and in-the-money.

1. An out-of-the-money written vertical spread consists of the purchase of a call with a strike price below the spot exchange rate and a sale of another call with the same expiration date and a higher strike price. In fact, each individual call is in-the-money because the strike prices are below the current exchange rate. The spread, however, is out-of-the-money because the exchange rate must fall for the investor to make a profit. The investor's maximum gain is the income from the spread. His maximum loss is the difference between the strike prices minus the income from the spread.

EXAMPLE:

Sell a CHF 54 JUL and buy a CHF 54 1/2 JUL. The income is 1.12 – 0.75 = 0.37.
On the expiration date, the most the investor can pay out is 0.50, the difference between
   the strike prices. Thus, his maximum loss is 0.50 – 0.37 = 0.13. If the exchange rate falls
   below 54, neither of the options will be exercised and his maximum profit is 0.37, the
   difference between the two premiums. If the exchange rate stays above 54.37, the
   investor loses. If the rate goes up to 54.5 or above, his loss is maximum and equal to
   0.50 – 0.37 = 0.13.

2. At-the-money written vertical spreads involve the sale of an in-the-money call
   and the purchase of an out-of-the-money call. For example, sell a CHF 55 AUG
   and purchase a CHF 55 1/2 AUG.

3. In-the-money written vertical spreads involve the purchase of an out-of-the-
   money call and the sale of an out-of-the-money call with a lower strike price.
   For example, purchase a CHF 56 JUL and sell a CHF 55 1/2 JUL.

Written vertical spreads are symmetrical with purchased vertical
spreads. Figure 4.8 shows the payoff profile of written vertical spreads.
Gains are limited to the income from the spread while losses are limited to
the difference in the strike prices less the income from the difference in the
premiums. The in-the-money spread is a bet against a big rise in the
exchange rate, which is profitable as long as the increase in the exchange
rate is small.

Combinations of Purchased and Written Vertical Spreads

Both the written and purchased in-the-money vertical spreads are bets
against large moves in the exchange rate, contrary to the market's anticipations reflected in the implied volatility. The spreads, then, have the
same goal and can be used together. In this case, the investor should buy
a call way in-the-money, the JUL 54, for example, and sell a call a little less
in-the-money, the JUL 54 1/2. This position corresponds to the purchased
in-the-money vertical spread. He should also sell a call out-of-the-money,
the JUL 55 1/2, and buy a call way out-of-the-money. This position corresponds to the written in-the-money vertical spread. The whole operation
is called a *condor*. Figure 4.9 shows the payoff profile. The position is profitable within the narrow band of stability and unprofitable everywhere
else. One advantage of this operation is that it has a low cost insofar as the
income from the written position helps to offset the outlay for the purchased position. Because of the multiple transactions, operations like this
can only be realized when costs for each transaction are low.

A well-known variation of the condor is called the *butterfly spread*. In
this situation, the two calls that are sold have the same strike price. For
example, buy JUL 54 1/2, sell two calls JUL 55, and buy one JUL 55 1/2.

Payoff

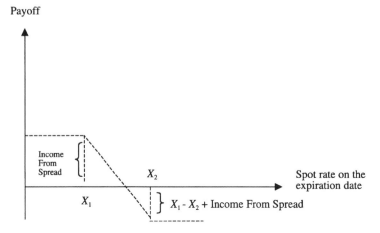

Figure 4.8   Payoff profile of a written vertical call spread

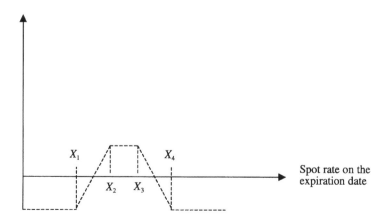

Figure 4.9   Payoff profile of a condor

This generates a cost of $0.75 - (2 \times 0.54) + 0.35 = 0.02$. Figure 4.10 shows the payoff profile. The maximum profit will be realized if the spot exchange rate is at 55. At this point income is 0.50 and profit is 0.48. The most that can be lost is 0.02, the initial cost of the position.

The condor and butterfly operations can be reversed so that the calls that were bought are sold and vice versa. The outcome diagram will be symmetric with Figure 4.10. In this position the investor is betting that the market's realized volatility will be higher than that implied by the options prices.

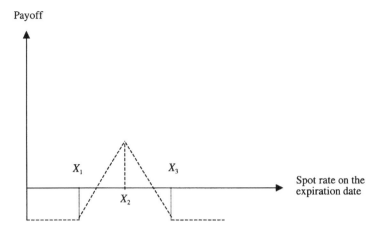

Figure 4.10 Payoff profile of a butterfly spread

Horizontal Spreads

As in the case of vertical spreads, three types of purchased horizontal spreads are available: In-the-money, at-the-money, and out-of-the-money. An in-the-money purchased horizontal spread involves buying and selling calls that are in-the-money; an at-the-money purchased horizontal spread involves calls that are at-the-money; and an out-of-the-money purchased horizontal spread involves calls that are out-of-the-money. In fact, only at-the-money horizontal spreads are pertinent because on the organized exchanges these are the only instruments with enough liquidity to make them feasible.

A purchased horizontal spread is speculation against big swings in the exchange rate and the fact that shorter term options have higher absolute thetas always lose time value faster than longer term options. The profit is derived from exploiting this phenomenon. The profit is at its maximum when the exchange rate remains stable.

The result will be quite different if the exchange rate undergoes a sharp rise or fall. A sharp fall in the exchange rate will cause the shorter term option to expire worthless while the value of the longer term call will not be worth much either because it has become way out-of-the-money. The larger the fall in the exchange rate, the closer the value of the spread comes to zero.

A sharp rise in the exchange rate will put both the calls way in-the-money. On the expiration date the shorter term call will be worth its intrinsic value and the longer term call will not be worth much more than its intrinsic value. Remember that the time value of an option is highest when the option is at-the-money. As the value of the exchange rate gets further

Payoff

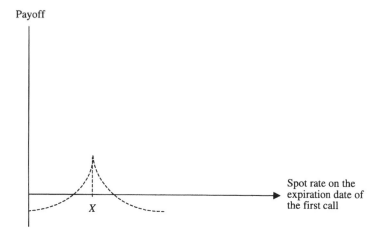

Spot rate on the
expiration date of
the first call

Figure 4.11   Payoff profile of a purchased horizontal call spread

from the strike price, the option's time value decreases. Figure 4.11 gives
the payoff pattern of a purchased horizontal spread if the longer term
option is sold when the shorter term option expires.

Thus, the at-the-money purchased horizontal spread is a bet on the stability of the exchange rate. Reversing the spread by buying the shortest
maturity and selling the longest would be the strategy to follow if the
investor feels that volatility will be higher than the premiums that are
implicit for the calls.

Other Combinations of Calls

It is obvious by now that the possible permutations of call combinations
are almost limitless. Most of them are not practical because of insufficient
liquidity, high transactions costs, or inadequate returns. There are two that
should be mentioned, though, because they can be useful for international
risk management: the diagonal spread and the ratio spreads.

1. In a *diagonal spread* one call is bought and another sold but with different strike
   prices and different expiration dates. In reality, a diagonal spread is a combination of a vertical spread and a horizontal spread. The investor buys a call with a
   relatively long time to expiration and sells another call with a shorter time to
   expiration and a higher strike price. The diagonal spread can be analyzed like a
   vertical spread with the advantage of a horizontal spread to back it up. Normally, the premium on the purchased call depreciates more slowly than the premium on the written call because, other things being equal, the absolute value
   of at-the-money thetas are higher for shorter term options. The longer term call
   costs more, but its resale value is higher.

A diagonal spread can also be analyzed like a horizontal spread with the advantage of a vertical spread. Since the strike price of the written call is higher, possible gains from an appreciation of the exchange rate are also higher. The disadvantage of the diagonal spread is that it is more costly. In fact, its cost is equal to the sum of the cost of a vertical spread and a horizontal spread.

From Table 4.1, for example, the purchase of an AUG 55 1/2 call and the sale of a JUL 56 call are an example of a diagonal spread. It can be analyzed as the sum of a horizontal spread [AUG 55 1/2 purchased, JUL 55 1/2 sold] and a vertical spread [JUL 55 1/2 purchased, JUL 56 sold].

2. A *ratio spread* involves taking any spread already encountered and augmenting it with the purchase or sale of one or more calls. Possible combinations are limited only by the imagination of the investor. Understanding how they work, however, is simple. One of the sides of the spread is doubled or tripled. For example, a purchased, out-of-the-money, vertical ratio spread could be composed of two JUL 55 1/2 purchased and one JUL 56 sold.

Because two calls are purchased, the cost is higher. The ratio is 2/1, two purchased against one sold. Thus, the payoff is doubled compared to a simple spread.

Either side of the spread could be augmented. For example, two JUL 56 could be sold and one JUL 55 1/2 bought. This 1/2 ratio is less bullish than the 2/1-ratio spread or the simple vertical spread, for that matter.

Strategies Based on Put Combinations

All the foregoing combinations using calls can be applied to puts where we find the four major spread categories—purchased vertical spreads, written vertical spreads, and written and purchased horizontal spreads. Put-based spreads can be out-of-the-money, at-the-money, and in-the-money.

1. *Purchased vertical spreads.* In a purchased vertical spread, the investor buys one put and simultaneously sells another with the same expiration date but a lower strike price. The spreads are in-the-money if both strike prices are higher than the spot exchange rate. They are at-the-money if the strike price of the purchased put is above the spot rate and the written put is below it. They are out-of-the-money if both strike prices are below the spot exchange rate. Where the out-of-the-money purchased vertical spread composed of calls was a bet on a rise in the exchange rate, the out-of-the-money purchased vertical spread composed of puts is a bet on a fall in the exchange rate. The maximum return is achieved when the exchange rate falls to the level of the lower strike price. Figure 4.12 shows the payoff profile of this type of spread.

2. *Written vertical spreads.* In a written vertical spread, the investor buys one put and sells another with the same expiration date but a higher strike price. The spreads can be in-the-money, at-the-money, or out-of-the-money. Where the written vertical spread composed of calls was a bet on a fall in the exchange rate, a written vertical spread composed of puts is a bet on a rise in the exchange rate. The maximum return is achieved when the exchange rate rises to the level of the higher strike price. Figure 4.13 illustrates the payoff profile.

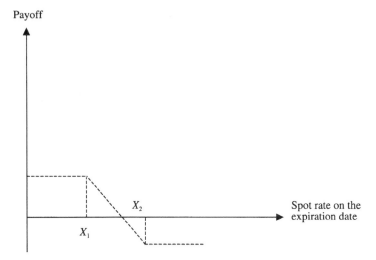

Figure 4.12   Payoff profile of a purchased vertical put spread

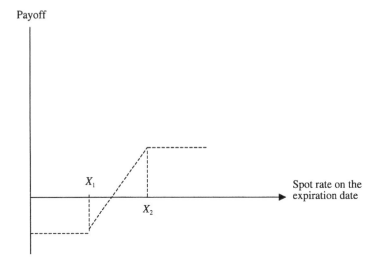

Figure 4.13   Payoff profile of a written vertical put spread

3. *Horizontal spreads.* In a horizontal spread, the investor buys a put with a relatively long time to expiration and simultaneously sells another with the same strike price but a shorter time to expiration. The spreads can be in-the-money, at-the-money, or out-of-the-money. Horizontal spreads with puts work like horizontal spreads with calls. They are a bet on the evolution of the time value of the two puts with a maximum return achieved when the exchange rate on the expiration date of the shortest term put is equal to its strike price.

Table 4.2
Call Spread and Put Spread Equivalencies

Call Spreads	Put Spreads
Out-of-the-money purchased vertical	Out-of-the-money written vertical
At-the-money purchased vertical	At-the-money written vertical
In-the-money purchased vertical	In-the-money written vertical
Out-of-the-money written vertical	Out-of-the-money purchased vertical
At-the-money written vertical	At-the-money purchased vertical
In-the-money written vertical	In-the-money purchased vertical
Out-of-the-money horizontal	In-the-money horizontal
At-the-money horizontal	At-the-money horizontal
In-the-money horizontal	Out-of-the-money horizontal

4. *Correspondence between call and put spreads.* Table 4.2 gives the correspondence between call spreads and put spreads. Although call spreads have their put spread equivalent, the two strategies are not always financially equivalent due to transaction costs and the possibility of early exercise. For example, an in-the-money purchased vertical call spread has a high probability of early exercise if the underlying currency is at a forward discount. Furthermore, in order to realize a profit (loss) on the expiration date, it will usually be necessary to repurchase the written option and sell the purchased one, thereby incurring incremental transaction costs. On the other hand, the equivalent put spread has little chance of being exercised early. Furthermore, if the operation succeeds, the puts will have a value of zero and will not have to be exercised on the expiration date for the investor to realize his profit, thereby eliminating the transaction costs associated with closing out his position. The saving in transaction costs and the low risk of early exercise make the put spread preferable to the call spread. Considerations such as this make it important for investors to have a clear theoretical and practical understanding of the ins and outs of the strategies that they intend to implement.

Straddles and Strangles

Straddles and *strangles* involve the simultaneous purchase of a call and a put. A straddle is when the two options have the same strike price and expiration date. In the other cases a strangle results.

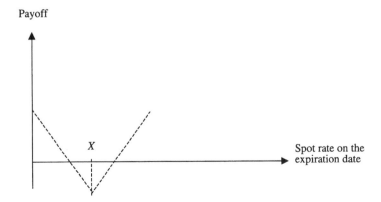

Figure 4.14   Payoff profile of a straddle

Straddles

The purchase of a straddle is a bet on a sudden large rise or fall in the underlying exchange rate. A sharp rise generates a profit from the call while the put becomes worthless. When a sharp fall occurs, the put generates a profit while the call becomes worthless. The rise or fall must be sharp enough to offset the cost of buying the options. If the rise is not sharp enough, the straddle will generate a loss. The loss is at its maximum when the exchange rate ends up at the strike price on the expiration date.

A trader could generate a straddle by purchasing a call and a put with a strike price of 55 and a July expiration date. Suppose the straddle costs 1.12, the sum of the two premiums. Its breakeven points are attained when the gain on one of the two options is high enough to offset the cost. This occurs at an exchange rate of 56.12 or 53.88. The possibility of a total loss is quite small. For a total loss to happen, the exchange rate would have to end up at exactly 55. More often than not, losses that do occur are only partial. In this sense, a straddle is less risky than the purchase of a simple put or call. On the other hand, possible returns are also more limited. Figure 4.14 shows a depiction of an outcome profile of a straddle.

Given that a straddle is a bet on a big move in the exchange rate, managing a straddle requires knowing when to close it out. Closing out the straddle before its expiration would be justified if a sharp upward or downward move takes place and one of the two options acquires a significant intrinsic value. Early closure would also be justified if a sharp increase in volatility causes an important rise in the time value of the two options. In this case, it would be better to take advantage of the gains before the passage of time wears them away.

Closing out the whole position, of course, is not always necessary. In the case where one of the two options acquires significant intrinsic value, it

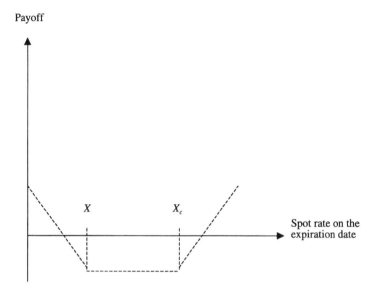

Figure 4.15   Payoff profile of a strangle

might be better to close out this side only, since most of the profit is here. The other option will be far out-of the-money with little time value and holding onto it will save transaction costs. Furthermore, something might be gained if the exchange rate starts to move the other way.

Strips and Straps

Strips and *straps* are like ratio spreads in that they augment one side of the straddle. A strip consists of a long position in one call and two puts with the same strike price and expiration date. It augments the gains if the exchange rate falls sharply. A strap consists of a long position in two calls and one put with the same strike price and expiration date. It augments the gains if the exchange rate rises sharply.

Strangles

The purchase of a call and a put with the same expiration date and different strike prices is called a *strangle*. The purchase of a strangle is like a straddle in that it is a bet on an expected sharp move in the exchange rate one way or the other. Figure 4.15 shows the payoff profile of this kind of position. The loss is total if the exchange rate stays between the two strike prices. The points that break even are therefore further apart than in the case of a straddle. The advantage of a strangle resides in the lower premiums due to the fact that the two options are out-of-the-money.

CAPS, FLOORS, COLLARS, AND SWAPTIONS

The foregoing section dealt with option packages in the form of spreads, straddles, strangles, and tunnels. In this section, we deal with other packages of standard vanilla options, called caps, floors, and collars.

Currency Caps

A currency cap is a portfolio of call options with different expiration dates designed to provide insurance against the exchange rate rising above a certain level, known as the *cap* price. It concerns a series of cash flows and the time between expiration dates called the *tenor*. The tenor could be monthly, quarterly, biannually, and so on. Each individual option is called a *caplet*.

Consider an airline company based in France with a contract to purchase 20,000 tons of kerosene per month. In order to hedge variations in the price of kerosene, it has organized a commodity swap whereby it pays $200 per ton for the next 12 months. In order to hedge the currency risk when it exchanges its dollars for euros, the company could purchase a currency cap in the United States with the same reset conditions as the swap. If the current exchange rate is EUR 1 = USD 0.90, the at-the-money cap price would be $0.90 and the tenor would be one month. The amount of the contract would be EUR 4,444,444 which is the euro equivalent of the $4,000,000 ($200 × 20,000 barrels = $4,000,000) it receives every month from the swap. On the first day of every month for the next 12 months, the company would compare the spot exchange rate, defined as the exchange rate recorded in New York on the last working day of the preceding month, with the cap price. If it is lower than the cap price, the option would not be exercised and the company would purchase the $4,000,000 worth of euros at the spot rate. If, however, the spot rate is higher than the cap price, the company will exercise the option and receive the difference between the two prices times the EUR 4,444,444 size of the contract. Suppose, for example, that on the last working day of the first month, the spot rate in London is $0.95. The bank will pay the company ($0.95 − $0.90) × EUR 4,444,444 = $222,222. The total income from the transaction will be the 4,444,444 euros less the cost of the caplet. The same procedure will be repeated on each reset date.

The Cap as a Portfolio of Call Options

It is clear from the foregoing example that the cap is a contract composed of a portfolio of call options. Consider the following notation.

C_t^i = value of the caplet with expiration date i
X = cap price

S_t = the price of the underlying commodity at time t
Q = the amount of the contract
F_{t,T_i} = the forward price of S at time t on a contract with maturity T_i.

On the exercise dates $T_1, T_2 \ldots T_n$ the payoff will be:

$$Q\max(S_{T_i} - X, 0); i = 1, 2 \ldots n. \tag{4.1}$$

To value each caplet we assume risk neutrality so that $E(S_{T_i}) = F_{t,T_i}$ and that S_{T_i} has a lognormal distribution.

$$C_t^i = Qe^{-r(T_i-t)}E\max(S_{T_i} - X, 0). \tag{4.2}$$

We then make the substitution $E(S_{T_i}) = F_{t,T_i}$ and compute the true expectation as we did in Appendix 3.2. This gives the Black formula (equation 3.22)

$$C_t^i = Qe^{-r(T_i-t)}[F_{t,T_i}N(d_1) - XN(d_2)], \tag{4.3}$$

where

$N(d)$ = the value of the cumulative normal distribution evaluated at d.

$$d_1 = \frac{\ln(F_{t,T_i}/X) + \sigma^2/2(T_i - t)}{\sigma\sqrt{T_i - t}}$$

$$d_2 = \frac{\ln(F_{t,T_i}/X) - \sigma^2/2(T_i - t)}{\sigma\sqrt{T_i - t}} = d_1 - \sigma\sqrt{T_i - t}$$

The total value of the cap is

$$\text{Cap} = \sum_{i=1}^{n} C_t^i. \tag{4.4}$$

Using these formulas, we can price a three-month currency cap purchased by the aviation company consuming 20,000 tons of kerosene per month.

X = $0.90
S_0 = the current spot rate in London = $0.90
Q = the amount of the contract = $4,000,000/$0.90 = EUR 4,444,444
r = the riskless rate on the USD = 5%
σ = 20%
r^* = the riskless rate on the euro = 3%

There will be three resets: at the end of Month 1, the end of Month 2, and the end of Month 3. We use equation 2.2 to calculate the spot rate as[1]

$F_{0,1/12} = \$0.90e^{(0.05-0.03)\times 1/12} = \$0.9015$
$F_{0,1/6} = \$0.90e^{(0.05-0.03)\times 2/12} = \$0.9030$
$F_{0,1/4} = \$0.90e^{(0.05-0.03)\times 3/12} = \$0.9045$

Using this information in equation 4.3 gives:

$C_0^1 = \$4,444,444 \times 0.02127 = \$95,533.32$
$C_0^2 = \$4,444,444 \times 0.03066 = \$136,266.65$
$C_0^3 = \$4,444,444 \times 0.03775 = \$167,777.76.$

From equation 4.4, the value of the cap is:

$$\text{cap} = \sum_{i=1}^{3} C_t^i = \$399,577.73.$$

Thus, the premium represents about 3.33 percent of the current $12,000,000 that will be received over the three months.

Currency Floors

A *floor* is similar to a cap except that it is designed to provide insurance against the price of the underlying commodity falling below a certain level, known as the *floor price*. A floor is equivalent to a series of put options, called *floorlets*.

For example, consider a small oil producer in Canada who produces 50,000 barrels of oil per month. To hedge against a fall in the price of oil he has arranged a commodity swap based on the price of Brent crude reported by Platt's on the last working day of the preceding month whereby he receives $25 per barrel for 50,000 barrels on the first working day of every month for the next 24 months. In order to hedge the currency risk, the company could purchase a currency floor with the same reset conditions as the swap. If the current exchange rate is CAD 1 = USD 0.70, the at-the-money floor exchange rate would be $0.70, the tenor would be one month and the amount of the contract would be CAD 1,785,714; which is the Canadian dollar equivalent of the $1,250,000 ($25 × 50,000 barrels = $1,250,000) it will receive each month. On the first day of every month for the next 24 months, the company would compare the spot exchange rate, defined as the exchange rate recorded in New York on the last working day of the preceding month, with the floor price. If it is higher than the floor price, the option would not be exercised and the company would receive the spot rate for the $1,250,000. If, however, the spot rate is lower than the cap price, the company will exercise the option and receive the difference between the two prices times the CAD 1,785,714 size of the contract. Suppose, for example, that on the last working day of the first month, the spot rate in New York is $0.65. The bank will pay the company ($0.70 − $0.65) × CAD 1,785,714 = $89,285.70. This procedure would be repeated on each reset date over the life of the floor.

Using the same assumptions and notation as above, each floorlet can be valued with the following equation.

$$p_t^i = Qe^{-r(T_i - t)}[XN(-d_2) - F_{t,T_i}N(-d_1)], \tag{4.5}$$

where d_1 and d_2 are defined above.

The value of the floor is:

$$\text{floor} = \sum_{i=1}^{n} p_t^i. \tag{4.6}$$

Suppose, for example, that the company decides to hedge its currency risk for the next three months by purchasing an at-the-money, three-month floor with the same reset conditions as the swap. To price the floor we have the following information.

$X = \$0.70$
S_0 = the current spot exchange rate = $0.70.
Q = the amount of the contract = CAD 1,785,714
$r = 8\%$
$\sigma = 20\%$
r^* = the riskless rate on the USD = 4%

There will be three resets: at the end of Month 1, the end of Month 2, and the end of Month 3. From equation 2.2, we calculate the futures price as:[2]

$F_{0,1/12} = \$0.70e^{-(0.08-0.04)\times 1/12} = \$0.6977$
$F_{0,1/6} = \$0.70e^{-(0.08-0.04)\times 2/12} = \$0.6953$
$F_{0,1/4} = \$0.70e^{-(0.08-0.04)\times 3/12} = \$0.6930$

Using this information in equation 4.5 gives:

$p_0^1 = \$1,785,714 \times \$0.01704 = \$30,438.57$
$p_0^2 = \$1,785,714 \times \$0.02484 = \$44,357.14$
$p_0^3 = \$1,785,714 \times \$0.03075 = \$54,910.70.$

From equation 4.6 the value of the floor is:

$$\text{floor} = \sum_{i=1}^{3} p_t^i = \$129,696.42.$$

This represents about 1.7 percent of the current value of $3,750,000.

Collars

A *collar* is an instrument designed to guarantee that the exchange rate always lies between two given levels. It is the multi-period equivalent of the tunnel presented in chapter 3. A collar consists of a long position in the cap and a short position in the floor when hedging against price rises. It consists of a short position in the cap and a long position in the floor when hedging against price falls. A collar is usually constructed so that the price of the cap is initially equal to the price of the floor. In this case, the initial cash outlay of entering into the collar is zero. Although there is no cash outlay, the collar is not free. The cost comes in the potential gains that have been surrendered in the option that was sold.

Swaptions

European options on swaps or *swaptions* are another increasingly popular innovation. They give the holder the right to enter into a swap at a given time in the future. With a *call* swaption, the purchaser has the right to pay the fixed price. In a put swaption, the purchaser has the right to receive the fixed price. Most swaptions refer to options on interest rate swaps and they can be used to lock in the fixed interest rate that will be paid (a call) or received (a put).

Consider a swaption where we have the right to pay the fixed rate X on a swap that will last n years beginning in T_0 years. There are m payments per year and the amount of the swap is Q. For an interest rate swap, Q is equal to the notional amount of the swap divided by the number of payments per year: $Q = \{notional\ principal/m.\}$ On the exercise date at time T_0, the fixed rate X of the swaption will be compared with the fixed rate that could be obtained on a similar swap initiated at that time. If it is higher than X, the swaption will be exercised and the holder obtains a swap with the rate equal to X. If it is lower than X, the option will expire worthless and the holder will negotiate the swap at the lower swap price. Thus, a swaption is similar to a cap or a floor in that it involves a series of options. However, where the individual caplets and floorlets are evaluated at different values of the underlying asset corresponding to the different expiration dates, the individual options in a swaption all have the same value for the underlying asset, the current fixed rate of the swap on the swaption's expiration date. Let T_0 represent the expiration date. The payoff is calculated from the value of the variable at time t based on the fixed interest rate prevailing at T_0, but the payoffs of the individual options refer to the reset dates in the swap itself. Let $T_1, T_2 \ldots T_{mn}$ represent the other dates on which the payments are made in the swap contract (a payment may or may not be made at T_0) and X_{T_0} the swap price on the date when the payoff is calculated. The expected payoff from each call is discounted from T_i rather than T_0 and each call can be evaluated as

$$C_t^i = Qe^{-r(T_i-t)}E\max(X_{T_0} - X, 0). \tag{4.7}$$

Substituting the futures price at time t for delivery at time T_0 for $E(X_{T_0})$, $F_{t,T_0} = E(X_{T_0})$, we can evaluate equation 4.7 using the Black formula on a futures contract.

$$C_t^i = Qe^{-r(T_i-t)}[F_{t,T_0}N(d_{1F}) - XN(d_{2F})] \tag{4.8}$$

$$d_{1F} = \frac{\ln(F_{t,T_0}/X) - \sigma^2/2(T_0 - t)}{\sigma\sqrt{T_0 - t}}$$

$$d_{2F} = \frac{\ln(F_{t,T_0}/X) - \sigma^2/2(T_0 - t)}{\sigma\sqrt{T_0 - t}} = d_{1F} - \sigma\sqrt{T_0 - t}$$

The total value of the call swaption is:

$$\sum_{i=0}^{mn} C_t^i = Q\left[F_{t,T_0}N(d_{1F}) - XN(d_{2F})\right]\sum_{T_i=T_0}^{T_{mn}} e^{-r(T_i-t)}.$$

As an example, suppose the LIBOR yield curve is flat at a continuously compounded rate of 7.7 percent per year. The discrete rate is thus equal to $e^{0.0777} - 1 = 0.08$. Consider a swaption that gives the buyer the right to pay 8 percent in a three-year swap starting in one year. The volatility of the swap rate is 40 percent, payments are made every six months, and the notional principal is $200 million.

$X = 8\%$
S_0 = the current swap rate = 8%
$m = 2$
Q = the amount of the contract = \$200 million$/2$ = \$100 million
$\sigma = 40\%$
$F_{0,1} = 8\%$ (because the yield curve is flat)

From equation 4.9, the total value of the call swaption is:

$$\sum_{i=1}^{3} C_0^i = \frac{\$200}{2} \times \left[0.08N(d_{1F}) - 0.08e^{-0.07}N(d_{2F})\right] \times$$

$$\left[e^{-1.5\times0.077} + e^{-2\times0.077} + e^{-2.5\times0.077} + e^{-3\times0.077} + e^{-3.5\times0.077} + e^{-4\times0.077}\right]$$

$$= \$100 \times 0.01268 \times 4.8655 = \$6.17 \text{ million.}$$

The equivalent price of a put swaption (the right to receive the fixed price) can be calculated in the same way. The value of each put is

$$p_t^i = Qe^{-r(T_i-t)}[XN(-d_{2F}) - F_{t,T_0}N(-d_{1F})], \tag{4.10}$$

and the total value of the put swaption is:

$$\sum_{i=0}^{mn} p_t^i = Q[XN(-d_2) - F_{t,T_0}N(-d_1)] \sum_{T_i=T_0}^{T_{mn}^n} e^{-r(T_i-t)} \tag{4.11}$$

EXOTIC OPTIONS

As traders and investors have learned to use options, they have also become aware of their limits and disadvantages. Based on this, the banks have sought innovative new products as a means of developing new markets. The fruits of their effort gave birth to what is called *exotic options*. Exotic options, sometimes referred to as second generation options, are standard options that have been modified in one way or another to serve a specific purpose or client need. There are many kinds of exotic options. Some are path dependent, such as Asian options and lookback options. Others depend on correlations with other assets such as basket options and quanto options. Besides these options, there are a multitude of other exotics such as compound options, binary options, power options, rainbow options, and many others. Some exotic options have proven to be highly complex and lacking any real market. Others have proven more successful. Without going into an exhaustive survey of the second generation options, we will present several features and uses of some of the most popular contracts for foreign currency management.

Asian Currency Options

Asian options, which are also called average-price or average-rate options, are path dependent options whose payoff depends on the average exchange rate calculated over a predetermined part of the option's life. This type of option makes it possible to hedge a series of daily cash inflows over a given period in one single contract. Since an average price is generally less volatile than the price itself, Asian options are generally cheaper than the corresponding vanilla options.[3] Consequently, they offer reasonably priced hedging instruments adapted to periodic cash flows resulting from commercial transactions. For example, a company with regular cash flows in foreign currency spread evenly over the year is likely to be interested in insuring that the average exchange rate is below some level. An Asian call option can achieve this more cheaply and effectively than a series of vanilla call options on each cash flow.

The two types of Asian options are the average price option and the average strike option. For the average price option, the strike price is fixed and the payoff depends on the average price of the underlying instrument. Payoffs for average price options are $\max(S_{ave} - X, 0)$ for a call and $\max(X - S_{ave}, 0)$ for a put. As an example, consider a company treasurer who changes his foreign currency income day by day at the spot rate. He wants to make sure that he gets a rate at least as good as the current spot rate so he purchases an Asian put with a strike price equal to the current spot rate. On the expiration date, if the average rate is lower than the strike price, he exercises the option and gets the difference between the two. With the put option, he has effectively changed all his foreign income at the strike price less the value of the premium. If the average rate is higher than the strike price, the option expires worthless. His effective exchange rate is the average rate diminished by the value of the premium.

It is important to note that an average rate option is not the same thing as the purchase of a series of options with the same strike price, each one expiring on a different day over the period to be covered. In this case, some options would be exercised while others would expire worthless. Consequently, the average effective rate would be higher than the strike price. Since the outcome for this strategy is higher than the outcome for the average rate option, its premium should be higher.

For the average strike option, the strike price is determined by the average price of the underlying asset. Payoffs for average strike options are $\max(S_T - S_{ave}, 0)$ for a call and $\max(S_{ave} - S_T, 0)$ for a put. Consider, for example, a treasurer who makes periodic purchases of foreign currency. He wants to guarantee that his purchase price will not be higher than the average exchange rate since his last purchase. Thus, he purchases an average strike call. If the spot exchange rate on the expiration date is higher than the average over the period, he exercises and receives the difference. His rate will be the average plus the option premium. If the spot rate is under the strike price on the expiration date, the option expires worthless. His rate is the spot rate plus the option premium.

An average price option can be advantageous for a company with regular foreign currency cash flows, whereas an average strike option can be used to guarantee an average rate for cash flows that are only exchanged periodically.

Kemna and Vorst (1990) developed a pricing formula for average price options when the underlying asset is lognormally distributed and the average price in question is a geometric average. This gives:

$$C = S_t e^{-(r+r^*+\sigma^2/6)(T-t)/2} N(d_{1,A}) - X e^{-r(T-t)} N(d_{2,A}) \qquad (4.12)$$

and

$$p = Xe^{-r(T-t)}N(-d_{2A}) - S_t e^{-(r+r^*+\sigma 2/6)(T-t)/2}N(-d_{1,A}),$$ (4.13)

where

$$d_{1A} = \frac{\ln\frac{S_t}{X} + (r - r^* + \frac{\sigma^2}{6})\frac{(T-t)}{2}}{\sigma\sqrt{\frac{T-t}{3}}}$$ (4.14)

$$d_{2A} = \frac{\ln\frac{S_t}{X} + (r - r^* - \frac{\sigma^2}{2})\frac{(T-t)}{2}}{\sigma\sqrt{\frac{T-t}{3}}}.$$ (4.15)

In practice, most Asian options are on arithmetic rather than geometric averages. There are no analytical pricing formulas for arithmetic averages because the distribution of the arithmetic average of a set of lognormal distributions does not have analytically tractable properties. This obstacle can be overcome in several ways. One methodology involves calculating an approximation coefficient that adjusts for the difference between the arithmetic and geometric means.[4] Another methodology uses the fact that the distribution of the arithmetic is approximately lognormal. It involves calculating the first two moments of the probability distribution of the arithmetic average in a risk neutral world and then assuming that the distribution is lognormal.[5] The option can then be priced as an option on a futures contract using equations 3.22 and 3.23.

To give an application of the moment methodology mentioned above, consider an Asian option just issued with maturity at time T based on the arithmetic average from 0 to T with n observations. The first moment M_1 and the second moment M_2 of the average in a risk neutral world calculated between time 0 and T are equal to: [6]

$$M_1 = \frac{1}{n}\sum_{i=1}^{n} F_{0,T_i}$$ (4.16)

and[7]

$$M_2 = \frac{1}{n^2}\left[\sum_{i=1}^{n} F_{0,T_i}^2 e^{\sigma_i^2 T_i} + 2\sum_{i<j} F_{0,T_i} F_{0,T_j} e^{\sigma_i^2 T_i}\right].$$ (4.17)

The variance of the arithmetic average can thus be approximated as:

$$\hat{\sigma}^2 = \frac{1}{T} ln \frac{M_2}{M_1^2}. \tag{4.18}$$

The option can be priced using equations 3.22 and 3.23 where $F_{t,T} = \frac{M_i}{n}$ and $\sigma = \hat{\sigma}$.

Basket Currency Options

Basket currency options are written on portfolios, or baskets, of currencies. The payoff depends on the value of the portfolio of currencies. Since the assets are imperfectly correlated, basket options have lower volatility and therefore cost less than straight options. They can be useful for companies that are confronted by foreign exchange exposure in a number of currencies. In this case, there might be an advantage to grouping the exposure and negotiating a *basket* option. For example, a basket put option might be used to cover a long position of $30 million worth of yen, $25 million worth of euros, $20 million worth of pounds, $15 million worth of francs, and $10 million worth of the Italian lira. The premium will be based on a contract for $100. Suppose the strike price is $98 million. If the weighted average exchange rate yields less than $98 million, the option is exercised. If it yields more, the option expires.

The purchase of five different puts for the different amounts in question in each separate currency at a strike price 2 percent below the exchange rate being covered is an alternative strategy to the basket put. However, neither the results nor the costs would be the same. The puts do not have to be exercised or abandoned together. Some can be exercised while others can be abandoned. Thus, the strategy of individual puts has a good chance of getting a better outcome than the basket option, which only guarantees the average rate. The average of the exchange rates has less volatility than each individual currency and, consequently, its cost should be lower than the cost of the strategy composed of individual puts.

Basket options can be priced in a manner similar to the Asian option methodology presented in the preceding paragraph. The methodology involves calculating the first two moments of the probability distribution of the value of the basket at maturity in a risk-neutral world and then assuming that the distribution is lognormal. The option can then be priced as an option on a futures contract using equations 3.22 and 3.23.

Look Back Currency Options

A *lookback* currency option is an option whose payoff depends on the maximum or minimum exchange rate within the life of the option. For a call the payoff is max$[S_T - S_{min}, 0]$ and for a put it is max $[S_{max} - S_T, 0]$. A lookback currency option gives its holder the right to purchase or sell foreign exchange at the most favorable exchange rate realized over the life of the option. The buyer of a lookback call, for example, has the right to purchase a certain amount of foreign exchange at the lowest exchange rate realized between the creation of the call and its expiration date. The buyer of a lookback put has the right to sell foreign exchange at the highest exchange rate realized between its creation and its expiration date. In other words, the strike price of a lookback option is not known until the expiration date. This is the fundamental difference between a traditional option and a lookback. Since the new twist is favorable to the owner, the premium of a lookback is higher than the premium on a traditional option. Historically the premium has been approximately twice as high. Lookbacks, however, are a worthwhile strategy only in certain conditions.

If the exchange rate never drops below (rises above) the spot rate on the day the option is purchased, the strike for a lookback call (put) will be the first exchange rate. A traditional at-the-money call (put) written at the same time as the lookback would have the same strike price and would, therefore, give the same result. Since the cost would be much lower, the traditional call (put) would give a better result than the lookback. Lookbacks are not appropriate instruments for situations when the exchange rate is in a period of expected regular appreciation (depreciation).

Now consider the opposite case where the exchange rate depreciates (appreciates) regularly over the period. The strike price for the lookback call (put) will be the last exchange rate. Here again, the lookback is less attractive than a traditional at-the-money call (put). The traditional at-the-money call (put) would cost much less than the lookback. Although on the expiration date it would be out-of-the-money and would expire worthless, the investor could still obtain the foreign exchange at the spot rate, the same rate as the strike price for the lookback. Since the premium for the traditional call is lower than for the lookback, the overall cost of the foreign exchange would be lower for the traditional call holder. Lookbacks are not appropriate instruments for situations when the exchange rate is in a period of expected regular depreciation.

From this we can conclude that the lookback is the best strategy only if the exchange rate goes far enough below (above) the exchange rate registered on the first and last days of the option's life. Thus, it would be lower (higher) than the strike price of the traditional call option. For the lookback to be preferred to the traditional call option, the difference between the minimum (maximum) rate over the life of the option and the beginning rate must be larger than the difference between the premium of the lookback and the traditional at-the-money call.

In general, lookback options are especially attractive during periods of relatively high volatility for firms unable or unwilling to pay a higher price than their competitors for their foreign currency. This would be the case, for example, for a company with a payment to be made at the beginning of a period when the exchange rate is expected to experience a temporary decline. A lookback would make it possible to take advantage of the decline even after the payment has been made.

Garman (1989) extended the Goldman, Sosin, and Gatto (1979) lookback pricing formula to currency options. The formulas for European lookback calls and puts at time zero is

$$C = S_0 e^{-r^*T} N(d_{1LBC}) - S_0 e^{-r^*T} \frac{\sigma^2}{2(r-r^*)} N(-d_{1LBC}) - S_{\min} e^{-rT}$$

$$\left[N(d_{2LBC}) - \frac{\sigma^2}{2(r-r^*)} e^{y_{LBC}} N(-d_{3LBC}) \right], \tag{4.19}$$

where

$$d_{1LBC} = \frac{\ln(\frac{S_0}{S_{\min}}) + (r - r^* + \frac{\sigma^2}{2})T}{\sigma\sqrt{T}} \tag{4.20}$$

$$d_{2LBC} = \frac{\ln(\frac{S_0}{S_{\min}}) + (r - r^* - \frac{\sigma^2}{2})T}{\sigma\sqrt{T}} \tag{4.21}$$

$$d_{3LBC} = \frac{\ln(\frac{S_0}{S_{\min}}) + (-r + r^* + \frac{\sigma^2}{2})T}{\sigma\sqrt{T}} \tag{4.22}$$

$$y_{LBC} = -\frac{2(r - r^* - \sigma^2/2)\ln(S_0/S_{\min})}{\sigma^2} \tag{4.23}$$

and

$$p = S_{\max} e^{-rT} \left[N(d_{1LBp}) - \frac{\sigma^2}{2(r-r^*)} e^{y_{LBp}} N(-d_{3LBp}) \right]$$

$$+ S_0 e^{-r^*T} \frac{\sigma^2}{2(r-r^*)} N(-d_{2LBp}) - S_0 e^{-r^*T} N(d_{2LBp}), \tag{4.24}$$

where

$$d_{1LBp} = \frac{\ln(\frac{S_{max}}{S_0}) + (-r + r^* + \frac{\sigma^2}{2})T}{\sigma\sqrt{T}}$$

$$d_{2LBp} = \frac{\ln(\frac{S_{max}}{S_0}) + (-r + r^* - \frac{\sigma^2}{2})T}{\sigma\sqrt{T}}$$

$$d_{3LBp} = \frac{\ln(\frac{S_{max}}{S_0}) + (r - r^* - \frac{\sigma^2}{2})T}{\sigma\sqrt{T}}$$

$$y_{LBp} = -\frac{2(r - r^* - \sigma^2/2)\ln(S_{max}/S_0)}{\sigma^2}.$$

The foregoing formulas are derived under the assumption that the asset price is observed continuously. In fact, as with Asian options, the price is sensitive to how frequently the price is observed for computing the maximums and minimums. If the maximums and minimums are observed on a discrete basis, these formulas can be adjusted to take the observation frequency into consideration.[8]

Compound Options

A *compound* option is an option on an option. In this case, the underlying instrument is itself an option. This kind of instrument is useful for managing risks associated with conditional cash flows. The four main types of compound options are: a call on a call, a call on a put, a put on a call, and a put on a put. Compound options have two separate exercise dates and two separate strike prices. The first exercise date-and-strike price refers to the compound option itself. The second exercise date-and-strike price refers to the option that is the underlying instrument. This kind of instrument is useful for managing risks associated with conditional cash flows. The classic example is that of a company preparing to tender a bid for a contract. The deadline for the bid is three months in the future, and the results will be known six months after that, a total of nine months in the future. The currency risk takes effect only when the bid has been submitted, that is, in three months time. Once the bids are submitted, the company is sure to want to hedge its exposure with the purchase of an option. However, it might want to know immediately how much that coverage will cost. A three-month compound option on the cost of the six-month option that it might want to buy if it wins the contract would do it.

Robert Geske (1979) developed the original formulas for European style compound calls and puts. Appendix 4.1 gives the formulas for some European compound options.

Barrier Options

Barrier options are options where the payoff depends on whether the price of the underlying asset reaches a pre-specified level over a given time period. In fact, barrier options are one of the oldest types of exotic options, having traded in the United States as far back as 1967. Barrier options are cheaper than corresponding standard calls and puts. They also make it possible for users to restrict their hedging to price ranges that they consider feasible. Thus, risk managers can hedge their exposures without paying for price ranges that they believe are unlikely to occur.

Barrier options can be classified as either *knock-out* or *knock-in*. A knock-out option ceases to exist when the price of the underlying asset reaches a barrier. A knock-in option comes into existence when a barrier is reached. The standard knock-out option entitles its owner to receive a rebate when a barrier is hit and a European option payout if it is not hit. The standard knock-in option entitles its owner to receive a European option if a barrier is hit and a rebate at expiration if it is not hit. The price of the option depends on whether the barrier is hit from above or below. Depending on whether the price of the underlying asset is above or below the barrier, there are basically four kinds of barrier options for calls and for puts: down-and-outs, down-and-ins, up-and-outs, and up-and-ins.

Barriers can be added to almost any kind of option. Thus, besides the standard barrier options, there are Asian barriers, forward-start barriers, dual barriers, correlation-binary barriers, spread barriers, lookback barriers, and so on. The common feature of all these barrier options is that their payoffs depend on whether or not one or more barriers are breached during the life of the option. The diversity of this family of options makes it impossible to go into much detail on pricing formulas.[9]

NOTES

1. The equation is given as $F_{t,T} = S_t e^{(r-r^*)\tau}$.
2. See note 1.
3. Because the payoff depends on an average, these options are less susceptible to possible spot price manipulation on the settlement date as well.
4. See Zhang (1998), pp. 135–154.
5. See Turnbull and Wakeman (1991). In this section we follow Hull (2000) pp. 468–469.

6. The equivalent moments for continuous sampling are $M^1 = \{(e^{(r-\delta)T} - 1)/(r-\delta)T\}S_0$ and $M_2 = \{2e^{[(r-\delta) + \sigma^2]T}S_0^2/((r - \delta - \sigma^2)(2r - 2\delta + \sigma^2)T^2)\} + \{2S_0^2/((r - \delta)T^2)\}[\{1/(2(r - \delta) + \sigma^2)\} - \{e^{(r-\delta)T}/(r - \delta + \sigma^2)\}]$.

7. Remember that $V = \bullet_{i=1}^{n} S_{T_i}$ and $V^2 = \bullet_{i=1}^{n} \bullet_{j=1}^{n} S_{T_i} S_{T_j} \cdot E(S_{T_i} S_{T_j}) = F_{0,T_i} F_{0,T_j} e^{\rho_{ij}}$ $\sigma_i \sigma_j \sqrt{T_i T_j}$. When $i < j$, $\rho_{ij} = \sigma_i \sqrt{T_i}/\sigma_j \sqrt{T_j}$ so that $E(S_{t_i} S_{T_j}) = F_{0,T_i} F_{0,T_j} e^{\rho_{ij}\sigma_i^2 T_i}$.

8. See Broadie, Glasserman, and Kou (1998).

9. See Zhang (1998) pp. 203–335 for an in-depth treatment of barrier options.

REFERENCES

Broadie, M., P. Glasserman, and S.G. Kou. (1998). "connecting Discrete and Continuous Path-Dependent Options," Finance and Stochastics, 2, 1–28.

Garman, M. (1989). "Recollection in Tranquility," Risk, 2 (3), 16–19.

Geske, R. (1979). "The Valuation of Compound Options," Journal of Financial Economics, 7, 63–81.

Goldman, B., H. Sosin, and M.A. Gatto. (1979). "Path Dependent Options: Buy at the Low, Sell at the High," Journal of Finance, 34, 1111–1127.

Hull, J.C. (2000). Options, Futures, and Other Derivatives. London: Prentice Hall International.

Kemna, A., and A. Vorst. (1990). "A Pricing Method for Options Based on Average Asset Values," Journal of Banking and Finance, 14, 113–129.

Turnbull, S.M., and L.M. Wakeman. (1991). "A Quick Algorithm for Pricing European Average Options," Journal of Quantitative and Financial Analysis, 26, 377–389.

Zhang, P.J. (1998). Exotic Options. Singapore: World Scientific Publishing.

Appendix 4.1

Compound Options

COMPOUND OPTION FORMULAS

$$C_{cc} = S_0 e^{-r^*T_2} N_2 (d_{1CC}, a_{1CC}, \sqrt{T_1/T_2}) - X_2 e^{-rT_2} N_2$$

$$(d_{2CC}, a_{2CC}, \sqrt{T_1/T_2}) - e^{-rT_1} X_1 N(d_{2CC}), \tag{A.2}$$

where

> S = the price of the exchange rate on which the underlying option is written
>
> X_1 = the exercise price on the compound option
> X_2 = the exercise price on the underlying option
> T_1 = the exercise date on the compound option
> T_2 = the exercise date on the underlying option
> $N_2(\cdot)$ = the cumulative bivariate normal distribution function

$$d_{1CC} = \frac{\ln\frac{S_0}{S} + (r - r^* + \frac{\sigma^2}{2})T_1}{\sigma\sqrt{T_1}}$$

$$a_{1CC} = \frac{\ln\frac{S_0}{X_2} + (r - r^* + \frac{\sigma^2}{2})T_2}{\sigma\sqrt{T_2}}$$

$$d_{2CC} = d_{1CC} - \sigma\sqrt{T_1}$$

$$a_{2CC} = a_{1CC} - \sigma\sqrt{T_2}$$

The variable $\overline{S}$ is the exchange rate at T_1 for which the option price at T_1 equals X_1. Thus, $\overline{S}$ must satisfy the equation:

$$\overline{S}e^{-r^*(T_2-T_1)}N(d_1) - X_2 e^{-r(T_2-T_1)}N(d_2) - X_1 = 0 \tag{A.3}$$

where

$$d_1 = \frac{\ln\dfrac{\overline{S}}{X_2} + (r - r^* + \dfrac{\sigma^2}{2})(T_2 - T_1)}{\sigma\sqrt{T_2 - T_1}}$$

and

$$d_2 = d_1 - \sigma\sqrt{T_2 - T_1}.$$

Obtaining equation A.2 involves solving equation A.3 by trial and error to obtain $\overline{S}$ and then applying the bivariate normal density function to the payoff at T_1, the exercise date of the compound option. With similar methodology and notation, the formula of a European style put on a call is:

$$P_{pC} = X_2 e^{-rT_2}N_2(-d_{2CC}, a_{2CC}, -\sqrt{T_1/T_2}) - S_0 e^{-r^*T_2}N_2$$
$$(-d_{1CC}, a_{1CC}, -\sqrt{T_1/T_2}) + e^{-rT_1}X_1 N(-d_{2CC}). \tag{A.4}$$

The value of a European style call on a put is:

$$C_{Cp} = X_2 e^{-rT_2}N_2(-d_{2CC}, -a_{2CC}, -\sqrt{T_1/T_2}) - S_0 e^{-r^*T_2}N_2$$
$$(-d_{1CC}, -a_{1CC}, \sqrt{T_1/T_2}) - e^{-rT_1}X_1 N(-d_{2CC}). \tag{A.5}$$

The value of a European put on a put is:

$$P_{pp} = S_0 e^{-rT_2}N_2(d_{1CC}, -a_{1CC}, -\sqrt{T_1/T_2}) - X_2 e^{-rT_2}N_2$$
$$(d_{2CC}, a_{2CC}, -\sqrt{T_1/T_2}) + e^{-rT_1}X_1 N(d_{2CC}). \tag{A.6}$$

Chapter 5

Arbitrage and Hedging with Spot and Forward Contracts

INTRODUCTION

Arbitrage, as noted in chapter 1, is the exploitation of market misalignment, and hedging is the cover against any open risk-exposed positions of a participant in the marketplace. Academic research has taken us to two interesting ends on this issue of arbitrage with hedging. At one end, we find that theoretical explorations of market potential have opened the eyes of actual traders and made them realize the fruits of the mechanics of financial markets. Asset markets in general—and currency market in particular—have created conditions in which players make money without even taking any risk through arbitrage, and on many occasions they generate large amounts of profits by taking speculative positions—sometimes covered and sometimes naked.[1] On the other end of the spectrum, we note that it is the academic maxim mostly that intrigues others by letting them believe that markets are so well-aligned that arbitrage opportunity can hardly exist in the real world, and hence risk-free profit-taking is a mere illusion. In this chapter, an attempt is made to examine how correct that analytical view is against the setting of real markets, how much academic research helps us understand the behavior of real traders, and to what extent the impression or belief that there is no scope for arbitrage holds ground. We shall attempt to check into the foreign exchange market in which currencies are traded for spot and forward contracts almost 24 hours a day, where traders hardly get out of trading rooms. The plan of this chapter is as follows: In the following next five sections under the heading "Arbitrage Profits," we bring out the conditions for profitable arbitrage with full hedging with and without transaction costs, and ascertain the *minimum* and *maximum* (possible) gains (profits) out of trading acts under admissible situations. The theoretical designs of operational schemes are discussed under different possible scenarios with and without leveraged market moves. Each scenario is then tested with real-time data, taken mostly from *Reuters*, and rechecked with bankers and dealers. In the section under "Arbitrage and Leverage," arbitrage with leverage and arbitrage-induced total profits are measured when the trader operates with transaction costs. The next section reexamines the arbitrage profits without transaction costs once again. The following sections discuss covered interest triangular arbitrage profits, followed by observations on micro-structure and dynamics of market competition. Some empirical evidence, taken from the *Reuters* real-time data screen, is examined in the context of the scope for arbitrage, and profit measures and profit multipliers are computed. These results are then presented in Table 5.1. Finally, in the last section, we conclude the work with some observations. Many comments in regard to the speed of transaction, logistics, and the feasibility of the operational success, execution jam, limit order, and so on are made at appropriate points in our discussion.

ARBITRAGE PROFITS: LOWER AND UPPER BOUNDS

In currency markets throughout the world, active participants trade around the clock, going long and/or short often enough and making foreign exchange trading the most voluminous structure of asset-market transactions. This market has various facets, and here we plan to take up the trading in spot and forward contracts along with participation in money market. A significant research along the line has been done by Keynes (1923), Aliber (1973), Frenkel and Levich (1975), and Deardorff (1979). More recently, Blenman (1992a, 1992b, 1996), Blenman and Thatcher (1995), Rhee and Chang (1992), Callier (1981), Clinton (1988), Ghosh (1991, 1994, 1997), McCormick (1979), Roll and Solnik (1979), Tsiang (1959, 1973), and a few others have extended the discussions somewhat further.[2] Our approach here is to take stock of the research to date in some measure, then attempt to assess the degree to which we have been or have not been able to exploit the market to its full potential by our financial engineering.

Arbitrage Profits without Transactions Costs

Assume that transaction costs are so low that one can virtually ignore them as nonexistent. Later in this chapter, we discard this simplifying assumption, and enter into the world in which transactions costs are significant. The presence of transaction costs is introduced in the way they appear in trade transactions. For now, let S be the current spot rate of exchange of, say, one French franc in terms of U.S. dollar(s), F the currently traded forward rate with T-day maturity ($T = 30, 60, 90, 180, 360$, etc.), r and r^*, the U.S. and French interest rates, respectively, for the period matching the forward contract we are considering here.[3]

When an investor has the quotations of these exchange rates and interest rates either from her computer screen in real time or from her broker or from bank telephone calls, she has, for our examination, basically two alternative investment strategies: (i) borrow, for instance, M dollars in the U.S. market at the rate r, convert the borrowed amount in French francs at the spot rate of exchange S, invest the converted French franc amount (M/S) at r^* and get the following amount $(M/S)(1 + r^*)$ at the end of T days; (ii) borrow the equivalent amount of French francs, say N French francs at r^*, convert into M dollars (that is, $M = N \cdot S$), invest these M dollars at the rate r, and get $M(1 + r)$ dollars at the end of T days. But that is not all. Under alternative (i), the investor sells $(M/S)(1 + r^*)$ francs at the forward rate at the very moment she buys francs in the spot market, and thus turns her initial investment dollars into the amount of $(M/S)(1 + r^*)F$ without entering into risk anywhere in the process. At this stage, she must subtract $M(1 + r)$ from $(M/S)(1 + r^*)F$, and compute her T-day profits (π_1) in this play of covered arbitrage as follows:

$$\pi_1 = \frac{M}{S}(1+r^*)F - M(1+r) = M\{(\frac{F}{S})(1+r^*) - (1+r)\}. \tag{5.1}$$

If $\pi_1 > 0$, the investment strategy (i) is profitable. By going through the similar algebraic steps, one may easily see that $\pi_1 < 0$ (which yields loss under strategy (i)) signifies the profitable condition under alternative (ii), as outlined above. Obviously, $\pi_1 = 0$ means the zero-profit situation under the given parametric environment.

It is now instructive that we explore further into the conditions in which $\pi_1 = 0$. For economy of space, we deal with $\pi_1 > 0$, and the sign reversal (if that happens to be the case) should simply be construed as taking the other alternative investment strategy for positive profit condition.

Profit Multiplier in the Absence of Transaction Costs

It has been already shown that if, for instance, $\pi_1 > 0$ holds, then the investor makes the following amount of total profits at the end of T days:

$$\pi_1 = M\{(\frac{F}{S})(1+r^*) - (1+r)\}. \tag{5.2}$$

The present value of this profit π_1 is then as follows:

$$\pi_1^0 = \frac{M}{(1+r)}\{(\frac{F}{S})(1+r^*) - (1+r)\}. \tag{5.3}$$

This is the measure of the *minimum* bound of the investor's profits now in the risk-free activities in the currency market under the given situation. Since this is the amount the investor owns *now,* she should make use of this amount instantly to play the market still with the same quotations in the exchange and money markets. Here is then the second round of profits:

$$\pi_2 = ((\frac{\pi_1^0}{S})(1+r^*)F - \pi_1^0(1+r) = \pi_1^0\{(\frac{F}{S})(1+r^*) - (1+r)\},$$

which is readily reduced to the expression:

$$\pi_2 = [\frac{M}{(1+r)}]\{(\frac{F}{S})(1+r^*) - (1+r)\}^2,$$

the present value of which then is:

$$\pi_2^0 = [\frac{M}{(1+r)^2}]\{(\frac{F}{S})(1+r^*) - (1+r)\}^2. \tag{5.4}$$

The present value of profits upon *i*th iteration ($i = 1, 2, \ldots, n$) is then:

$$\pi_i^0 = [\frac{M}{(1+r)^i}]\{(\frac{F}{S})(1+r^*) - (1+r)\}^i,$$

$$= (\frac{M}{1+r})\{(\frac{F}{S})(1+r^*) - (1+r)\}.[\frac{1}{(1+r)^{i-1}}\{(\frac{F}{S})(1+r^*) - (1+r)\}^{i-1}]. \tag{5.5}$$

Let $\mu(i) \equiv [1/(1+r)^{i-1}\{(F/S)(1+r^*) - (1+r)\}^{i-1}]$ be the arbitrage profit multiplier of the initial profits at the *i*th round of arbitrage ($i = 1, 2, 3, \ldots n, \ldots, 4$). From equation 5.5, one can get for *n* successive iterations of covered arbitrage:

$$\pi_{(16n)}^{\ \ 0} \equiv \sum_{i=1}^{n} \pi_i^0 = M \sum_{i=1}^{n} (\frac{1}{(1+r)^i})\{(\frac{F}{S})(1+r^*) - (1+r)\}^i$$

$$= M\alpha\beta\left[\frac{1-(\alpha\beta)^n}{1-\alpha\beta}\right] \tag{5.6}$$

where $\alpha \equiv \frac{1}{(1+r)}$ and $\beta/\{(\frac{F}{S})(1+r^*) - (1+r)\}.$

For $n = \infty$, $\pi_{(164)}^{\ \ 0} = M\alpha\beta\left[\frac{1}{1-\alpha\beta}\right]$ (if $\alpha\beta < 1$); otherwise $\pi_{(164)}^{\ \ 0} = \infty.$ \tag{5.7}

Equation 5.7 defines the *maximum* bound of profits the investor can make out of the given situation. One can see now that $M\alpha\beta = \{M/(1+r)\}\{(F/S)(1 + r^*) - (1 + r)\}$ is the present value of the first round of

Profits (π^0)

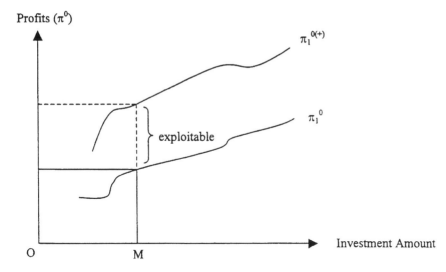

Figure 5.1   Investment and profits on single and cumulative iterations

her arbitrage profits, and $\mu^+(n)/\{1-(\alpha\beta)^n\}/\{1-\alpha\beta\}$ is the profit multiplier for n *successive* rounds of (arbitrage) profits. Figure 5.1 portrays the boundaries.

In Figure 5.1, the horizontal axis measures the initial investment funds of the investor, and the vertical axis measure the present value of cumulative profits for first i rounds of arbitrage ($i = 1, 2, 3, \ldots, n, \ldots, \infty$). If the initial amount invested is M dollars, then upon first round of arbitrage, the investor makes a net profit of $_M\pi_1^0$ now, and on first n rounds of arbitraging she makes the amount of $_M\pi_n^{(+)0}$. The rays π_1^0 and $\pi_n^{(+)0}$ in Figure 5.1 define the relationship between initial investment amount and total profit levels at different cumulative arbitrage rounds. As Figure 5.1 shows, if the initial amount instead were Z ($> M$), then those profit measures would be different. At this point, a point should be noted: if the investor does not go beyond the first round of arbitrage with initial amount, say, M dollars, her unexploited profit is the difference between $_M\pi_n^{(+)0}$ and $_M\pi_1^0$.

To comprehend the significance of our analysis, let us examine the amount of profits (a rational trader can generate) and the magnification thereof upon different iteration of covered arbitrage operations, and on that score, consider the following data taken out of *The Wall Street Journal* and *Financial Times* as an illustration: $M = \$1,000,000$, $S = 0.2022$, $F = 0.2035$, $r = 0.0447$, and $r^* = 0.0445$, $T = 360$ days, and $\theta = 0$. With this market data, the arbitrageur makes a profit of \$4,612.91 on her first round, \$5,816.88 on her 25th round; but for 25 successive rounds, she earns a net profit of \$129,815.40. As it is evident now, it is easy to ignore any one round of arbitrage profits, but any rational investor can hardly ignore the cumulative amount at a given instant of time. If the investor can make it to the round 100 in this illustrative case, then her cumulative profits amount to $773,505.90. When we admit 25 percent borrowing against the equity position (that is, $\theta = 25\%$), one can find that the computed values of profits—at individual round and at cumulative rounds—change (increase), but not very significantly until higher levels of iterations are made.

Arbitrage-Induced Total Profits without Transactions Costs

Thus far, we have dealt with the repeat exploitations of the foreign exchange market admitting of arbitrage opportunities, and arbitrage profits at each round of play have been computed. But note that in the first round the investor has played the borrowed funds either from a bank or from herself at the going market rate r (which must be construed as the opportunity cost for her own money in the event the initial amount was taken out of her own purse), and hence $M(1 + r)$ must be subtracted from the money made in the first round. But from second round onward, she should *stop* deducting interest expenses. What it all means is that, from second round on, profit calculations should be as follows:

$$\pi_{T(2)}^+ = (\frac{\pi_1^0}{S})(1+r^*)F,$$

and therefore,

$$\pi_{T(2)}^{(+)0} = \frac{\frac{\pi_1^0}{S}(1+r^*)F}{(1+r)}$$

$$= [\frac{M}{(1+r)}]\{(\frac{F}{S})(1+r^*)-(1+r)\}\{\frac{1}{(1+r)^2}\}[(\frac{F}{S})(1+r^*)], \tag{5.8}$$

and similarly,

$$\pi_{T(3)}^{(+)0} = [\frac{M}{(1+r)}]\{(\frac{F}{S})(1+r^*)-(1+r)\}\{\frac{1}{(1+r)^2}\}[(\frac{F}{S})(1+r^*)]^2 \tag{5.9}$$

and

$$\pi_{T(i)}^{(+)0} = [\frac{M}{(1+r)}]\{(\frac{F}{S})(1+r^*)-(1+r)\}\{\frac{1}{(1+r)^{i-1}}\}[(\frac{F}{S})(1+r^*)]^{i-1} \tag{5.10}$$

Here the superscript $+$ in π denotes the cumulative magnitude of profits, superscript 0 refers to the present value of the profit, and subscript $T(i)$ refers to the ith iteration of arbitrage in the calculation of total arbitrage-induced profits as opposed to pure total arbitrage profits ($i = 1, 2, 3,\ldots n,\ldots, 4$). The summation over first n rounds then yields:

$$\pi_{T(1\to n)}^{(+)0} \equiv \sum_{i=1}^{n} \pi_{T(i)}^{(+)0}$$

$$\equiv \sum_{i=1}^{n} [\frac{M}{(1+r)}]\{(\frac{F}{S}) \times (1+r^*) - (1+r)\}\{\frac{1}{(1+r)^{i-1}}\}[(\frac{F}{S})(1+r^*)]^{i-1}, \tag{5.11}$$

$$= [\frac{M}{(1+r)}]\{(\frac{F}{S})(1+r^*) - (1+r)\}\left[\frac{1-\left(\dfrac{F}{S}\dfrac{1+r^*}{1+r}\right)^n}{1-\left(\dfrac{F}{S}\dfrac{1+r^*}{1+r}\right)}\right] \tag{5.12}$$

and, for $n = \infty$, if $\dfrac{F}{S}\left(\dfrac{1+r^*}{1+r}\right) < 1$

$$\pi_{(1\to\infty)}^{(+)0} \equiv \left(\frac{M}{1+r}\right)[\frac{F}{S}(1+r^*) - (1+r)] \times \left(\frac{1}{1-\left(\dfrac{F}{S}\dfrac{1+r^*}{1+r}\right)}\right) \tag{5.13}$$

When $\dfrac{F}{S}\left(\dfrac{1+r^*}{1+r}\right) > 1$ infinite iterations result in infinite amount of profits. So the bounds for profits—lower and upper—are defined as follows:

$$\pi_{T(1)}^0 = [\frac{M}{(1+r)}]\{(\frac{F}{S})(1+r^*) - (1+r)\}: \qquad \text{lower bound;}$$

$$\pi_{T(1\to\infty)}^{(+)0} = [\frac{M}{(1+r)}]\{(\frac{F}{S})(1+r^*) - (1+r)\}\left[\frac{1}{1-\left(\dfrac{F}{S}\dfrac{1+r^*}{1+r}\right)}\right]: \quad \text{upper bound,}$$

$$\left(\text{when } (\frac{F}{S})\frac{(1+r^*)}{(1+r)} < 1\right),$$

$$\pi_{T(1\to\infty)}^{(+)0} = \infty \qquad\qquad \left(\text{when } (\frac{F}{S})\frac{(1+r^*)}{(1+r)} > 1\right).$$

One may note that $\mu^+(n) \equiv \{1 - (\alpha\beta)^n\}/\{1 - \alpha\beta\}$ is the *(pure arbitrage) profit multiplier*, and $\mu^+_T(n) = [1 - \{(F/S)(1 + r^*)/(1 + r)\}^n]/\{1 - (F/S)(1 + r^*)/(1 + r)\}$ is the *arbitrage-induced profit multiplier* for n rounds $(1 \leqslant n \leqslant 4)$. Similarly, $\pi_{(1\to\infty)}^{(+)0}$ and $\pi_{T(1\to\infty)}^{(+)0}$ are the *pure* arbitrage and *arbitrage-induced* total profits for the first n rounds.

Arbitrage Profits with Transactions Costs

Now, ease up the assumption that transactions costs are nonexistent, and introduce those costs indeed in the way they factor in—that is, by way of their appearing in the form of *bid* (buy) and *ask* (sell) quotations in foreign exchange rates. Let S^B and S^A be the spot *bid* and *ask* prices (of dealers or banks) of, say, 1 French franc in terms of U.S. dollars, F^B and F^A be the T-day forward *bid* and *ask* quotations. Next, denote the bank's deposit rate (or its borrowing rate—the investor's earnings rate on her deposits) and lending rate (which is the investor's borrowing rate) in the United States by r_D and r_L, and r_D^* and r_L^* in France, respectively. With these notations in place, the investor makes the following amount of profits when she enters into the investment strategy (i), as outlined earlier:

$$\pi_{t(1)} = \frac{M}{S^A}(1 + r_D^*)F^B - M(1 + r_L)$$

$$= M\{\frac{F^B}{S^A}(1 + r_D^*) - (1 + r_L)\} \tag{5.14}$$

whence the present value is:

$$\pi_{t(1)}^0 = \left(\frac{M}{1 + r_L}\right)\{\frac{F^B}{S^A}(1 + r_D^*) - (1 + r_L)\}. \tag{5.15}$$

Here $\pi_{t(1)}$ stands for profits for the first round of arbitrage with transaction costs, and $\pi_{t(1)}^0$ is the present value of first-round arbitrage profits. Under transactions costs this is the *minimum* amount of arbitrage profits for the investor. The present value of the ith iteration of the market play with the same data is then measured by the following:

$$\pi_{t(1)}^0 = \left(\frac{M}{1 + r_L}\right)\{\frac{F^B}{S^A}(1 + r_D^*) - (1 + r_L)\}^i, \tag{5.16}$$

and hence the sum total of the present value of profits from round 1 through n is:

$$\pi_{t(1\to n)}^{(+)0} \equiv M \sum_{i=1}^{n} \frac{1}{(1+r_L)^i} \{ \frac{F^B}{S^A}(1+r_D^*) - (1+r_L) \}^i = M\alpha_t\beta_t \left(\frac{1-(\alpha_t\beta_t)^n}{1-\alpha_t\beta_t} \right), \tag{5.17}$$

where $\alpha_t \equiv 1/(1 + r_L)$ and $\beta_t \equiv (F^B/S^A)(1 + r_D^*) - (1 + r_L)$. As before, for $n = \infty$, and $\alpha_t\beta_t < 1$,

$$\pi_{t(164)}^{(+)0} = M\alpha_t\beta_t \left(\frac{1}{1-\alpha_t\beta_t} \right), \text{ and for } \alpha_t\beta_t > 1, \ \pi_{t(164)}^{(+)0} = \infty. \tag{5.18}$$

Note that subscript t signifies the presence of transaction costs. Here $M\alpha_t\beta_t$ is the present value of the first round of riskless profits in currency markets, and $1/(1 - \alpha_t\beta_t)$ is the multiplier for $n = \infty$ (if $\alpha_t\beta_t < 1$). This is the *maximum* amount of profits attainable under transactions costs under investment strategy (i).[4]

Following the procedure outlined in an earlier section, one can easily get the following expressions of arbitrage-induced total profits for the ith iteration and the cumulative value of arbitrage-induced total profits up to and inclusive of the ith iteration in the presence of transaction costs:

$$\pi_{Tt(i)}^{(+)0} = \left(\frac{M}{1+r_L} \right) \{ \frac{F^B}{S^A}(1+r_D^*) - (1+r_L) \} \cdot \left(\frac{F^B}{S^A} \frac{1+r_D^*}{1+r_L} \right)^{i-1} \tag{5.19}$$

$$\pi_{Tt(1\to n)}^{(+)0} \equiv \sum_{i=1}^{n} \pi_{Tt(i)}^{(+)0} \left(\frac{M}{1+r_L} \right)$$

$$\equiv \sum_{i=1}^{n} \{ \frac{F^B}{S^A}(1+r_D^*) - (1+r_L) \} \left(\frac{F^B}{S^A} \frac{1+r_D^*}{1+r_L} \right)^{i-1}. \tag{5.20}$$

So, the bounds for profits—lower and upper—are defined in this instance (under transactions costs) as follows:

$$\pi_{Tt(1)}^0 = \frac{M}{(1+r_L)} \{ \left(\frac{F^B}{S^A} \right)(1+r_D^*) - (1+r_L) \} : \qquad \text{lower bound;}$$

$$\pi_{Tt(1\to n)}^{(+)0} = \left(\frac{M}{1+r_L} \right) \{ \left(\frac{F^B}{S^A} \right)(1+r_D^*) - (1+r_L) \} \frac{\left[1 - \left(\frac{F^B}{S^A} \frac{1+r_D^*}{1+r_L} \right)^n \right]}{\left[1 - \left(\frac{F^B}{S^A} \frac{1+r_D^*}{1+r_L} \right) \right]} : \quad \text{upper bound.}$$

When $n = \infty$, the upper bound is equal to:

$$\pi_{Tt(1\to\infty)}^{(+)0} = \left(\frac{M}{1+r_L}\right)\left\{\left(\frac{F^B}{S^A}\right)(1+r_D^*)-(1+r_L)\right\}\left[\frac{1}{1-\left(\frac{F^B}{S^A}\frac{1+r_D^*}{1+r_L}\right)}\right]: \text{ upper bound}$$

$$\text{(when } (F^B/S^A)(1+r^{*D})/(1+r_L)<1),$$

$$\pi_{Tt(1\to\infty)}^{(+)0} = \infty \qquad\qquad \text{(when } (F^B/S^A)(1+r^{*D})/(1+r_L)>1).$$

ARBITRAGE WITH LEVERAGE: TOTAL (ARBITRAGE-INDUCED) PROFITS WITH TRANSACTIONS COSTS

Leverage refers to the extent of debt the investor uses in her total investable funds for arbitrage in the foreign exchange market. In this analytical structure, borrowed funds have indeed been introduced as the initial investment dollars (or francs) for the investor. Now, consider the scenario in which leverage is further utilized by our investor at every step of her market moves. It is assumed now that the investor has the ability to borrow θ percent of every dollar amount of equity (or its equivalent amount in another currency) she has at the going market rate r_L (or at r_L^* in case of the other currency). This additional feature then requires the necessary modifications in the previous derivations, and upon those modifications, one must get the following present value of profits at the first round:

$$\pi_{Tt(1)}^0 = \left(\frac{M}{1+r_L}\right)\left\{\frac{F^B}{S^A}(1+r_D^*)-(1+r_L)\right\}, \qquad\qquad (5.21)$$

which is exactly the same value as (5.15). Since this much profit is the present value of the investor's total (pure and arbitrage-induced) profits, she can borrow $\theta\pi_{Tt(1)}^0$ from her bank, and thus put $\pi_{Tt(1)}^0(1 + \theta)$ in arbitrage process to generate the following amounts of arbitrage-induced total profits in the next round (second round in this instance):

$$\left(\frac{\pi_{Tt(2)}^0(1+\theta)}{S^A}\right)(1+r_D^*)F^B - \pi_{Tt(1)}^0\theta(1+r_L),$$

the present value of which is then:

$$\pi^0_{Tt(2)} = \left(\frac{M}{1+r_L}\right)\left\{\frac{F^B}{S^A}(1+r_D^*)-(1+r_L)\right\}\cdot$$

$$\left[\left(\frac{1}{1+r_L}\right)\left\{\frac{F^B}{S^A}(1+r_D^*)+\theta\left\{\frac{F^B}{S^A}(1+r_D^*)-(1+r_L)\right\}\right\}\right] \tag{5.22}$$

and then, for round i ($i = 1, 2, \ldots, n$),

$$\pi^0_{Tt(i)} = \left(\frac{M}{1+r_L}\right)\left\{\frac{F^B}{S^A}(1+r_D^*)-(1+r_L)\right\}\cdot$$

$$\left[\left(\frac{1}{(1+r_L)^{i-1}}\right)\cdot\left\{\frac{F^B}{S^A}(1+r_D^*)+\theta\left\{\frac{F^B}{S^A}(1+r_D^*)-(1+r_L)\right\}\right\}^{i-1}\right] \tag{5.23}$$

The summation over the first n consecutive iterations of arbitrage then yields the following amount of total profits:

$$\pi^{(+)0}_{Tt(16n)} \equiv \sum_{i=1}^{n}\pi^0_{Tt(i)} = \left(\frac{M}{1+r_L}\right)\left\{\frac{F^B}{S^A}(1+r_D^*)-(1+r_L)\right\}\times$$

$$\sum_{i=1}^{n}\left(\frac{1}{(1+r_L)^{i-1}}\right)\left\{\frac{F^B}{S^A}(1+r_D^*)+\theta\left\{\frac{F^B}{S^A}(1+r_D^*)-(1+r)\right\}\right\}^{i-1} \tag{5.24}$$

Note here that the sum total of n rounds of consecutive arbitrage in the market gives rise to the magnification of the initial arbitrage profits by the factor of:

$$\sum_{i=1}^{n}\left(\frac{1}{(1+r_L)^{i-1}}\right)\left\{\frac{F^B}{S^A}(1+r_D^*)+\theta\left\{\frac{F^B}{S^A}(1+r_D^*)-(1+r)\right\}\right\}^{i-1}\cdot$$

If $0 < [1/(1 + r_L)][(F^B/S^A)(1 + r_D^*) + \theta\{(F^B/S^A)(1 + r_D^*) - (1 + r_L)\}] < 1$, the profit function is convergent to its upper bound, which is defined by:

$$\pi^{(+)0T}_{t(164)} = \left(\frac{M}{1+r_L}\right)\frac{F^B}{S^A}\{(1+r_D^*)-(1+r_L)\}\cdot\left(\frac{1}{1-\hat{\alpha}_t\hat{\beta}_t}\right),$$

where $\hat{\alpha}_t = \dfrac{1}{1+r_L}$ and $\hat{\beta}_t = \left[\dfrac{F^B}{S^A}(1+r_D^*)+\theta\left[\dfrac{F^B}{S^A}(1+r_D^*)-(1+r_L)\right]\right].$

Table 5.1a

Arbitrage-induced total profits with no transaction costs and no borrowing against the equity positions: profit multiplier in each round (column 3), profits in each round (column 4), cumulative profit multiplier (column 5), and cumulative profits (column 6).

i	θ	$\mu_{(i)}$	$\pi^0_{(n)}$	$\mu^*_{(n)}$	$\pi^{(+)0}_{T t\,(1 \to n)}$
1	0	1.00	$6,236.60	1.00	$6,236.60
2	0	1.01	6,275.50	2.01	12,512.10
3	0	1.01	6,314.64	3.02	18,826.74
4	0	1.02	6,354.02	4.04	25,180.76
5	0	1.03	6,393.65	5.06	31,574.41
6	0	1.03	6,433.52	6.09	38,007.93
7	0	1.04	6,473.65	7.13	44,481.58
8	0	1.04	6,514.02	8.18	50,995.59
9	0	1.05	6,554.64	9.23	57,550.24
10	0	1.06	6,595.52	10.29	64,145.76
20	0	1.13	7,018.60	21.23	132,406.20
25	0	1.16	7,240.21	26.96	168,161.26
100	0	1.85	11,541.42	138.24	862,135.12
∞	0	∞	∞	∞	∞

Following the earlier procedure, let $\mu_{T t}(i)/(1/(1+r_L)^{i-1}$. $\{F^B/S^A)(1+r^*_D)+\theta\{F^B/S^A(1+r^*_D)-(1+r)\}\}^{i-1}$, and $\mu^+_{T t}(n)/(1-(\hat{\alpha}\hat{\beta})^n/1-(\hat{\alpha}_t\hat{\beta}_t)$ the profit multipliers at ith round and cumulatively for first n rounds, respectively. The numerical values of these multipliers are given in Table 5.1.

ARBITRAGE PROFITS WITHOUT TRANSACTIONS COSTS ONCE AGAIN

Here we resurrect the earlier section that dealt with profit multiplier in the absence of transaction costs, once again with further modification and obvious generalization. We have already noted that once the present value of first round of profit (π_1^0) is recognized, the investor puts π_1^0 into arbitrage and then generates the following amount of profits in the second round:

Table 5.1b
Arbitrage-induced total profits with no transaction costs, and 25 percent borrowing against the equity positions: profit multiplier in each round (column 3), profits in each round (column 4), cumulative profit multiplier (column 5), and cumulative profits (column 6).

i	θ	$\mu_{(i)}$	$\pi^0_{(n)}$	$\mu^+_{(n)}$	$\pi^{(+)0}_{T\tau\,(1\to n)}$
1	0.25	1.00	$6,236.60	1.00	$6,236.60
2	0.25	1.01	6,285.22	2.01	12,521.83
3	0.25	1.02	6,334.22	3.02	18,856.05
4	0.25	1.02	6,383.60	4.05	25,239.65
5	0.25	1.03	6,433.37	5.08	31,673.02
6	0.25	1.04	6,483.52	6.12	38,156.54
7	0.25	1.05	6,534.06	7.17	44,690.60
8	0.25	1.06	6,585.00	8.22	51,275.60
9	0.25	1.06	6,636.34	9.29	57,911.94
10	0.25	1.07	6,688.07	10.36	64,600.01
20	0.25	1.16	7,228.13	21.55	134,416.48
25	0.25	1.20	7,514.30	27.48	171,411.21
100	0.25	2.16	13,453.28	150.59	939,171.82
∞	0.25	∞	∞	∞	∞

$$\pi_2 = \left(\left(\frac{\pi^0_1}{S}\right)(1+r^*)F - \pi^0_1(1+r)\right) = \pi^0_1\left\{\left(\frac{F}{S}\right)(1+r^*) - (1+r)\right\},$$

the present value of which is then:

$$\pi^0_2 = \left[\frac{M}{(1+r)^2}\right]\left\{\left(\frac{F}{S}\right)(1+r^*) - (1+r)\right\}^2 \qquad (5.25)$$

if pure arbitrage profit scenario is considered. Otherwise, the investor computes the total profit level (in the arbitrage-induced sense) to be:

$$\pi^+_{T(2)} = \left(\frac{\pi^0_1}{S}\right)(1+r^*)F,$$

Table 5.1c
Arbitrage-induced total profits with transaction costs, and no borrowing against the equity positions: profit multiplier in each round (column 3), profits in each round (column 4), cumulative profit multiplier (column 5), and cumulative profits (column 6).

i	θ	$\mu_{Tt(i)}$	$\pi^0_{Tt(i)}$	$\mu^*_{Tt(n)}$	$\pi^{(+)0}_{Tt(1\cdots n)}$
1	0	1.00	$931.20	1.00	$931.20
2	0	1.05	974.59	2.00	1,863.26
3	0	1.09	1,020.02	3.00	2,796.58
4	0	1.15	1.067.56	4.01	3,729.99
5	0	1.20	1,117.31	5.01	4,664.66
6	0	1.25	1,169.38	6.01	5,600.19
7	0	1.31	1,223.89	7.02	6,536.60
8	0	1.37	1,280.93	8.03	7,473.89
9	0	1.44	1,340.63	9.03	8,412.04
10	0	1.50	1,403.11	10.04	9,351.07
20	0	2.37	2,212.71	20.18	18,789.58
25	0	2.97	2,778.69	25.28	23,541.88
100	0	88.92	84,642.91	104.75	97,545.35
∞	0	∞	∞	∞	∞

which, as noted earlier, is:

$$\pi^{(+)0}_{T(2)} = \frac{\frac{\pi^0_1}{S}(1+r^*)F}{(1+r)}$$

$$= \left[\frac{M}{(1+r)}\right]\left\{\left(\frac{F}{S}\right)(1+r^*)-(1+r)\right\}\left\{\frac{1}{(1+r)}\right\}\left[\left(\frac{F}{S}\right)(1+r^*)\right], \tag{5.26}$$

and similarly,

$$\pi^{(+)0}_{T(3)} = \left[\frac{M}{(1+r)}\right]\left\{\left(\frac{F}{S}\right)(1+r^*)-(1+r)\right\}\left\{\frac{1}{(1+r)^2}\right\}\left[\left(\frac{F}{S}\right)(1+r^*)\right]^2 \tag{5.27}$$

Table 5.1d
Arbitrage-induced total profits with transaction costs, and 25 percent borrowing against the equity positions: profit multiplier in each round (column 3), profits in each round (column 4), cumulative profit multiplier (column 5), and cumulative profits (column 6).

i	θ	$\mu_{\pi t\,(i)}$	$\pi^0_{\pi t\,(i)}$	$\mu^+_{\pi t\,(n)}$	$\pi^{(+)\,0}_{\pi t\,(1\,-n)}$
1	0.25	1.00	\$931.20	1.00	\$931.20
2	0.25	1.05	974.59	2.00	1,863.47
3	0.25	1.10	1,020.02	3.00	2,796.84
4	0.25	1.15	1,067.56	4.01	3,731.29
5	0.25	1.20	1,117.31	5.01	4,666.83
6	0.25	1.26	1,169.38	6.02	5,603.45
7	0,25	1.31	1,223.89	7.02	6,541.17
8	0.25	1.38	1,280.93	8.03	7,479.98
9	0.25	1.44	1,340.63	9.04	8,419.88
10	0.25	1.51	1,403.11	10.05	9,360.88
20	0.25	2.39	2,212.71	20.22	18,831.29
25	0.25	3.00	2,778.69	25.35	23,607.97
100	0.25	92.92	4,642.91	105.99	98,694.75
∞	0.25	∞	∞	∞	∞

and

$$\pi^{(+)0}_{T(i)} = \left[\frac{M}{(1+r)}\right]\left\{\left(\frac{F}{S}\right)(1+r^*)-(1+r)\right\}\left\{\frac{1}{(1+r)^{i-1}}\right\}\left[\left(\frac{F}{S}\right)(1+r^*)\right]^{i-1}$$

(5.28)

Note that in all these arbitrage activities, the investor thus far only puts in the present value of the generated arbitrage profits into the next round of covered arbitrage. In reality, she can (and rationally should) use the original amount M and $\pi_i^0(1 + \theta)$ for the $(i + 1)$ round of arbitrage ($i = 1$, 2, 3,..., n). It is instructive, therefore, that we modify the earlier section that dealt with profit multiplier in the absence of transaction costs. The first round of arbitrage profits is obviously the same as before, but let it be rewritten (in this modified environment) as follows:

$$\hat{\pi}_1^0 = M\left[\frac{F}{S}\frac{1+r^*}{1+r} - 1\right] = M\alpha$$

$$\text{where } \alpha \equiv \left[\frac{F}{S}\frac{1+r^*}{1+r} - 1\right],$$

and now, the second round is as follows:

$$\hat{\pi}_2 = \left(\frac{M + \hat{\pi}_1^0(1+\theta)}{S}\right)(1+r^*)F - (M + \theta\hat{\pi}_1^0)(1+r),$$

whence:

$$\hat{\pi}_2^0 = M + \theta\hat{\pi}_1^0\left[\frac{F}{S}\frac{1+r^*}{1+r} - 1\right] = M\alpha[1 + \{1 + \alpha(1+\theta)\}].$$

Similar operations yield in the third round of iterative arbitrage:

$$\hat{\pi}_3^0 = M + \theta\hat{\pi}_2^0\left[\frac{F}{S}\frac{1+r^*}{1+r} - 1\right] = M\alpha[1 + \{1 + \alpha(1+\theta)\}^2] + \{1 + \alpha(1+\theta)\}, \quad \text{and in the}$$

ith round of iterative arbitrage:

$$\hat{\pi}_i^0 = M + \theta\hat{\pi}_{i-1}^0\left[\frac{F}{S}\frac{1+r^*}{1+r} - 1\right] = M\alpha[1 + \{1 + \alpha(1+\theta)\}^{i-1}] + \{1 + \alpha(1+\theta)\}^{i-2}.$$

Let $A \equiv \{1 + \alpha(1 + \theta)\}$. A close look at the expressions of π_1^0 for $i = 1, 2, 3,$ $4, \ldots, n$ reveals the following:

$$\hat{\pi}_1^0 = M\alpha(A^0),$$
$$\hat{\pi}_2^0 = M\alpha(A^0 + A^1)$$
$$\hat{\pi}_3^0 = M\alpha(A^0 + A^1 + A^2)$$
$$\hat{\pi}_4^0 = M\alpha(A^0 + A^1A^2 + A^3), \text{ and}$$

.

.

$$\hat{\pi}_n^0 = M\alpha(A^0 + A^1A^2 + A^3 + \ldots + A^{n-1}).$$

The successive n rounds of iteration in arbitrage in the currency market then create the cumulative profits in the amount of:

$$\hat{\pi}(1 \to n) \equiv \sum_{i=1}^{n} \hat{\pi}_i^0 = M\alpha\left[n + (n-1)A + (n-2)A^2 + (n-3)A^3 + \ldots A^{n-1}\right]$$

for $n - i \geqslant 0$ and $i \geqslant 1$. Here $M\alpha$ is the initial profit ($\pi_i^0 \equiv \pi_i^0$), and $[n + (n - 1)A + (n - 2)A^2 + (n - 3)A^3 + \ldots + A^{n-1}]$ is the cumulative multiplier $\mu(1 \to n)$ in this modified analytical framework.

Now all the previous sections can be appropriately modified with and without transaction costs.

Covered Interest Triangular Arbitrage (CITA):

(Pure Arbitrage) Profits under CITA

Next, we examine the scope of the covered interest arbitrage in triangularity. For the sake of simplicity, assume away transaction costs in currency and capital (or money) market. We again start off with a scenario like the following: an investor begins the process with U.S. dollars (let it be the first currency), which he converts into British pound (second currency), invests the converted pound amount in U.K. at the British rate of interest r_2. The pound amount generated in the investment process is then converted into Japanese yen (third currency), and the yen amount is then invested in the Japanese market. Finally, the newly created yen value is then converted back into U.S. dollars. Let us denote different terms as follows:

M = (original) amount of, say, U.S. dollars borrowed for investment;

r_1 = U.S. interest rate;

r_2 = British interest rate;

r_3 = Japanese interest rate;

S_{21} = spot rate of exchange of British pounds in terms of U.S. dollars (second currency in terms of first currency);

S_{32} = spot rate of exchange of Japanese yens in terms of British pounds (third currency in terms of second currency);

S_{31} = spot rate of exchange of Japanese yens in terms of U.S. dollars (third currency in terms of first currency);

F_{31} = forward rate of exchange of Japanese yen in terms of U.S. dollars.

Under the scenario, the investor's present value of covered interest triangular arbitrage profits ($P^+_{1(0:CITA)}$) can be computed as follows:

$$P^+_{1(0:CITA)} = \left(\frac{M}{S_{21}}\left[(1+r_2)\frac{1}{S_{32}}(1+r_3)F_{31} - M(1+r_1)\right]\frac{1}{1+r_i}\right) =$$

$$M\frac{1}{(1+r_1)}\left[\frac{F_{31}}{S_{32}S_{21}}(1+r_2)(1+r_3)-(1+r_1)\right], \tag{5.29}$$

and then,

$$P^+_{i(0:CITA)} = M\frac{1}{(1+r_1)^i}\left[\frac{F_{31}}{S_{32}S_{21}}(1+r_2)(1+r_3)-(1+r_1)\right]^i, \ i=1, 2,...n. \tag{5.30}$$

The cumulative profit in the first n rounds is then defined by ($P^{+*}_{n:CITA}$):

$$P^{+*}_{n:CITA} = \sum_{i=1}^{n}P^+_{i(0:CITA)} = M\frac{1}{(1+r_1)^i}\left[\frac{F_{31}}{S_{32}S_{21}}(1+r_2)(1+r_3)-(1+r_1)\right]^i = M\lambda\left[\frac{1-\lambda^n}{1-\lambda}\right],$$

where $\lambda \equiv \frac{1}{1+r_1}\left[\frac{F_{31}}{S_{32}S_{21}}(1+r_2)(1+r_3)-(1+r_1)\right]$. Here $\left[\frac{1-\lambda^n}{1-\lambda}\right]$ is the pure

arbitrage profit multiplier under CITA ($\mu^+_{\infty(0:CITA)}$). Since $0 < \lambda < 1$, for n = ∞,   (5.31)

$$\mu^+_{\infty(0:CITA)} = \frac{1}{1-\lambda}.$$

Let us now use some hypothetical market data: $r_1 = 10\%$, $r_2 = 9.5\%$, $r_3 = 9.75\%$, $S_{21} = 2.00$, $S_{31} = 0.0098$, $S_{32} = 0.0049$, $F_{31} = 0.0105$, and $M = \$1,000,000$. With these data then, one gets the following computed values: $P^+_{1(0)} = \$170,547.90$ (as compared to $P_{1(0)} = \$70,113.50$), $\mu^+_{\infty(0:CITA)} = 1.2056151$ (compared to $\mu_\infty = 1.0754001$). It appears that magnification effect of arbitrage profit under covered interest triangular arbitrage (CITA) usually is more pronounced than it is under simple covered interest arbitrage (CIA). It is intuitively clear that if there is an additional gain from a movement from a two-currency to three-currency in arbitrage context, CITA must be superior to CIA. To ascertain the general validity of such ranking, one must compare CITA with n currencies *vis-a-vis* CITA with $(n - 1)$ currencies where $n \geq 3$. If the former is superior to the later, one should use CITA instead of CIA in exploiting market opportunities.

Arbitrage-Induced Profits under CITA:

As in an earlier section, we can now eliminate the interest deductions from round two onward in the total profit calculation under covered interest triangular arbitrage. The first round, of course, remains the same as (5.31). It is easily then computed that the present value of the profit level on ith iteration $(i > 1)$ under CITA $(\tilde{P}_{i(0:CITA)})$ is as follows:

$$\tilde{P}_{i(0:CITA)} = \frac{1}{(1+r_1)^{i-1}} \left[\frac{F_{31}}{S_{32}S_{21}}(1+r_2)(1+r_3) \right]^{i-1} \cdot \theta,$$ (5.32)

where $\theta = M \dfrac{1}{(1+r_1)} \left[\dfrac{F_{31}}{S_{32}S_{21}}[(1+r_2)(1+r_3)-(1+r_1)] \right].$

The cumulative profits over n iterations $(\tilde{P}^+_{n:CITA})$ are measured then by the following:

$$\tilde{P}^+_{n(CITA)} = M \frac{1}{1+r_1} \left[\frac{F_{31}}{S_{32}S_{21}}(1+r_2)(1+r_3)-(1+r_1) \right] \sum_{i=1}^{n} \frac{1}{(1+r_1)^{i-1}} \left[\left[\frac{F_{31}}{S_{32}S_{21}}(1+r_2)(1+r_3) \right]^{i-1} \right].$$ (5.33)

Here, (pure) profit multiplier $(\mu^+_{n(0:CITA)})$, profit level $(P^+_{n(0:CITA)})$ under CITA, (arbitrage-induced) profit multiplier $(\tilde{\mu}^+_{n(0:CITA)})$, and profit levels $(\tilde{P}^+_{n(0:CITA)})$ under different values of n under CITA are given by Table 5.2: Next, one may wonder why an investor should begin the arbitrage process with \$1 million in place of \$1 billion or \$10 trillion if the arbitrage opportunities exist. In this chapter, that is not the issue for discussion. We must, however, point out that we never attempt to measure the optimum

Table 5.2
Pure arbitrage profits, arbitrage-induced profits, and different multipliers under CITA with M = \$1,000,000; r_1 = 10%; r^2 = 9.5%; r_3 = 9.75%; S_{21} = 2.000; S_{31} = 0.0098; S_{32} = 0.0049; F_{31} = 0.0105.

n	$\mu^+_{n(o:CITA)}$	$P^+_{n(0:CITA)}$	$\tilde{\mu}^+_{n(o:CITA)}$	$\tilde{P}^+_{n(0:CITA)}$
1	1	\$170,547.70	1	\$170,547.70
2	1.1705477	\$199,634.20	2.2151139	\$377,782.58
3	1.1996341	\$204,594.84	3.6917016	\$629611.21
4	1.2045948	\$205,440.87	5.4859309	\$935,612.89
5	1.2054409	\$205,585.17	7.6661683	\$1,307,447.30
10			27.976086	\$4,771,257.10
20			224.33316	\$38,259,504
25			601.99015	\$120,668,035
∞	1.2056148	\$205,614.84	4	4

level of investment. One may look at it factually that the amount the investor begins with is the maximum amount he has (or can borrow from a bank) at the point when he engages in his arbitrage operation, and thus one can take that amount as M in this theoretical paradigm. Another point must be raised here next. It is often stated that since interest rate parity exists as a condition for market equilibrium, and hence the arbitrage profit does not exist in the very first round, then arbitrage profit as well as its multiplier must be zero. Having seriously considered this point, we have noted almost always that at any point in time, there exists a set of interest rates, different from a pair that is consistent with interest rate parity.[5] In other words, one can almost surely find a constellation of interest rates for which covered interest arbitrage veritably exists.

At a more general level, we must now suggest that one may follow the earlier procedure to bring all types of transaction costs into the analytical framework. With several experiments with real-market data collected in several periods, we note that covered interest triangular arbitrage (CITA) appears to be a better investment strategy than simple design of covered interest arbitrage (CIA), although further econometric testing should be performed to put real emphasis to our tentative conclusion in the real world. Further extensions are left for the readers and interested practitioners who may decide to play in foreign exchange markets. One should note that although, in this paper, we have worked out CITA activities with three currencies, it is neither difficult nor less useful to deal with any arbitrary number of currencies (greater than three) with this analytical procedure outlined here. In fact, the mathematical generalization of equation 5.33 is as follows:

$$\tilde{P}^{+}_{n:CITA} = \tilde{\theta} \sum_{i=1}^{n} \frac{1}{\left(1+r_j\right)^{i-1}} \left[\frac{F_{mj}}{\prod\limits_{j=1,j\neq m}^{m} S_{j+1,j}} \prod_{j=1}^{m}\left(1+r_{j+1}\right) \right],$$

$$\text{where } \tilde{\theta} = M \frac{1}{\left(1+r_j\right)} \left[\frac{F_{mj}}{\prod\limits_{j=1,j\neq m}^{m} S_{j+1,j}} \prod_{j=1,j\neq m}^{m}\left(1+r_{j+1}\right) - \left(1+r_j\right) \right],$$

(5.34)

$S_{j+1,j}$ is the rate of exchange of the $(j + 1)$th currency in terms of the jth currency. Empirical testing of this multidimensional profit formula is one as complicated as it may appear at first sight.

SOME OBSERVATIONS

Although it is often contended that the dynamics of market competition wipe out arbitrage opportunities very quickly, and hence iterative arbitrage does not make much sense in view of the physical speed of each transaction, in the context to today's technology, it should be noted that one can make about one million calculations and 10,000 evaluations in 1 second through a computer. One should also note that market quotations last, on average, between 10 seconds and 4 minutes, depending on the time of the day, trading volume, and the currencies concerned. Having factored in all this information, it is quite feasible that multiple rounds of arbitrage operations can be performed with any market data remaining frozen for a few seconds or minutes. At this stage we must bring out the fact that to make such a series of transactions the arbitrageur must have the arrangement with her bank for digitized signature even though it requires a side collateral commitment of the arbitrageur's line of credit, which she knows she will not tie up in any real sense. A prior discussion with the bank is a good step in the logistical design for such market play.

One may contend that since profits out of the first round of arbitrage are obtained only at the end of, say, one year from that day, how is this investor getting funds for the second, the third, and other rounds of market plays? Note here that π_1 is a sure amount of money made by the investor without taking any risk, and any bank should recognize this amount the investor makes at the end of one year from now. If that is a common knowledge of the investor as well as that of the bank, it is equally recognizable that this investor has $\pi_1^0 / \pi_1 / 1 + r$ now—and it is now her equity position, which she can legitimately utilize with a prior discussion with her banker. Finally, it is worth noting, particularly against the backdrop of the common belief that markets are so well aligned that scope for arbitrage is nonexistent in reality, that in the currency market almost always one can find arbitrage opportunity. Note that although spot and forward rates are *usually* defined at a point in time, and corresponding to those defined rates a set of domestic and foreign interest rates will yield π_1 = 0, one can always find another set of interest rates, which generates π_1 ? 0. This clearly signifies that arbitrage opportunity is a viable and feasible strategy in the foreign exchange market more often than not. Additionally, it should be pointed out that one who watches real-time data can easily recognize that quotations on spot and forward rates by different banks and/or dealers are not always same at the same instant. So, on that front one may find the scope for arbitrage. Finally, we should note that if one round of arbitrage act is undertaken, it may appear that arbitrage profit is negligible, and in that sense one may conclude that arbitrage opportunity is virtually nonexistent. But as the Table 5.1 shows, iterations, and cumulation make arbitrage trading very significant in real life.

EMPIRICAL EVIDENCE

Using *Reuters* real-time data screen and checking many of their quotes with number of banks, the values of π's and μ's for different iteration i and different values of leverage θ have been computed. We compiled data for six weeks from June 19, 1995 through July 31, 1995. Out of those intra-day data, randomly chosen usually three times a day from *Reuters* data screen, we have made 100 sets of computations. As expected, computed values are different for different sets, and here we choose the set that lies within the median set of 5, and the geometric mean of these median sets has been used to calculate the entries in Tables 5.1c and 5.1d under different assumed values of θ.

Tables 5.1c and 5.1d presents the computed profits and profit multipliers in the presence of transaction costs in both currency and money markets. *Ask* and *bid* quotes in the foreign exchange markets and *deposit* and *lending* rates of interest were taken from the *Reuters* screen three times a day (around 10:00 A.M., 11:30 A.M., and 2:30 P.M.) within the same time period (June 19, 1995 through July 31, 1995), and almost a third of these intra-day quotes were verified with a number of banks. Here we have S^A = 0.2028, F^A = 0.2037, r_B = 0.0454, r_D = 0.0444, r^*_B = 0.0440, r^*_D = 0.0438, M = $1,000,000, T = 360, θ = 0, 0.25, 0.5, 0.75, and i = 1, 2, 3, 4, 5, 6, 7, 8, 9, 10, 20, 25, 100, ∞. In the presence of transaction costs, profit measures are substantially reduced at each level of iteration, and hence cumulative measures are reduced as a result also.

CONCLUSION

We note through our computations with real-time data that the standard academic prognosis that arbitrage is hardly profitable because the markets are very well-aligned stands to be partly correct and partly incorrect. If $1,000,000 generates $931.20, which is not a significant profit (see Table 5.1a), one can hardly consider arbitrage as a meaningful investment instrument. Under transaction costs, both strategy (i) and strategy (ii) give negative profits 20 percent of the time in our data sample with deutsche mark *vis-a-vis* U.S. dollar. Of course, in those situations, no trader would engage in arbitrage, and hence, profit possibilities would simply be zero (not negative). It is in this sense one may agree with the existing academic research that tends to suggest that arbitrage is more of an illusion than a veritable reality. Yet, arbitrage-induced cumulative total profits, which are significant in magnitudes, have not been pointed out earlier. We find that arbitrage still provides a very meaningful window of opportunity for profit making without risk in currency market, where iterative arbitrage activities are undertaken under a skillful programming hand with maximum speed of transactions. Cumulative profits in Table 5.1 are quite eloquently demonstrative of that reality.

NOTES

The authors express their sincere appreciation to the referee, and Peter Zhang, C.F. Lee, Geoffrey Booth, Michael Sullivan, and Shmuel Hauser for useful and constructive comments on the previous draft. They are also indebted to K.C. Han, Philippe Givry, and David Suk for their computational assistance.

1. See, for instance, Ghosh (1997) on this issue.

2. See other citations in the *References* on this score.

3. Here r and r^* are the annual interest rates. If one has to get to the interest rate matching, say, a forward contract maturing in 90 days, then the investor should divide annual interest rates by 4 to arrive at the three-month interest rate of the United States and of the other country. One should note that the investor can choose any compounding or discounting interval, even continuous compounding or discounting for computations, and profit measures as a result will get modified.

4. It should be clearly noted at this point that if equation 5.14 assumes negative value, it does not automatically signify positive profit condition under investment strategy (ii). It is instructive therefore that we define profit measures under different arbitrage iterations when the investor is borrowing, say, N French francs at r^*_L, converting the amount into U.S. dollars at the spot rate of exchange (S^B), investing the converted dollar amount in the U.S. market at r_D, selling the dollars at the forward rate, and finally paying off the original debt and the accrued interest on that debt. In this case, her profits in the first round of arbitrage ($\pi^*_{t(1)}$) are computed as follows:

$$\pi^*_{t(1)} = NS^B(1 + r_D)/F^A - N(1 + r^*_L)$$
$$= N\{(S^B/F^A)(1 + r_D) - (1 + r^*_L)\}, \tag{5.34}$$

and therefore, the present value of the amount is:

$$\pi^{*(0)}_{t(1)} = [N/(1 + r_L)]\{(S^B/F^A)(1 + r_D) - (1 + r^*_L)\}. \tag{5.35}$$

On the ith iteration, then profits are defined by:

$$\pi^{*(0)}_{t(i)} = [N/(1 + r^*_L)^i]\{(S^B/F^A)(1 + r_D) - (1 + r^*_L)\}^i. \tag{5.36}$$

Note here that (5.14) and (5.34) are not *necessarily* of opposite signs[3].

5. In real life, some of these results have been used, and it is inappropriate to mention anything beyond this simple statement.

REFERENCES

Aliber, R.G. (1973). "The Interest Rate Parity Theorem: A Reinterpretation," *Journal of Political Economy*, 81 (November/December).

Blenman, L.P. (1992a). "The Interest Rate Parity: Seven Expressions: A Reply," *Financial Management*, Autumn.

Blenman, L.P. (1992b). "A Model of Covered Interest Arbitrage under Market Segmentation," *Journal of Money, Credit, and Banking*, 23 (4).

Blenman, L.P. (1996). "Contemporaneous, Non-contemporaneous Currency Exchanges and Arbitrage Activity," *The International Journal of Finance*, 8 (1).

Blenman, L.P., and J.S. Thatcher. (1995). "Arbitrage Opportunities in Currency and Credit Markets: New Evidence," *The International Journal of Finance*, 7 (1).

Callier, P. (1981). "One Way Arbitrage, Foreign Exchange and Securities Markets: A Note," *Journal of Finance,* 36 (December).

Clinton, K. (1988). "Transaction Costs and Covered Interest Arbitrage: Theory and Evidence," *Journal of Political Economy,* 96 (April).

Deardorff, A. V. (1979). "One-Way Arbitrage and Its Implications for the Foreign Exchange Markets," *Journal of Political Economy,* 87 (2).

Frenkel, J. A., and R. M. Levich. (1975). "Covered Interest Arbitrage: Unexploited Profits?" *Journal of Political Economy,* 83 (April).

Ghosh, D. K. (1991). "The Interest Rate Parity: Seven Expressions," *Financial Management,* Winter.

Ghosh, D. K. (1994). "The Interest Rate Parity, Covered Interest Arbitrage and Speculation under Market Imperfection." In D. K. Ghosh and E. Oritz (Eds.), *Changing Environment of International Financial Markets: Issues and Analysis.* London: Macmillan.

Ghosh, D. K. (in press). "Naked and Covered Speculation in the Foreign Exchange Market." In D. K. Ghosh and E. Oritz (Eds.), *The Global Structure of Financial Markets.* London: Routledge.

Keynes, J. M. (1923). *A Tract on Monetary Reform.* London: Macmillan.

McCormick, F. (1979). "Covered Interest Arbitrage: Unexploited Profits?—A Comment," *Journal of Political Economy,* 87 (April).

Rhee, S. G., and R. P. Chang. (1992). "Intra-day Arbitrage Opportunities in Foreign Exchange and Eurocurrency Markets," *Journal of Finance,* 47 (2).

Roll, R. W., and B. Solnik. (1979). "On Some Parity Conditions Frequently Encountered in International Finance," *Journal of Macroeconomics,* 1 (Summer).

Tsiang, S.-C. (1959). "The Theory of Forward Exchange and Effects of Government Intervention on the Forward Exchange Market," *International Monetary Fund Staff Papers,* 7 (April), 75–106.

Tsiang, S.-C. (1973). "Spot Speculation, Forward Speculation, and Arbitrage: A Clarification and Reply," *American Economic Review,* 63, 999–1002.

Chapter 6

Arbitrage and Hedging with Options

INTRODUCTION

In chapter 5 we have explored arbitrage and hedging with spot and forward contracts and derived profit measures under different strategic scenarios. In this chapter, we study the feasibility and opportunity of arbitrage with the underlying cover of currency options. Theoretical exploration and market analysis of derivative securities have colored the landscape of financial economics and investment practice over the past two decades. Ever since the publication of the seminal papers by Black and Scholes (1972, 1973) and Merton (1973), and a few years later by Cox, Ross, and Rubinstein (1979), analysts and practitioners have virtually revolutionized investment strategies in financial markets worldwide. Options, futures, forward, swaps, and so on—in their simple and synthetic forms—have provided various opportunities for covering risk and increasing speculative interests. Following the lead of earlier research, Garman and Kohlhagen (1983), Biger and Hull (1983), Giddy (1983), Grabbe (1983), and Yang (1985), to name a few, have extended options in the domain of foreign currencies. A rich and extremely useful literature, for example, Geske and Johnson (1984), Brennan (1979), and Black (1975), has been developed on the way—examining, enunciating, and illustrating many aspects of investment through the use of derivative securities. Merton, Scholes, and Gladstein (1978) provide a simulation of risk and returns of alternative-option portfolio strategies. Mueller (1981), Pounds (1978), and Pozen (1978), Grube, Panton, and Terrell (1979), Jones (1984), Yates and Kopprasch (1980), among others, examine covered call-and-put options and other facets of these instruments in investment strategies.

Options, futures, and other derivative securities have been extensively used as a consequence to hedge and/or speculate in financial markets, and the scope of the use of these securities has been the subject of continuous studies.

In this chapter, we attempt to use currency options—puts and calls—to derive conditions under which a trader can make profits from his trading strategy without assuming any risk, and how he can compound his profits via option-covered arbitrage upon iterative plays in the marketplace. For the derivation of the basic results, we first simplify the analytical structure by assuming away transaction costs. Once the results are derived in this simplified structure, we bring out transactions costs by way of introducing *ask* and *bid* quotes in the foreign exchange rates, and *deposit* and *borrowing* rates of interest that banks give and charge when investors deposit their funds in banks and borrow funds from banks, respectively.

In the existing literature, arbitrage operations in foreign exchange markets have been defined conspicuously with spot and forward contracts in terms of foreign and domestic interest rates. The classic research in this area must be attributed to Frenkel and Levich (1975) and Deardorff (1979). Using proportional costs of transactions, Frenkel and Levich (1975) show that interest-rate parity is bound by a neutral band, which is defined by:

$$\left[\frac{F - S\left(\frac{1+r}{1+r^*}\right)}{S\left(\frac{1+r}{1+r^*}\right)} \right] = t + t^* + t_s + t_f,$$

where S, F = spot; forward rate of exchange r, r^* = domestic; foreign rate of interest t, t^* = proportional transaction costs in domestic and foreign money markets; and t_s, t_f = proportional transaction costs in spot and forward exchange markets, respectively. Deardorff (1979) illustrates that in one-way arbitrage, the neutral band becomes narrower, as shown below:

$$\left[\frac{F - S\left(\frac{1+r}{1+r^*}\right)}{S\left(\frac{1+r}{1+r^*}\right)} \right] = t + t^* - t_s - t_f.$$

Callier (1981), Bahmani-Oskooee and Das (1985), and Clinton (1988) illustrate further narrowing of the neutral band under different market conditions. Rhee and Chang (1992) attempt to measure arbitrage profitability and its persistence over time in the foreign currency market with spot and forward contracts. More recently, Blenman (1992a, 1992b), Blenman and Thatcher (in press), and Ghosh (in press-a, in press-b) have examined arbitrage profitability and the minimum and maximum bounds for such profits under conditions of market imperfection where market imperfection is captured directly by bid and ask quotes in the foreign exchange market, and deposit and borrowing rates in money markets (as opposed to proportional transaction costs in those markets as envisaged in earlier works).[1]

In this chapter, however, we move away from both of the approaches in the existing literature. Instead, we introduce options in the currency market as the instruments to cover risk in arbitrage activities, then analyze the feasibility of profitable arbitrage and the compounding of derivable profits under alternative operational frameworks. In the sections dealing with option covered currency without transaction costs, we enunciate the conditions under which arbitrage with option cover available in the market place admits of profits and the compounding of that initial profit level to a rational and active investor. Three distinct investment scenarios and measures of profits are presented in this section. The first scenario depicts what can be termed pure arbitrage profits when the investor plays with the profits alone (generated in the initial stage) from round two onward. The second scenario extends the analytical framework envisioned in the first scenario to churn in pure arbitrage profits with full utilization of all the funds that are potentially available to the investor. In the third scenario we extend the second scenario with further appeal to practical notion of cost consideration. The following sections introduce transaction costs by way of bringing out ask and bid quotes of the foreign exchange rates, deposit and borrowing rates of interest in the money market, and brokerage, fee-inclusive option premiums.

OPTION COVERED CURRENCY ARBITRAGE WITHOUT TRANSACTION COSTS

Before we begin to develop the analytical vehicle, let us introduce the notations that will be used in this section:

S = spot rate of exchange (of, say, 1 French franc in terms of U.S. dollar(s));

X_p = exercise price of 1-month put option;

P = put premium (as observed in the market);

X_C = exercise price of 1-month call option;

C = call premium (as observed in the market);

r = domestic interest rate for one month;

r^* = foreign interest rate for one month.

Pure Arbitrage Profits with Newly Created Profits

Consider an investor who has M dollars at his disposal (or can borrow M amount from his bank at the interest rate of r) to begin investing in the currency market. He converts his M dollars into, say, French francs at the spot rate and gets M/S French francs, which he can invest in the French market at r^*, and thus make $(M/S)(1 + r^*)$ at the end of one month. There is no risk involved in the French franc amount. This investor who starts off with M dollars can hedge his position by exercising his put option (which we assume he has bought) by selling $(M/S)(1 + r^*)$ French francs at the rate X_p, thus retrieving $(M/S)(1 + r^*)(X_p - P(1 + r))$ amount in U.S. dollars. Since the investor has purchased the put option for P, which at the end of one month equals $P(1 + r)$, and his original amount of investable funds M dollars are worth $M(1 + r)$, his profits at the end of one month, in this instance, is then measured by π_1:[2]

$$\pi_1 = \frac{M}{S}\left(1+r^*\right)(X_p - P(1+r)) - M(1+r)$$

$$= M\left[\frac{X_p}{S}\left(1+r^*\right) - (1+r)\left(\frac{P}{S}\left(1+r^*\right)+1\right)\right] \tag{6.1}$$

If $\pi_1 > 0$, the investor should borrow funds domestically, convert domestic funds into foreign funds and invest overseas, and reconvert his foreign currency-denominated amount into his home currency by exercising the put option. If $\pi_1 < 0$, he should probably do the opposite—that is, he should borrow funds from a foreign bank, convert the borrowed funds into home currency at spot market, invest in the home market, and reconvert the home currency-denominated amount by exercising the call option, then take the profit. If the put premium is exactly equal to the call premium, the converse strategy will certainly hold good. Only in the case in which $\pi_1 = 0$ should the investor be indifferent. It is a case of option-based covered interest rate parity, simply defined by the following expression:

$$\frac{X_p}{S}\left(1+r^*\right) = (1+r)\left(\frac{P}{S}\left(1+r^*\right)+1\right),$$

which can be alternatively shown to be as follows:

$$\left(\frac{X_p - S}{S}\right)\left(1+r^*\right) = \left(r-r^*\right) + \frac{P}{S}(1+r)\left(1+r^*\right) \tag{6.2}$$

Note now that if $P = 0$ and $X_p = F$ (the forward rate of exchange, matching the expiration of the option), then equation 6.2 collapses into the celebrated interest rate parity in international finance. Obviously, for $P = 0$ (or, more correctly, for $P > 0$), $X_p > F$.

So far, we have correctly considered the option premium that the investor picks up in the marketplace for his actual transactions. However, theoretically, P is equal to its value, which, *à la* Black and Scholes (1972), is defined by:

$$e^{-rT}P_x\left[1-N\left(d-\sigma\sqrt{T}\right)\right]-e^{r^*T}S[1-N(d)],$$

where

$$d=\left\{\left[\ln(S/X_p)+\left(r-r^*+(\sigma^2/2)\right)T\right]/\sigma\sqrt{T}\right\},$$

σ is the instantaneous standard deviation of the returns on holding of the foreign currency, T is the option's maturity expressed in annualized terms, and $N(\cdot)$ is the standard normal cumulative distribution function. Here if a put-call parity holds good, then

$$P = C + X_p e^{-rT} - Se^{-r^*T}.$$

From this, it is obvious that if $X_p = S$ and/or $T = 0$, $P = C$, and in that event, as noted earlier, $\pi_1 > 0$ means that the investor converts his dollar (*numeraire* currency) into foreign currency and buys put options for the amount generated in the foreign currency, and if $\pi_1 < 0$, he obtains call options as a hedging device. In this exposition further to follow, since multiple rounds of option-covered arbitrage plays are exercised virtually within the time frozen for transactions (in the sense that the market quotes remain unchanged), T, σ, r, r^*, S, X_p, and hence d remains constant, and most likely X_p and S continue to assume the same value. Yet, we must recognize that in any arbitrarily chosen moment, spot-forward parity or put-call parity is not necessarily true, and hence some of these observations should be taken with a grain of salt. Most likely, however, as one may note from real-time data, the parity statements are not empirically observable most of the time, which means that arbitrage opportunities do surface more often than we tend to believe.

As already pointed out, if $\pi_1 \neq 0$, then profit opportunities exist in a risk-free fashion. For the economy of space, let us consider here $\pi_1 > 0$, and let the reader work out the opposite scenario.[3]

$$\pi_1 = M\left[\frac{X_p}{S}(1+r^*)-(1+r)\left(\frac{P}{S}(1+r^*)+1\right)\right], \tag{6.3}$$

measures the profit made by the investor that will come to his bank account a month from today, which means that he has earned an amount now equal to $\pi_1/(1+r) \equiv \pi_{1(0)}$. That is,

$$\pi_{1(0)} = \left(\frac{M}{1+r}\right)\left[\frac{X_P}{S}(1+r^\bullet) - (1+r)\left(\frac{P}{S}(1+r^\bullet)+1\right)\right]. \tag{6.4}$$

This is the legitimate equity position of this investor right now, immediately after the instant execution of his menu of investment strategies already described, and his banker should not have any problem in recognizing this amount. So, here we assume that in this age of technological speed $\pi_{1(0)}$ is realized and recognized by the transaction-endorsing bank for use by the investor for another round while the market quotes are still unchanged. Since this amount is on hand, the investor seizes the market data to play another round (second round) of arbitrage with his newly created equity $\pi_{1(0)}$. On this second round of play, he makes the amount π_2, which is equal to:

$$\pi_2 = \left(\frac{M}{1+r}\right)\left[\frac{X_P}{S}(1+r^\bullet) - (1+r)\left(\frac{P}{S}(1+r^\bullet)+1\right)\right]^2,$$

whence:

$$\pi_{2(0)} = \left(\frac{M}{(1+r)^2}\right)\left[\frac{X_P}{S}(1+r^\bullet) - (1+r)\left(\frac{P}{S}(1+r^\bullet)+1\right)\right]^2$$

$$= \left(\frac{M}{(1+r)}\right)\left[\frac{X_P}{S}(1+r^\bullet) - (1+r)\left(\frac{P}{S}(1+r^\bullet)+1\right)\right] \times$$

$$\left[\frac{\frac{X_P}{S}(1+r^\bullet) - (1+r)\left(\frac{P}{S}(1+r^\bullet)+1\right)}{1+r}\right]^{2-1} \tag{6.5}$$

Similar algebraic manipulations yield then upon the ith iteration:

$$\pi_{i(0)} = \left(\frac{M}{(1+r)}\right)\left[\frac{X_P}{S}(1+r^\bullet) - (1+r)\left(\frac{P}{S}(1+r^\bullet)+1\right)\right] \times$$

$$\left[\frac{\frac{X_P}{S}(1+r^\bullet) - (1+r)\left(\frac{P}{S}(1+r^\bullet)+1\right)}{1+r}\right]^{i-1} \tag{6.6}$$

The summation over all successive iterations ($i = 1, 2, 3, \ldots, n$) results in the following expression:[4]

$$\sum_{i=1}^{n} \pi_{i(0)} = \sum_{i=1}^{n} \left\{ \left(\frac{M}{(1+r)} \right) \left[\frac{X_P}{S}(1+r^*) - (1+r)\left(\frac{P}{S}(1+r^*)+1 \right) \right] x \right.$$

$$\left. \left[\frac{\frac{X_P}{S}(1+r^*) - (1+r)\left(\frac{P}{S}(1+r^*)+1 \right)}{1+r} \right]^{i-1} \right\}$$

$$= \left(\frac{M}{(1+r)} \right) \left[\frac{X_P}{S}(1+r^*) - (1+r)\left(\frac{P}{S}(1+r^*)+1 \right) \right] \left(\frac{1-\alpha^n}{1-\alpha} \right),$$

$$\text{where } \alpha \equiv \left[\frac{\frac{X_P}{S}(1+r^*) - (1+r)\left(\frac{P}{S}(1+r^*)+1 \right)}{1+r} \right].$$

$$(6.7)$$

As it is obvious now, the investor can arbitrage iteratively, and make a total profit of π_0^* in n rounds ($n = 1, 2, 3, \ldots$). Here $(1-\alpha^n)/(1-\alpha)$ is the n-round multiplier of the present value of the first round of arbitrage profit, which has already been expressed as follows:

$$\pi_{1(0)} \equiv \left(\frac{M}{1+r} \right) \left[\frac{X_P}{S}(1+r^*) - (1+r)\left(\frac{P}{S}(1+r^*)+1 \right) \right] \qquad (6.8)$$

The nth round (as opposed to n-round) arbitrage multiplier is defined, as one can immediately see from equation i, by the expression:

$$\left[\frac{\frac{X_P}{S}(1+r^*) - (1+r)\left(\frac{P}{S}(1+r^*)+1 \right)}{1+r} \right]^{n-1}.$$

From these two multipliers, one can note, profit levels may converge to its upper limit:

$$\lim_{n \to \infty} \pi_0^* \equiv \pi_0^{**} = \pi_{1(0)} \left(\frac{1}{1-\alpha} \right).$$

More clearly,

$$\pi_0^{**} = \left(\frac{M}{(1+r)} \right) \left[\frac{X_P}{S}(1+r^*) - (1+r)\left(\frac{P}{S}(1+r^*)+1 \right) \right] \left(\frac{1}{1-\alpha} \right), \qquad (6.9)$$

if $\alpha < 1$ and $n \to \infty$. If $\alpha > 1$ and $n \to \infty$, profit level asymptotically approaches infinity,—that is, arbitrage profits become unbounded.

Pure Arbitrage Profits with Total Available Funds

Remember in Scenario A, the investor puts back only $\pi_{1(0)}$ into second round of iterative arbitrage with option cover, and in the *i*th round only the profits made in the $(i-1)th$ round. More rational and profitable strategy in the second round of play, if correctly conceived, should be the one in which the investor uses his strategy with $(M + \pi_{1(0)})$ amount of funds (instead of $\pi_{1(0)}$ amount), which then churns into the following level of profits in the second round:

$$\hat{\pi}_{2(0)} = \left(\frac{1}{1+r}\right)\left[(M+\pi_{1(0)})/S\right]\left\{\frac{M}{S}(1+r^*)(X_P - P(1+r))\right\}$$
$$-(M+\pi_{1(0)})(1+r) = M\alpha(1+\alpha), \tag{6.10}$$

and on the *i*th round, the profit level amounts to:

$$\hat{\pi}_{i(0)} = \left(\frac{1}{1+r}\right)\left[(M+\pi_{1(0)}+\pi_{2(0)}+...\pi_{i-1(0)})/S\right].$$
$$\left\{\frac{M}{S}(1+r^*)(X_P - P(1+r))\right\} - (M+\pi_{1(0)}+\pi_{2(0)}+...\pi_{i-1(0)})(1+r)$$
$$= M\alpha(1+\alpha)^{i-1} \tag{6.11}$$

The summation over all the successive iterations $(i = 1, 2, 3, ..., n)$ results in the following expression in this modified situation:

$$\hat{\pi}_0^* = \sum_{i=1}^n \hat{\pi}_{i(0)} = \sum_{i=1}^n M\alpha(1+\alpha)^{i-1} = M\alpha\left[\frac{1-(1-\alpha)^n}{1-(1+\alpha)}\right]. \tag{6.12}$$

Since $\alpha > 0$, $(1 + \alpha) > 1$, and hence $\hat{\pi}_0^{**} (\equiv \lim_{n\to\infty} \hat{\pi}_0^*)$ is unbounded. In simple terms, the investors can generate unlimited amount of profits by fully exploiting market misalignment.

Arbitrage Profits with Total Available Funds: True Measure

In the earlier section dealing with pure arbitrage with total available funds, we have measured profit level in round 2 as follows:

$$\hat{\pi}_{2(0)} = \left(\frac{1}{1+r}\right)\left[(M+\pi_{1(0)})/S\right]\left\{\frac{M}{S}(1+r^*)(X_P - P(1+r))\right\} - (M+\pi_{1(0)})(1+r).$$

Note that since $\pi_{1(0)}$ is the investor's money just made, he may not feel like including interest cost on this amount in the calculation of capital costs to be subtracted in profit computation—that is, his profit measure in second round should *truly* be equal to $(\tilde{\pi}_{2(0)})$:

$$\tilde{\pi}_{2(0)} = \left(\frac{1}{1+r}\right)\left[(M+\pi_{1(0)})/S\right]\left\{\frac{M}{S}(1+r^*)(X_P - P(1+r))\right\} - M(1+r)$$

$$= M\alpha^2 \tag{6.13}$$

and similarly, on his *i*th round, profits must be measured by:

$$\tilde{\pi}_{i(0)} = \left(\frac{1}{1+r}\right)\left[(M+\pi_{1(0)}+\pi_{2(0)}+\ldots\pi_{i-1(0)})/S\right].$$

$$\left\{\frac{M}{S}(1+r^*)(X_P - P(1+r))\right\} - M(1+r) = M\alpha^i \tag{6.14}$$

The cumulative profits for *n* rounds then must be as follows:

$$\pi_0^* = \sum_{i=1}^{n}\tilde{\pi}_{i(0)} = M\alpha\left(\frac{1-\alpha^n}{1-\alpha}\right) \tag{6.15}$$

OPTIONS COVERED CURRENCY ARBITRAGE WITH TRANSACTION COSTS

Here we introduce transaction costs exactly in the way these costs appear in a trading structure. Let us bring out then *ask* and *bid* quotes in the exchange rates, and *deposit* and *borrowing* rates of interest in home and foreign markets as follows:

S^A = *ask* spot rate of exchange (of, say, 1 French franc in terms of U.S. dollar(s));

S^B = *bid* spot rate of exchange (of, say, 1 French franc in terms of U.S. dollar(s));

X^T_P = exercise price of 1-month put option inclusive of brokerage fee;

P^T = put premium inclusive of brokerage fee, which is usually equal to $P(1 + t)$, where *t* measures the *ad valorem* fee on transaction;

X^T_C = exercise price of a one-month call option inclusive of brokerage fee;

C^T = call premium inclusive of brokerage fee, which is usually equal to $C(1 + t)$, where *t* measures the *ad valorem* fee on transaction;

r_D = (domestic *deposit*) interest rate for one month;

r_B = (domestic *borrowing*) interest rate for one month;

r^*_D = (foreign *deposit*) interest rate for one month;

r^*_B = (foreign *borrowing*) interest rate for one month.

If the investor borrows *M* dollars and performs the same operations he does in the section dealing with pure arbitrage profits with newly created profits, his first round profits should be measured by the following expression:

$$\pi_1^T = M\left[\frac{X_P^T}{S^B}(1+r_D)-(1+r_B)\left(\frac{P^T}{S^B}(1+r_D^{\cdot})+1\right)\right],$$ (6.16)

where π_1^T denotes arbitrage profits in the first round with transaction costs. $\pi_1^T/(1+r_B)\equiv\pi_{1(0)}^T$ is the present value of the first round of arbitrage profits under transaction costs. Now, following the same procedure as in the earlier section, one can get the following expression for the ith round of arbitrage profits under transaction costs:

$$\pi_{i(0)}^T = \left(\frac{M}{(1+r_B)^i}\right)\left[\frac{X_P^T}{S^B}(1+r_L^{\cdot})-(1+r_B)(1+r_L^{\cdot})\left(\frac{P^T}{S^B}\right)\right]^i$$

$$= \left(\frac{M}{(1+r_B)}\right)\left[\frac{X_P^T}{S^B}(1+r_L^{\cdot})-(1+r_B)\left(\frac{P^T}{S^B}(1+r^{\cdot})+1\right)\right]\times$$

$$\left[\frac{\frac{X_P^T}{S^B}(1+r_L^{\cdot})-(1+r_B)\left(\frac{P^T}{S^B}(1+r^{\cdot})+1\right)}{1+r}\right]^{i-1},$$

and hence,

$$\pi_0^{T^*} =$$

$$\sum_{i=1}^{n}\pi_{i(0)}^{T^*} = \left(\frac{M}{1+r_B}\right)\cdot\left\{\left(\frac{M}{(1+r_B)}\right)\left[\frac{X_P^T}{S}(1+r_D^{\cdot})-(1+r_B)\left(\frac{P^T}{S^B}(1+r_D^{\cdot})+1\right)\right]\left(\frac{1-(\alpha^T)^n}{1-\alpha^T}\right)\right\},$$

where $\alpha^T\equiv(X_P^T/S^B)(1+r_D^{\cdot})-(1+r_B)((P^T/S^B)+1)$. The derivations with transaction costs in Scenario B and in Scenario C are straightforward, and since it will simply consume too much space and give rise to some tedium, although the final forms are very significant for the investor, we leave those chores for the interested readers.

It is not difficult to realize that profits at each iteration under transaction costs are reduced, and collective rounds yield reduced levels of profits as a result. It also becomes quite comprehensible that in some instances profits may completely disappear or even turn into losses.

MICROSTATICS AND MACRODYNAMICS OF THE
MARKET: SOME OBSERVATIONS

It is a fundamental reality that if arbitrage opportunity exists in the marketplace, it soon disappears by the dynamics of competition, and in that sense it may appear quite questionable if the second, and third, and the nth round of arbitrage activities of our investor can ever take place. A careful reflection of this point is absolutely essential, and upon that reflection and comprehension of market forces, one should realize the following points. First of all, if the investor finds that arbitrage opportunity exists, say, by the satisfaction of the condition, given by equation 6.1, he ascertains profits *instantly* for all the n rounds of arbitrage. The market data are the same for round 1 and round n within 20 seconds or 2 minutes in which quotes do not change from the investor's screen. If his first finger presses a key on his first computer, his 10th finger presses the same programmed key on his 10th computer *almost* at the very same instant. The first and the 10th round differ, however, only by the amounts of arbitrage funds—in the first round the amount is M dollars, and on the nth round the amount is $\pi_n/(1+r)^n$ and the time involved in these 10 successive rounds may be less than a second with digitized signatures of approval by the bank(s) in the middle with today's technology and speed. The moment the market data are factored in, and π_1 (? 0) is ascertained, one computes $\pi_{1(0)}$, $\pi_{2(0)}$, $\pi_{3(0)}$, ..., $\pi_{n(0)}$, and so on. If the investor can exploit the market one time via arbitrage, he can exploit the same market several times, since the moment is *virtually* frozen, and the data for market exploitation remain the same. Note that the investor is a micro agent operating in the marketplace in which even the speediest adjustment cannot deprive him of the opportunity to take advantage of the market misalignment. We know for sure that arbitrage exists in the market, and many players subsist on it. Therefore, arbitrage and iterations are valid plays in the market. One should also note that in the trillion-dollar market, a million or even a few billions by a micro agent may not throw the market into any state of concussion. However, if a large number of participants act in the same moment, there may be an execution jam, and nobody is likely to make any profits out of arbitrage. In the situation of multiple players, the macrodynamics of the market set in and force arbitragers into a zero-profit condition. One more point should be made. Since too many iterations are involved in this investment strategy, one should realize that before some iteration is executed, some quotes may change. So in order to guard against this possibility, an appropriate limit order should be put in with each iteration of covered arbitrage, and it should guarantee nonnegative profit conditions in the repeated arbitrage acts.

Market dynamics and market efficiency are of paramount significance. Cornell (1977) examines these concerns quite efficiently. For further exam-

ination of our analytical framework, let us consider the adjustment process in the dynamic macrostructure of the market, which can be captured
in the following way:

$$d\omega/dt = \lambda(\omega - \omega^*),$$

where $\omega/X_p/S$, ω^* is the value of in which option-based covered interest
rate parity, as defined earlier by equation (6.2), holds, and $\lambda > 0$ is the
speed of adjustment. The solution to this differential equation is given by:

$$\omega(t) = \omega^* + (\omega_0 - \omega^*)e^{-\lambda t}$$

Here ω_0 is the initial value of X_p/S. As $t\to\infty$, $\omega\to\omega^*$. One should note then
that in the frozen (static) moment, no adjustment is possible, and micro-
level arbitrage is an exploitable opportunity.

At this point, a few more issues should be addressed as well. One may
wonder why an investor who sees an arbitrage opportunity will start off
with $1 million instead of hundreds of millions or billions of dollars. The
answer is simple. If the investor has $1 million as the maximum amount
available to him, he only has to begin with that much money. M dollars, in
our paradigm, is the maximum available initial fund. Of course, if the
investor has more, he will initiate his moves with more funds. The issue
here is not what the optimal amount of initial investment funds for arbitrage should be; the issue is: if an initial amount—be it M dollars or Z dollars—is available for arbitrage, what amount of money can potentially be
generated out of that initial situation? Two other issues should be brought
to light in this context. One may argue that since profits out of the first
round of arbitrage are obtained only at the end of one month from that
day, how is this investor getting funds for second, and third, and other
rounds of market plays? Note here that π_1 is a sure amount of money
made by the investor without taking any risk, and any bank should recognize this amount the investor makes at the end of one month. If this is a
common knowledge of the investor as well as that of the bank, it is equally
recognizable that this investor has $\pi_{1(0)}/\pi_1/1 + r)$ now—and it is his
equity position, which he can legitimately utilize (probably with a prior
discussion with his banker). It is worth noting, particularly against the
backdrop of the common belief that markets are so well-aligned that scope
for arbitrage in reality is nonexistent, that in the currency market one can
almost always find arbitrage opportunity. Note that although spot rate
and option prices are *usually* defined at a point of time, and corresponding to those defined quotes a set of domestic and foreign interest
rates will yield $\pi_1 = 0$, one can always find another set of interest rates
from the available spectrum of interest rates, which generates $\pi_1 \geqslant 0$. This
clearly signifies that arbitrage opportunity is a viable and feasible strategy

in the foreign exchange market more often than not. Additionally, it should be pointed out that one who watches real-time data can easily recognize that the quotations on spot rate and options prices by different banks and/or dealers are not always the same at the same instant. So on that front one may also find the scope for arbitrage. Finally, we should note that if one round of arbitrage act is undertaken, it may appear that arbitrage profit is negligible, and in that sense one may conclude that arbitrage opportunity is virtually nonexistent.

NOTES

1. See other citations in the references at the end.

2. Here r and r^* are the interest rates for one month—not the annual interest rates. If one has annual interest rates available, the investor should divide those rates by 12 to get to the (acceptable) one-month interest rates matching, say, an option maturing in a month. Since one-month options are being considered here, we have chosen one-month compounding/discounting in this work. But, technically one should note that the investor can choose any compounding or discounting interval, even continuous compounding or discounting for computations, and profit measures as a result will get modified. The author would like to acknowledge his indebtedness to the participants in the seminar in Marseille who suggested this point.

3. It should be clearly noted at this point that if equation (6.1) assumes negative value, it does not automatically signify positive profit condition under investment strategy in which the investor borrows funds from a foreign country and starts from the other end. It is instructive, therefore, that we define profit measures under different arbitrage plays when the investor is borrowing, say, N French francs at r^*, converting the amount into U.S. dollars at the spot rate of exchange (S), investing the converted dollar amount in the U.S. market at r, exercising call option and buying French francs, and finally paying off the original debt and the accrued interest on that debt. In this case, his profits in the first round of arbitrage $^f\pi_1$ are computed as follows:

$$^f\pi_1 = NS(1 + r)\{(1/X_C) - (1/C)(1 + r^*)\} - N(1 + r^*)$$
$$= N[(S/X^C)(1 + r) - (1 + r^*)\{(S/C)(1 + r) + 1\}], \qquad (6.17)$$

and therefore, the present value of the amount is:

$$^f\pi_{1(0)} = (N/(1 + r))[(S/X^C)(1 + r) - (1 + r^*)\{(S/C)(1 + r) + 1\}], \qquad (6.18)$$

and on the ith iteration, then profits are defined by:

$$^f\pi_{i(0)} = (N/(1 + r^*)^i)[[(S/X^C)(1 + r) - (1 + r^*)(1 + r)(S/C)]^i$$
$$- [(S/X^C)(1 + r) - (1 + r^*)(1 + r)(S/C)]^{i-1}(1 + r^*)]. \qquad (6.19)$$

Note here that (1) and (^{f}1), and, in more general situations, (i) and ($^f i$) are not *necessarily* of opposite signs.

4. It should be noted, as the reviewer pointed out aptly, that there may be an institutional ceiling on the amount an investor can go after with these iterations. A

creative design may be in order to circumvent such institutional restriction if it exists.

REFERENCES

Bahmani-Oskooee, M., and S. P. Das. (1985). "Transactions Costs and Interest Parity Theorem," *Journal of Political Economy*, 93.

Biger, N., and J. Hull. (1983). "The Valuation of Currency Options," *Financial Management*, Spring.

Black, F. (1975). "Fact and Fantasy in the Use of Options," *Financial Analysts Journal*, 44.

Black, F., and M. Scholes. (1972). "The Valuation of Option Contracts and a Test of Market Efficiency," *Journal of Finance*, 27.

Black, F., and M. Scholes. (1973). "The Pricing of Options and Corporate Liabilities," *Journal of Political Economy*, 81.

Blenman, L. P. (1992a). "The Interest Rate Parity: Seven Expressions: A Reply," *Financial Management*, Autumn.

———. (1992b). "A Model of Covered Interest Arbitrage under Market Segmentation," *Journal of Money, Credit, and Banking*, 23 (4).

Blenman, L. P., and J. S. Thatcher. (in press). "Arbitrageur Heterogeneity, Investor Horizon and Arbitrage Opportunities," *Financial Review*.

Brennan, M. J. (1979). "The Price of Contingent Claims in Discrete Time Models," *Journal of Finance*, 34 (1).

Callier, P. (1981). "One Way Arbitrage, Foreign Exchange and Securities Markets: A Note," *Journal of Finance*, 36 (December).

Clinton, K. (1988). "Transaction Costs and Covered Interest Arbitrage: Theory and Evidence," *Journal of Political Economy*, 96 (April).

Cornell, B. (1977). "Spot Rates, Forward Rates and Market Dynamics," *Journal of Political Economy*, 5 (1).

Cox, J., S. Ross, and M. Rubinstein. (1979). "Option Pricing: A Simplified Approach," *Journal of Financial Economics*, 7 (September).

Deardorff, A. V. (1979). "One-Way Arbitrage and Its Implications for the Foreign Exchange Markets," *Journal of Political Economy*, April.

Frenkel, J. A., and R. M. Levich. (1975). "Covered Interest Arbitrage: Unexploited Profits?" *Journal of Political Economy*, 83 (April).

Garman, M. B., and S. W. Kohlhagen. (1983). "Foreign Currency Option Values," *Journal of International Money and Finance*, December.

Geske, R., and H. E. Johnson. (1984). "The American Put Valued Analytically," *Journal of Finance*, 39 (5).

Ghosh, D. K. (published 1997a, Vol. 3, 349–361). "Arbitrage with Hedging: Exploited and Exploitable Profits," *The European Journal of Finance*.

———. (published 1997b, Vol. 32, 391–409). "Profit Multiplier in Covered Currency Trading with Leverage," *Financial Review*.

Ghosh, D. K. "Covered Arbitrage with Currency Options: A Theoretical Analysis," *Global Finance Journal* 2004 (in press).

Giddy, I. H. (1983). "Foreign Exchange Options," *Journal of Futures Markets*, Summer.

Grabbe, J. D. (1983). "The Pricing of Call and Put Options on Foreign Exchange," *Journal of International Money and Finance*, 2.

Grube, R., D. Panton, and J. Terrell. (1979). "Risks and Rewards in Covered Call Positions," *Journal of Portfolio Management*, 5 (Winter).

Jones, P. (1984). "Option Arbitrage and Strategy with Large Price Changes," *Journal of Financial Economics*, 13.

Merton, R. (1973). "Theory of Rational Option Pricing," *Bell Journal of Economics and Management Science*, 4 (Spring).

Merton, R., M. Scholes, and M. Gladstein. (1978). "A Simulation of Returns and Risk of Alternative Option Portfolio Investment Strategies," *Journal of Business*, 51 (April).

Mueller, P. (1981). "Covered Call Options: An Alternative Investment Strategy," *Financial Management*, 10 (Winter).

Pounds, H. (1978). "Covered Call Option Writing: Strategies and Results," *Journal of Portfolio Management*, 5 (Winter).

Pozen, R. (1978). "The Purchase of Protective Puts by Financial Institutions," *Financial Analysts Journal*, 34.

Rhee, S. G., and R. P. Chang. (1992). "Intra-day Arbitrage Opportunities in Foreign Exchange and Eurocurrency Markets," *The Journal of Finance*, 47 (1).

Yang, H. (1985). "A Note on Currency Option Pricing Models," *Journal of Business Finance and Accounting*, 12 (Autumn).

Yates, J., and R. Kopprasch. (1980). "Writing Covered Call Options: Profits and Risks," *Journal of Portfolio Management*, 6 (Fall).

Chapter 7

Arbitrage and Hedging with Forward Forward Contracts in Interest Rates

INTRODUCTION

In this chapter, we discuss arbitrage and hedging, but the hedging instruments used here are forward contracts in interest rates. As noted in earlier chapters, the interest rate parity and discussions on arbitrage in foreign exchange market have been existing in literature for a long period. Ever since the classic treatment of the issue by Keynes (1923), several attempts have been made to reexamine and reinterpret this subject. All existing works, as it appears, revolve around the covered interest rate parity involving spot and forward contracts in currency exchange rates, with domestic and foreign interest rates matching the maturity of the chosen forward contract. It has been pointed out that in the absence of interest rate parity where transaction costs do not exist, an investor can make profits from appropriate currency market transactions without assuming any risk. Frenkel and Levich (1975, 1977), Deardorff (1979), and later a host of researchers (see, for instance, Blenman, 1991; Ghosh, 1994, 1997; and many others[1]) have discussed the feasibility of arbitrage profits or the absence thereof with and without transaction costs. That literature has been recognized duly for the proper setting of this work in relation to its discussion of arbitrage. An attempt is thus made here to open up a new branch in which a new interest rate parity can be derived, and, more importantly, it brings out the conditions where covered arbitrage can profitably arise in the market in which forward contract on interest rate exists in this age of financial engineering. In the section titled "The Analytical Structure: A New Parity and Covered Arbitrage," the analytical framework that provides another version of interest rate parity is introduced, then the scope for covered arbitrage profits for an investor is explored. In the section "The Parity and Covered Arbitrage with Transaction Costs," the framework to cover the case of transaction costs is brought out, and the condition for arbitrage profits is enunciated. In section "Compounding of Covered Arbitrage Profits," the possibility of compounding profit levels in the event that profits are feasible in the first instance under the initial scenario is thrown into relief. In the last section, concluding remarks are offered regarding the possibility of extending the work under other scenarios.

THE ANALYTICAL STRUCTURE: A NEW PARITY AND COVERED ARBITRAGE

In this section, a time line is drawn for an investor with a menu of available choices that he can use in his design of investment strategies. First, assume that the investor, at the present, has the quotations on the spot rate of exchange S_0, three-month forward rate of exchange F_{01}, and three-month domestic and foreign rates of interest r_{01}, r^*_{01}, respectively. He also has six-month quotations on all of those rates: F_{02}, r_{02}, and r^*_{02}. In this situation, with a three-month and a six-month data set, the investor must check if the interest rate parity exists for both maturity levels (that is, for three and six months). If the interest rate parity exists for, say, a three-month situation, but it fails to exist for a six-month period, or vice versa, it is obvious that the investor will engage in covered arbitrage in the situation that admits of deviation from parity. If, however, both the three-month and six-month quotations provide the scope for arbitrage opportunity, the investor should get involved with the case that yields the higher rate of return. So far, the case is simple with these two sets of quotations. But, in financial markets where new instruments have already entered in the form of forward contracts (forward rate agreements FRAs on interest rates), the investment design may become a bit more sophisticated.

Consider forward contracts on interest rates, and examine their impact on interest rate parity and the absence thereof in an effort to measure arbitrage profits and profit multipliers. Before going further, it is first useful to explain what a forward contract on interest rate is. A forward contract is one that fixes an interest rate at that present time for a deposit or a loan starting at a future date, say, three months from that given day and expiring at a further future date, say, six months from that day.[2] Therefore, a three to six month forward contract on interest rate is immediately established between the investor and the bank, and the terms of the contract are binding to both parties. Since these contracts are currently available in financial markets, one may encounter the scenarios defined by the following time line:

In Figure 7.1, the left end of the time line represents the present time (or today), the midpoint shows the period of three months from that day, and

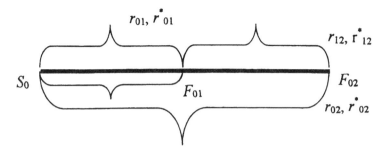

Figure 7.1 Arbitrage with forward contracts in interest rates and forward exchange rates

the right end shows the period of six months from that day. S_0 is the currently quoted spot rate of exchange of, say, £1 in terms of U.S. dollars ($S_0 =$ $/£1), F_{01}, and F_{02}, the forward rates of exchange for three-month and six-month maturities. r_{01} and r_{02} are three-month and six-month interest rates in the domestic market. Similarly, r^*_{01}, and r^*_{02} are foreign market interest rates for three and six months, respectively. Now, let r_{12}, and r^*_{12} be three-to six-month domestic and foreign forward interest rates, which an investor can lock into immediately. The whole spectrum of quotations now available for our investor is then exhibited as follows:

S_0 = the spot rate of exchange of one British pound in terms of U.S. dollars;

F_{01} = three-month forward rate of exchange of one British pound in terms of U.S. dollars;

F_{02} = six-month forward rate of exchange of one British pound in terms of U.S. dollars;

r_{01} = three-month interest rate in domestic U.S. money market;

r^*_{01} = three-month interest rate in foreign money market;

r_{02} = six-month interest rate in domestic money market;

r^*_{02} = six-month interest rate in foreign money market;

r_{12} = three-month forward interest rate in domestic money market, effective three months from the present day, but the contract can be made immediately;

r^*_{12} = three-month forward interest rate in foreign British money market, effective three months from the present day, but the contract can be made immediately.

Under the given menu of market data, the question is: can the investor make arbitrage profits? In this chapter, the answer to this question is given, along with a general conclusion about the conditions in which risk-free profit opportunities exists and the condition in which they do not.

Given the market situations with the quotations presented, the investor has a number of opportunities to consider. Since all the possible scenarios cannot be depicted for the paucity of space, and since all possible scenarios are not economically meaningful, we will consider a few alternatives. In the framework of this analysis, other scenarios can be easily worked out. Consider that our investor has all the information on his computer screen—real-time and on-line. He can borrow, say, M dollars from his bank at r_{01} for three months or at r_{02} for six months. He may then exchange M dollars at the spot rate for British pounds, invest the pound amount either at r_{01}^* or at r_{02}^*, and sell the amount $(M/S_0)(1 + r_{01}^*)$ at the three-month forward rate or sell the amount $(M/S_0)(1 + r_{02}^*)$ at the six-month forward rate. He can get the dollar amount $(M/S_0)(1 + r_{01}^*) \cdot F_{01}$ or $(M/S_0)(1 + r_{02}^*) \cdot F_{02}$, depending upon the initial choice of maturity. The arbitrage profit levels from three-month and six-month maturities must then be as follows, respectively:

$$\pi_{01} = M\left[\frac{F_{01}}{S_0}\left(1+r_{01}^*\right)-\left(1+r_{01}\right)\right] \tag{7.1}$$

$$\pi_{02} = M\left[\frac{F_{02}}{S_0}\left(1+r_{02}^*\right)-\left(1+r_{02}\right)\right] \tag{7.2}$$

From equation 7.1 we get that if:

$$\frac{F_{01}}{S_0}\left(1+r_{01}^*\right)-\left(1+r_{01}\right)=0,$$

the interest rate parity exists for three-month maturity whereby we have:

$$r_{01} - r_{01}^* = \left(\frac{F_{01}-S_0}{S_0}\right)\left(1+r_{01}^*\right). \tag{7.3}$$

Similarly, from equation 7.2, in the situation of interest rate parity, one can get:

$$r_{02} - r_{02}^* = \left(\frac{F_{02}-S_0}{S_0}\right)\left(1+r_{02}^*\right). \tag{7.4}$$

These are the expressions of interest rate parity long known in existing literature. In the event of inequality between the left-hand and the right-hand sides in equation 7.3 and/or equation 7.4, the investor has the scope for risk-free profit opportunity via what is popularly called *covered arbitrage*. If the left-hand side of equations 7.3 or 7.4 is greater than the right-hand side, the investor should borrow from the home market and invest in the foreign market. In an opposite situation, an opposite strategy must be used—that is, borrowing from the foreign market and investing in the home market will yield positive profits to the investor who is not exposed to risk. To make these statements more comprehensible, take equation 7.3 and assume that $r_{01} = 10\%$, $r_{01}^* = 9.5\%$, $S_0 = 2$, and $F_{01} = 2.15$. In this case, note that we have the following situation $(r_{01} - r_{01}^*) < (F_{01} - S_0)/S_0)(1 + r_{01}^*)$ (as, with this data, one can easily find that $(0.10 - 0.095) < (2.15 - 2.00/2.00)$ $(1 + 0.095)$. Under this situation, if the investor borrows $1,000,000 at 10 percent from a domestic bank, and he exchanges his borrowed $1,000,000 at the spot rate $2.00 = £1, he gets £500,000, which invested in the British market at 9.5 percent yields £500,000H1.095 = £547,500. This amount of pound sterling is sold forward at 2.15 to bring the U.S. dollar amount to the tune of $1,177,125, from which the investor must subtract the borrowed amount and the total interest accrued on it ($1,000,000H1.1 = $1,100,000). Note now that the investor finally ends up with the net amount of $77,125 as the fruits of his interim financial transactions.

Next, consider the following alternatives: (a) the investor exchanges his M dollars in the spot market, invests the converted amount in the foreign market for six months in this instance, sells the newly created amount in the forward market, and subtracts from there the original principal and the accrued interest; (b) he first borrows M dollars for three months (not six months), and at the same time enters into a three- to six-month forward contract with a bank to put his amount $(M/S_0)(1 + r_{01}^*)$ (three months from present day) in deposit at r_{12}^* for the next three months, which at the end of six months from that day then becomes $(M/S_0)(1 + r_{01}^*)(1 + r_{12}^*)F_{02}$ upon the forward sale of the foreign currency amount. The profit level in this instance then must be:

$$\pi_{0,1,2} = M\left[\frac{F_{02}}{S_0}(1 + r_{01}^*)(1 + r_{12}^*) - (1 + r_{01})(1 + r_{12})\right]. \tag{7.5}$$

Compare equations 7.2 and 7.5, and in the event of $\pi_{0,2} = \pi_{0,1,2}$, we have a new interest rate parity, which can be expressed as follows:

$$[(1 + r_{01})(1 + r_{12}) - (1 + r_{01}^*)(1 + r_{12}^*) - (r_{02} + r_{02}^*)]$$

$$= \left(\frac{F_{02} - S_0}{S_0}\right)[(1 + r_{01}^*)(1 + r_{12}^*) - (1 + r_{02}^*)]. \tag{7.6}$$

This is the new interest rate parity. If there is no rollover with forward contracts on interest rates, the original interest rate parity, which is defined by the following expression:

$$\left(r_{02} - r_{02}^{\cdot}\right) = \left(\frac{F_{02} - S_0}{S_0}\right)\left(1 + r_{02}^{\cdot}\right)\left(1.1^{\cdot}\right) \tag{7.7}$$

is once again smoothly rehabilitated.[3] Note that under the pure expectation hypothesis of the term structure on interest rates (which holds in equilibrium), one can observe the following relations:

$$(1 + r_{01})(1 + r_{12}) = (1 + r_{02}), \text{ and } (1 + r^*_{01})(1 + r^*_{12}) = (1 + r^*_{02}),$$

which means that parity holds and arbitrage profits do not arise. But in reality, market has a centripetal move toward equilibrium at any point of time, but it is not in equilibrium *necessarily* at every point in time, hence parity does not take place, and thus, 1^{**} becomes meaningful at many times. Grabbe correctly notes, "It is tempting to equate the implied forward rate $f(t + n, T - n)$ [that is, in our example, r_{12}] with the expected short-term interest rate that will prevail at time $t + n$ [that is, in our case, for three- to six-months from now]. The expectations theory should be considered a purely empirical proposition in the same way that the speculative efficiency hypothesis is a purely empirical proposition" (1991, p. 266).[4] If liquidity preference or market segmentation theory can precisely bring out the relations $(1 + r_{01})(1 + r_{12}) = (1 + r_{02})$, and $(1 + r^*_{01})(1 + r^*_{12}) = (1 + r^*_{02})$, then 1^* holds, and arbitrage profits become nonexistent. In this situation, it is useless to discuss further on 1^{**} (as 1^* and 1^{**} cannot hold simultaneously). Since one cannot theoretically establish that 1^* always holds (see Grabbe, 1991), and empirical evidence for the absence of parity does often exist, 1^{**} is a significant situation to work on and profit possibilities should be meaningfully explored.

Now, consider the following scenario:

$$\left[\left(1 + r_{01}\right)\left(1 + r_{12}\right) - \left(1 + r_{01}^{\cdot}\right)\left(1 + r_{12}^{\cdot}\right) - \left(r_{02} - r_{02}^{\cdot}\right)\right]$$
$$\neq \left(\frac{F_{02} - S_0}{S_0}\right)\left[\left(1 + r_{01}^{\cdot}\right)\left(1 + r_{12}^{\cdot}\right) - \left(1 + r_{02}^{\cdot}\right)\right]. \tag{7.8}$$

If the left-hand side of equation 7.8 is greater than the right-hand side, then it is evident that the investor should borrow from the home market at r_{01} and invest in the foreign market at r_{01}^* for the first three months, then rollover for the next three months with a currently available three- to six-month forward contracts on interest rates instead of taking a straight six-month position. If the left-hand side is less than the right-hand side, the investor should borrow from the foreign market, invest in the home economy, and take the opposite position in terms of the choice of investment horizon.

THE PARITY AND COVERED ARBITRAGE WITH TRANSACTION COSTS

In the previous section, the discussion is about the absence of transaction costs in both foreign exchange markets and in money markets. In this section, we move away from the assumption that there are no transaction costs and introduce those costs for the investor the way they appear. In the original conceptual environment postulated by Frenkel and Levich (1977) and Deardorff (1979), transaction costs are proportional. Recently, Rhee and Chang (1992), Ghosh (1991, 1994), Blenmann (1991, 1992, 1996), and Blenman and Thatcher (1995, 1997) have introduced *ask* and *bid* quotations that essentially capture foreign exchange transaction costs and *lend* and *borrow* rates of interest that capture those costs in money market operations. First, let us introduce the modified notations as follows:

S_0^A = spot *ask* rate of exchange of one British pound in terms of U.S. dollars;

S_0^B = spot *bid* rate of exchange of one British pound in terms of U.S. dollars;

F_{01}^A = three-month forward *ask* rate of exchange of one British pound in terms of U.S. dollars;

F_{01}^B = three-month forward *bid* rate of exchange of one British pound in terms of U.S. dollars;

F_{02}^B = six-month forward *bid* rate of exchange of one British pound in terms of U.S. dollars;

F_{02}^A = six-month forward *ask* rate of exchange of one British pound in terms of U.S. dollars;

$r_{0i(L)}$ = i-month *lend* rate of interest in domestic money market ($i = 3, 6$);

$r^*_{0i(L)}$ = i-month *lend* rate of interest in foreign money market ($i = 3, 6$);

$r_{0i(B)}$ = i-month *borrow* rate of interest in domestic money market ($i = 3, 6$);

$r^*_{0i(B)}$ = i-month *borrow* rate of interest in foreign money market ($i = 3, 6$);

$r_{12(V)}$ = three- to six-month forward interest rate in domestic money market, effective three months from the given day, but the contract can be made that given day (V = lend (L) or borrow (B));

$r^*_{12(V)}$ = three- to six-month forward interest rate in foreign (British) money market, effective three months from the given day, but the contract can be made that given day (V = lending (L) or borrowing (B)).

With these notations with which we capture transaction costs, we present π_{01}, π_{02}, and $\pi_{0.1,2}$, defined by equations 7.9, 7.10, and 7.11, modified as π_{01}^T, π_{02}^T, and $\pi_{0.1,2}^T$, respectively as follows:

$$\pi_{01}^T = M\left[\frac{F_{01}^A}{S_0^B}\left(1+r^*_{01(L)}\right)-\left(1+r_{01(B)}\right)\right] \tag{7.9}$$

$$\pi_{02}^T = M \left[\frac{F_{02}^A}{S_0^B} \left(1 + r_{02(L)}^*\right) - \left(1 + r_{02(B)}\right) \right] \tag{7.10}$$

$$\pi_{0,1,2}^T = M \left[\frac{F_{02}^A}{S_0^B} \left(1 + r_{01(L)}^*\right)\left(1 + r_{12(L)}^*\right) - \left(1 + r_{01(B)}\right)\left(1 + r_{12(B)}\right) \right]. \tag{7.11}$$

From the equality of equations 7.10 and 7.11, one can easily establish the following parity statement:

$$\left[\left(1 + r_{01(B)}\right)\left(1 + r_{12(B)}\right) - \left(1 + r_{01(L)}^*\right)\left(1 + r_{12(L)}^*\right) - \left(r_{02(B)} - r_{02(B)}^*\right) \right]$$
$$= \left(\frac{F_{02}^A - S_0^B}{S_0^B} \right) \left[\left(1 + r_{01(L)}^*\right)\left(1 + r_{12(L)}^*\right) - \left(1 + r_{02(L)}^*\right) \right]. \tag{7.12}$$

In the event of the inequality between these two sides of equation 7.12, the opportunity for arbitrage profit arises and persistence of that profitable scenario exists. In the subsequent section, we explore this possibility.

COMPOUNDING OF COVERED ARBITRAGE PROFITS

In the previous sections, we have delineated the conditions under which covered arbitrage profits can exist. It is now time to examine the possibility of compounding the original profits made in the arbitrage operation by exploiting the initial absence of parity. Consider the possibility:

$$\pi_{0,1,2}^T =$$
$$M \left[\frac{F_{02}^A}{S_0^B} \left(1 + r_{01(L)}^*\right)\left(1 + r_{12(L)}^*\right) - \left(1 + r_{01(B)}\right)\left(1 + r_{12(B)}\right) \right] > 0. \tag{7.13}$$

That means the investor, at the given day, first borrows M dollars for three months (not six months) at $r_{01}^{(B)}$ and at the same time enters into a three- to six-month forward contract with that or any other bank for the rate $r_{12(B)}$ to put his amount $M/S_0^B(1 + r_{01(L)}^*)$ in deposit at $r_{12(L)}^*$ three months from that day for the next three months, which at the end of six months from that day then becomes $M/S_0^B(1 + r_{01(L)}^*)(1 + r_{12(L)}^*)F_{02}^A$ upon the forward sale of the foreign currency amount. The present value of this amount of profit is obviously:

$$\pi_{0,1,2(0)}^{T(1)} \equiv \frac{\pi_{0,1,2}^T}{\left(1 + r_{01(B)}\right)\left(1 + r_{12(B)}\right)}.$$

Since this profit is made by the investor on the first opportunity, we designate it as the first round by assigning 1 as the superscript—that is, by modifying the notation suitably as $\pi_{0.1,2(0)}^{T(1)}$. By plugging in this profit level along with the original amount of M dollars, by putting in $(M + \pi_{0.1,2(0)}^{T(1)})$ dollar amount in, the same way as he did put in his initial amount of M dollars, the investor can make the following amount from the second replica of his play:

$$\pi_{0.1,2(0)}^{T(2)} = M\alpha^T(\alpha^T + 2)^{2-1},$$

and from his nth round of play after putting in all previous levels of profits—by plugging in $M + \sum_{i=1}^{n-1}\pi_{0.1,2(0)}^{T(1)}$, he gets the following amount of profits:

$$\pi_{0.1,2(0)}^{T(n)} = M\alpha^T(\alpha^T + 2)^{n-1},$$

$$\text{where } \alpha^T = \left[\frac{\left[\frac{F_{02}^A}{S_0^B}\left(1 + r_{01(L)}^*\right)\left(1 + r_{12(L)}^*\right) - \left(1 + r_{01(B)}\right)\left(1 + r_{12(B)}\right) \right]}{\left(1 + r_{01(B)}\right)\left(1 + r_{12(B)}\right)} \right].$$

It is a matter of simple verification that on the very first round of arbitrage play, the investor's level of profit can be shown to be equal to $\pi_{0.1,2(0)}^{T(1)} = M\alpha^T(\alpha^T + 2)^{1-1} = M\alpha^T$. It is now evident that $(\alpha^T + 2)^{i-1}$ is the multiplier of the initial covered arbitrage profit on the ith round ($i = 1, 2, 3, \ldots, n$). Next, the summation of $\pi_{0.1,2(0)}^{T(1)}$ over first n iterations measures the cumulative profits on first n successive plays in the market with the data frozen over the period of iterations, and this cumulative profit is then defined as follows:

$$\pi_0^{T^*} = M\alpha^T \left[\frac{1 - (\alpha^T + 2)^n}{1 - (\alpha^T + 2)} \right].$$

Similar results in other possible scenarios can be easily derived, but it will not be of profitable use to time or space to continue.

CONCLUDING REMARKS

Many interesting extensions of these results can be made by way of introducing other features with this trading strategy in this framework, but the most fruitful exercise in this context has to do with some useful empirical work along these lines. Since this paper is grounded on theoretical structure, we keep it the way it is. And empirical studies along this work are left for future attempts. We must make some concluding observations, however, on the microstatics and macrodynamics of the market in the context of this research.

It is fundamental reality that if arbitrage opportunity exists in the market-place, it will soon disappear by the dynamics of competition. In that sense it may be questionable if the second, the third, and the nth round of arbitrage activities of our investor can ever take place. A careful reflection on this point is absolutely essential, and upon that reflection and comprehension of market forces, one should realize a few points. First of all, if an investor finds that an arbitrage opportunity exists, he ascertains profits *instantly* for all the n rounds of arbitrage. The market data are same for round 1 and round n within 20 seconds or 2 minutes at which quotes do not change from the investor's screen. His first and his nth executions take place *almost* at the very same instant with programmed trading, the two rounds differing only by the amounts of arbitrage funds. In the first round the amount is M dollars and in the nth round the amount will be $M + \Sigma_{i=1}^{n-1} \pi^{T(i)}_{0.1,2(0)}$, and the time involved in these n successive rounds may be less than a second with digitized signatures of approval by the bank(s) in the middle of today's technology and speed. The moment the market data are factored in, and $\pi_{0.1,2}$ ($\neq 0$) is ascertained, one computes $\pi^1_{0.1,2(0)}$, $\pi^2_{0.1,2(0)}$, $\pi^3_{0.1,2(0)}, \ldots, \pi^n_{0.1,2(0)}$, and so on. If the investor can exploit the market one time via arbitrage, he can exploit the same market several times because the moment is *virtually* frozen and the data for market exploitation remain the same. Note the investor is a micro-agent operating in the marketplace in which even the speediest adjustment cannot deprive him of the opportunity to take advantage of the market misalignment. We know for sure that arbitrage exists in the market, and many players subsist on it. Therefore, arbitrage and iterations thereof are the valid plays in the market. One should also note that in the trillion-dollar market, a million or even a few billions by a micro-agent may not throw the market into any state of concussion. However, if a large number of participants act at the same moment, there may be an execution jam, and nobody is likely to take any profits out of arbitrage. In a situation of multiple players, the macrodynamics of the market set in and force arbitragers into a zero-profit condition. One more point should be made then. Since too many iterations are involved in this investment strategy, one should realize that before any iteration is executed, some quotes may change. So to guard against this possibility appropriate limit orders should be put in with each iteration of covered arbitrage, and that should guarantee nonnegative profit conditions in the repeated arbitrage acts.

Market dynamics and market efficiency are of paramount significance. Clinton (1976) and Dornbusch (1976) highlight and examine some of these concerns quite efficiently. One should note that in a frozen (static) moment, no adjustment is possible, and micro-level arbitrage is certainly an exploitable opportunity.

At this point, a few more issues should be addressed as well. One may wonder why an investor who sees an arbitrage opportunity will start off with $1 million instead of hundreds of millions or billions. The answer is simple. If the investor has $1 million as the maximum amount available to him, he has to begin only with that much money. M dollars, in our paradigm, is the maximum available initial fund. Of course, if the investor has more, he will initiate his moves with more funds. The issue here is not what the optimal amount of initial investment funds for arbitrage should be; the issue is: if an initial amount—be it M or Z dollars—is available for arbitrage, what amount of money can potentially be generated out of that initial situation? Two other issues should be brought to limelight in this context. One may argue that since profits out of the first round of arbitrage are obtained only at the end of six months from the given day, how is this investor getting funds for the second, the third, and other rounds of market plays? Note here that π_1 is the guaranteed amount of money made by the investor without taking any risk, and any bank should recognize this amount the investor makes at the end of six months. If this is common knowledge by the investor as well as the bank, it is equally recognizable that this investor has $\pi_{1(0)} / \pi_1/1 + r$ now—and it is his equity position that he can legitimately utilize (probably with a prior discussion with his banker). Next, it is worth noting, particularly against the backdrop of the common belief that markets are so well aligned that scope for arbitrage in reality is nonexistent, that in the currency market one can almost always find arbitrage opportunity. Note that although the spot rate and forward rate are *usually* defined at a point of time, and corresponding to those defined quotes a set of domestic and foreign interest rates will yield $\pi_{0.1.2}$ = 0, one can always find another set of interest rates from the available spectrum of interest rates, which generates $\pi_{0.1.2}$? 0. That clearly signifies that arbitrage opportunity is a viable and feasible strategy in the foreign exchange market more often than not. Additionally, it should be pointed out that one who watches real-time data could also easily recognize that quotations on spot and forward rates by different banks and/or dealers are not always the same at that instant. So on that front one may also find the scope for arbitrage. Finally, we should note that if one round of arbitrage act is undertaken, it may also appear that arbitrage profit is negligible. In that sense one can conclude that arbitrage opportunity is virtually nonexistent. But the replication of the same strategy over and over does not make arbitrage profits insignificant in reality at all.

NOTES

1. See other studies cited in the references at the end of this work.
2. The existing literature on this new instrument is almost nonexistent. Forward contracts on interest rates are a variant of forward rate agreements (FRAs) on

interest rates, which appear to have better vintage. This instrument is still only in the arsenal of practitioners in banking institutions. However, one may review Sercu and Uppal (1995, pp. 290–294).

3. Take equation (7.6). $\left[(1+r_{01})(1+r_{12})-(1+r_{01}^*)(1+r_{12}^*)-(r_{02}+r_{02}^*)\right]$

$$= \left(\frac{F_{02}-S_0}{S_0}\right)\left[(1+r_{01}^*)(1+r_{12}^*)-(1+r_{02}^*)\right],$$

and decompose it as follows:

$$\frac{r_{02}-r_{02}^*}{1+r_{02}^*} = \left(\frac{F_{02}-S_0}{S_0}\right)\left[1-\frac{(1+r_{01}^*)(1+r_{12}^*)}{(1+r_{02}^*)}\right]$$

$$+\frac{(1+r_{01})(1+r_{12})-(1+r_{01}^*)(1+r_{12}^*)}{(1+r_{02}^*)}$$

whence:

$$\frac{r_{02}-r_{02}^*}{1+r_{02}^*} = \left(\frac{F_{02}-S_0}{S_0}\right)-$$

$$\left(\frac{F_{02}-S_0}{S_0}\right)\left[1-\frac{(1+r_{01}^*)(1+r_{12}^*)}{(1+r_{02}^*)}\right]+\frac{(1+r_{01})(1+r_{12})-(1+r_{01}^*)(1+r_{12}^*)}{(1+r_{02}^*)}$$

If pure expectations theory holds in both home and domestic economies—that is, $(1+r_{01})(1+r_{12}) = (1+r_{02})$, and $(1+r_{01}^*)(1+r_{12}^*) = (1+r_{02}^*)$, then (7.6) reduces to the following:

$$\frac{r_{02}-r_{02}^*}{1+r_{02}^*} = \left(\frac{F_{02}-S_0}{S_0}\right)-\left(\frac{F_{02}-S_0}{S_0}\right)+\frac{(1+r_{01})(1+r_{12})-(1+r_{01}^*)(1+r_{12}^*)}{(1+r_{02}^*)}$$

The whole expression then reduces to: interest rate parity—deviation from interest rate parity. Since deviation from interest rate parity is zero in this case, interest rate parity theory holds.

4. Here we discuss the contextual relevance of the term structure of interest. It should be noted that if the relations $(1+r_{01})(1+r_{12}) = (1+r_{02})$, and $(1+r_{01}^*)(1+r_{12}^*) = (1+r_{02}^*)$ hold, scope for arbitrage profits does not exist. Empirically one often finds the following: $(1+r_{01})(1+r_{12}) ? (1+r_{02})$, and $(1+r_{01}^*)(1+\hat{r}_{12}^*) ? (1+r_{02}^*)$. See Grabbe [1991] on this issue.

REFERENCES

Aliber, R. G. (1973). "The Interest Rate Parity Theorem: A Reinterpretation," *Journal of Political Economy*, 81 (6), 1451–1459.

Blenman, L. P. (1991). "A Model of Covered Interest Arbitrage under Market Segmentation," *Journal of Money, Credit, and Banking*, 23 (4), no. 706–717.

———. (1992). "The Interest Rate Parity: Seven Expressions: A Reply," *Financial Management*, 21 (3), 10–11.

———. (1996). "Contemporaneous, Non-contemporaneous Currency Exchanges and Arbitrage Activity," *The International Journal of Finance*, 8 (1), 15–32.

Blenman, L.P., and J.S. Thatcher. (1995). "Arbitrage Opportunities in Currency and Credit Markets: New Evidence," *The International Journal of Finance*, 7 (1), 1123–1145.

———. (1997). "Arbitrageur Heterogeneity, Investor Horizon and Arbitrage Opportunities: An Empirical Investigation," *Financial Review*, 32.

Callier, P. (1981). "One-Way Arbitrage, Foreign Exchange and Securities Markets: A Note," *Journal of Finance*, 36 (5), 1177–1186.

Clinton, K. (1976). "Spot Rates, Forward Rates and Exchange Market Efficiency," *Journal of Financial Economics*, 5 (1), 55–65.

———. (1988). "Transaction Costs and Covered Interest Arbitrage: Theory and Evidence," *Journal of Political Economy*, 96 (2), 358–370.

Deardorff, A.V. (1979). "One-Way Arbitrage and Its Implications for the Foreign Exchange Markets," *Journal of Political Economy*, 87 (2), 351–364.

Dornbusch, R. (1976). "Expectations and Exchange Rate Dynamics," *Journal of Political Economy*, 84 (6), 1161–1176.

Frenkel, J.A., and R.M. Levich. (1975). "Covered Interest Arbitrage: Unexploited Profits?" *Journal of Political Economy*, 83 (2), 325–338.

———. (1977). "Transaction Costs and Interest Arbitrage: Tranquil Versus Turbulent Periods," *Journal of Political Economy*, 85 (6), 1209–1226.

Ghosh, D.K. (1991). "The Interest Rate Parity: Seven Expressions," *Financial Management*, 20 (4), 8–9.

———. (1994). "The Interest Rate Parity, Covered Interest Arbitrage and Speculation under Market Imperfection." In D.K. Ghosh and E. Oritz (Eds.), *Changing Environment of International Financial Markets: Issues and Analysis* (pp. 69–79). London: Macmillan.

———. (1997). "Naked and Covered Speculation in the Foreign Exchange Market." In D.K. Ghosh and E. Oritz (Eds.), *The Global Structure of Financial Markets* (pp. 119–143). London: Routledge.

Giddy, I.H. (1976). "Why It Doesn't Pay to Make a Habit of Forward Hedging," *Euromoney*, December, 96–100.

Grabbe, J.O. (1991). *International Financial Markets* (2nd ed.). New York: Elsevier Science.

Keynes, J.M. (1923). *A Tract on Monetary Reform*. London: Macmillan.

McCormick, F. (1979). "Covered Interest Arbitrage: Unexploited Profits?—Comment," *Journal of Political Economy*, 87 (2), 411–417.

Rhee, S.G., and R.P. Chang. (1992). "Intra-day Arbitrage Opportunities in Foreign Exchange and Eurocurrency Markets," *Journal of Finance*, 47 (1), 363–379.

Roll, R.W., and B. Solnik. (1979). "On Some Parity Conditions Frequently Encountered in International Finance," *Journal of Macroeconomics*, 1.

Sercu, P., and R. Uppal. (1995). *International Financial Markets and the Firm*. Cincinnati, OH: South-Western College.

Taylor, M.P. (1989). "Covered Interest Arbitrage and Market Turbulence," *The Economic Journal*, 99 (396), 376–391.

Tsiang, S.-C. (1959). "The Theory of Forward Exchange and Effects of Government Intervention on the Forward Exchange Market," *International Monetary Fund Staff Papers*, 7 (April), 75–106.

Woodward, R. S. (1988). "Some New Evidence on the Profitability of One-Way versus Round-Trip Arbitrage," *Journal of Money, Credit, and Banking*, 20 (4), 645–652.

Chapter 8

Speculations in the Foreign Exchange Market

INTRODUCTION

Speculation is an assumption of calculated risk expected to happen by an individual investor or a firm looking to make profits from future markets condition(s). Sometimes the investor takes a speculative market position without an underlying cover, which is called a *naked speculation*. If the expectations on the future unknown(s) are materialized, the investor makes the precalculated amount(s) of profit. Since expectations may prove incorrect, an investor sometimes or often tries to insure himself against financial fatality by way of holding some fallback positions. If the investor does speculate with such underlying protection, it becomes a *covered speculation*. In this chapter, an attempt is made to demonstrate how speculation yields profits to an investor in the foreign exchange markets with and without protective measures. In the following section, we present the analytical structure of naked speculation with and without transaction costs. In the section after that, we give an exposition of covered speculation with currency options and synthetic combinations thereof. In the last section, we make some concluding remarks.

NAKED SPECULATION

Investors are not alike. Some are risk averse and some are risk lovers. The risk-free investment strategies of a rational individual or institution in currency markets with spot and forward contracts with and without transaction costs are usually discussed under the rubric of arbitrage and hedging (see Ghosh, 1994). In this chapter, we attempt to explain the rational behavior of an economic agent, who chooses to assume risk in his investment strategies. Risk refers to an investor entering or plunging into uncertainty and unknown variables in the decision-making process in the expectation of generating positive rates of return. We confine our discussions here within the scope of operations in spot and forward markets in currency trading.

It is generally believed that in a financial world, the higher the risk one assumes, the higher the return one should expect in exchange. It is this general belief that drives an investor—individual or institution—into a choice of an investment menu with calculated risks. Empirical evidence often shows that an investor indeed does really well on the average in terms of returns by risky investment designs. We try to bring out the core of such risky investment, which is called *speculation*. Speculation, as already noted, is the act of assuming a calculated risk in expectation of higher rates of return on the invested amounts. The existing literature is replete with research pieces on speculation. Various aspects of this economic activity have been examined by the studies of Friedman (1953), Tsiang (1959), Grubel (1966), Kenen (1965), Spraos (1959), Neihans (1984), Feldstein (1968), Kohlhagen (1979), McKinnon (1979), and Wihlborg (1978), Ghosh (1997a, 1997b, 1998), and Ghosh and Arize (1993). Here, we plan to examine and explore the situations involving speculation for a rational investor in the currency markets. To do so, we first assume that the investor faces no transaction costs in his financial operations in the market. Later, we will move away from the assumption of no transaction costs in the calculation of rational speculation and profit measurement.

INVESTMENT STRATEGY WITH RISK

Forward Speculation and Spot Speculation without Transaction Costs

Consider the following data collected by an investor.

Current spot rate of exchange $\bar{S} = 2.00$
One-year forward rate of exchange $F = 2.15$
One-year domestic rate of interest $r = 10\%$
One-year foreign rate of interest $r^* = 9.5\%$

Assume that the investor believes that spot rate of foreign exchange a year from the given day $\tilde{s}$ will be $3.00 = £1$. This belief may come from a phone call or fax transmittal from the investor's advisor, from a forecasting service, or simply from his own sense. Now, if the investor acts on this predicted value of the foreign exchange rate, he will enter into either forward speculation or spot speculation.

Forward Speculation without Transaction Costs

Forward speculation involves either the purchase or sale of forward contracts by the investor to enable him to earn profits by taking exactly the opposite position on the maturity date of the forward contract in the foreign exchange market. Spot speculation similarly involves the purchase or sale of foreign exchange in the current spot market with a view to making a profit in the future by taking exactly the opposite position. If, as we have already assumed, the *expected* spot rate of exchange one year from that day is 3, the investor can make a profit of $3.00 − $2.15 = $0.85, *times* the value of the forward contract the investor now enters in. He simply buys pound sterling (the foreign currency in the example) at the rate of $2.15 = £1 currently in the forward market—that is, he agrees to deliver $2.15 for each British pound at the end of one year. On the settlement date of the agreed-upon forward contract, the investor gets a British pound for his $2.15 to the counterparty, then he sells his just-acquired British pound at $3.00 = £1. By doing so, that is, by buying the pound at the forward market on the spot and selling the pound at the future spot market at the then-spot rate, he makes a profit. If his forward contract size is £10,000,000, he makes a total profit of $0.85H10,000,000 = $8,500,000. If the future spot rate is predicted to be 1.20 (which is less than the forward rate of 2.15), the investor makes money by selling a forward contract on the pound. If he enters into a forward sale contract of British pound (that is, a forward purchase of U.S. dollars), he gets $2.15 for the sale of each British pound, then he buys back the pound in the future spot rate of $1.20 = £1. Effectively, the investor makes $0.95 per pound. If his forward contract size is £10,000,000, he obviously makes a total profit of $9,500,000. The rules are then as follows:

If $\tilde{S} > F$, buy foreign currency forward,
and total profit is $= (\tilde{S} − F).A_F$. (8.1)
If $\tilde{S} = F$, buy or sell foreign currency forward,
and total profit is zero $(= (\tilde{S} 2 F).AF)$. (8.2)
If $\tilde{S} < F$, sell foreign currency forward,
and total profit is $(F − \tilde{S}).A_F$. (8.3)

Here A_F is the amount of the forward contract (contract size) in foreign currency denomination. Now, the question is: what happens if the prediction of on-the-spot rate a year from the given day becomes incorrect? From the illustration it is clear that as long as the spot rate one year from the given day is not less than one-year forward rate, the forward *buy* contract of the foreign currency will not yield loss to the investor, and similarly, as long as the spot rate one year from the given day is not more than a one-year forward rate, forward *sell* contract of the foreign currency will not yield loss to the investor. The situation beyond the dividing line then obvi-

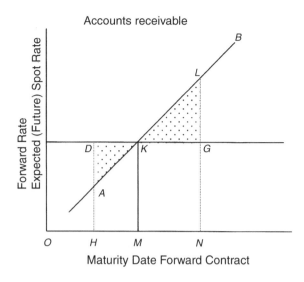

Figure 8.1 Profitable choice: forward buy or sell

ously creates loss for the speculator. Figure 8.1 portrays those results graphically.

Along the horizontal axis, we represent the forward contract maturity (settlement) date, and the vertical axis measures the forward rate and the spot rate of exchange on the date of forward contract maturity. In Figure 8.1, let *AKB* define the spot rate on the forward contract maturity date and *DKG* represent the forward rate of exchange. With this diagram, we exhibit the investor with a forward *buy* or *sell* contract of the foreign currency. If the contract maturity date is denoted by any point to the right of *M* (say, *N*) that corresponds to the spot rate above the forward rate (*NL* exceeds *NG*), he makes a profit on the forward *buy* contract (by *GL* times the amount of the contract size). If, on the other hand, the forward contract is a *sell* contract, and the maturity date of the forward is denoted by point to the left of *M* (say, *H*), he makes a profit to the tune of *AD* times the forward contract size. Exactly opposite happens, that is, loss is incurred by the investor, if at point *N*, he holds a forward *sell* contract, and at point *H*, he holds the forward *buy* contract. Since the investor does not have a crystal ball in his hand (and hence his prediction on future spot rate may prove significantly wrong), he may end up with a big loss for his speculative position with forward contract(s). In the situation of accounts payable, one gets exactly the opposite results.

Note now that forward speculation hardly involves any money being tied up until the settlement date arrives. It is a commitment (with probably a small percentage of the investor's line of credit attached to the contract). So, if the forward contract brings a fortune to the investor, he makes it virtually at the very instant he settles his forward contract and takes the opposite position in that instant spot market. The annualized rate of return in correct sense is more than finite.

Spot Speculation without Transaction Costs

Consider now the other alternative—spot speculation. In this case, the investor may choose to buy (or sell), for instance, pound sterling on the spot at the current spot rate to sell (or buy) the currency in the future spot market, depending on his prediction on the spot rate of exchange on the future date. Consider, once again, the same set of data we have presented earlier (this time forward rate is being ignored for the obvious reason).

Current spot rate of exchange $(S) = 2.00$

One-year domestic rate of interest $(r) = 10\%$

One-year foreign rate of interest $(r^*) = 9.5\%$

Assume that the investor believes that the rate of exchange one year from the present day is going to go up, and assume that he thinks that it will be 3. Under this assumption, if he has one British pound one year from the present, he will be able to sell that pound for $3.00. Since the present value of £1 a year from now will be £1$/(1 + r^*)$ (which is, in numerical example in this case, is equal to £0.9113242 = 1/1.095), the investor needs $S/(1 + r^*)$ dollars (that is, $2/1.095) now. The cost of borrowing (or the opportunity cost of) this dollar amount for one year from the present day being factored into the calculation, the dollar amount at the end of one year becomes equal to $S(1 + r)/(1 + r^*)$, or 2(1.1)/1.095. Then one may easily derive the following decision rules.

If $\tilde{S} > S(1 + r)/(1 + r^*)$, buy foreign currency spot, and total profit is defined by:

$$= \left[\tilde{S} - S\frac{(1+r)}{(1+r^*)} \right] \cdot A_S. \tag{8.4}$$

If $\tilde{S} = S(1 + r)/(1 + r^*)$, buy or sell foreign currency spot, and total profit is *zero:*

$$= \left[\tilde{S} - S\frac{(1+r)}{(1+r^*)} \right] \cdot A_S. \tag{8.5}$$

If $\tilde{S} < S(1 + r)/(1 + r^*)$, sell foreign currency spot, and total profit is measured by:

$$= \left[S \frac{(1+r)}{(1+r^*)} - \tilde{S} \right] \cdot A_S. \tag{8.6}$$

Here A_S is the size of the spot contract in foreign currency denomination. One should recognize that if the prediction on the one-year spot rate is proven incorrect, the investor may end up with a reduced profit from his original estimate or with a loss, depending upon the actual value of the future spot rate of exchange.

Take a close look at the spot speculation, forward speculation, and arbitrage, which is brought out in this context as well. Note the following profit measures out of these three operations in the currency market:

$$P_S = \tilde{S} - S \frac{(1+r)}{(1+r^*)} \tag{8.7}$$

is the measure of profit if the investor speculates in-the-spot market;

$$P_F = \tilde{S} - F \tag{8.8}$$

is the measure of profit if the investor speculates in the forward market;

$$P_A = F - S \frac{(1+r)}{(1+r^*)} \tag{8.9}$$

is the measure of (covered interest) arbitrage profit.

Combining these three measures of profit, one can easily rewrite equation 8.7 as follows:

$$P_S = \tilde{S} - S \frac{(1+r)}{(1+r^*)} = \left[\tilde{S} - F \right] + \left[F - S \frac{(1+r)}{(1+r^*)} \right] \tag{8.10}$$

Therefore, we find that:

$$P_S = P_F + P_A. \tag{8.11}$$

One may then conclude that spot speculation is equivalent to forward speculation and arbitrage altogether.

It is quite apparent at this stage that given the predicted value of the future spot rate of exchange, a speculator may engage in both spot and forward speculation. The speculator may find it profitable to engage in either of these speculative strategies. Look at Figure 8.2 in which the horizontal axis measures the predicted value of the future spot rate of exchange ($\tilde{S}$) and the vertical axis measures the forward rate of exchange (F). The distance OA measures the value $S(1 + r)/(1 + r^*)$ (in the illustrative case, it is equal to 2.0091324). The perpendicular ABC (which repre-

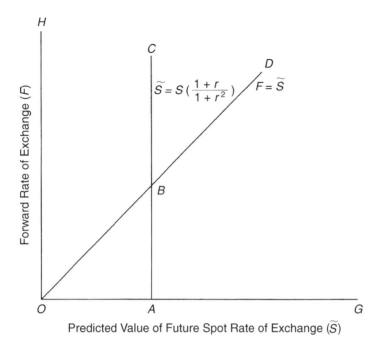

Figure 8.2 Profit (loss) possibilities with naked spot speculation

sents the condition of equality $\tilde{S} = S(1 + r)/(1 + r^*))$ is the dividing line between spot purchase and spot sell positions in the speculative strategy. The area to the left of this ABC line defines the condition in which $\tilde{S} < S(1 + r)/(1 + r)$—which signifies the spot sell of the foreign currency. The zone to the right of line ABC obviously earmarks the profitable area for speculative spot purchase of foreign currency. On line ABC, the investor is choice-neutral. Next, look at the 45° line OBD, which represents the equality between forward rate and future spot rate of exchange: $F = \tilde{S}$. Along this line, the investor should be indifferent between forward purchase and forward sale. But in the zone above this line, $\tilde{S} < F$, which means that the profit-seeking speculator will sell the foreign currency forward. In the opposite scenario—that is, below this line OBD (which depicts the condition: $\tilde{S} > F$), the investor will take the speculative position to buy foreign currency at the forward rate. Notice how this diagram has four distinct zones: (a) triangular area OAB, (b) open-ended area $GABD$, (c) cone-type area CBD, and (d) area $HOBC$. If the investor locates himself at point B (which is the intersection between OBD and ABC), he will find that speculation—both spot and forward—results in the zero-profit condition. Any other point of strategy in this diagram will offer some profitable situation. A close examination of this diagram reveals that in all of the zones carved out, there are two strategic speculative choices for the investor. In the triangular zone OAB, the investor has the following choices: (a.i) sell foreign currency spot and (a.ii) buy foreign currency forward. In zone $GABD$, he can choose either of the two: (b.i) buy foreign currency spot and (b.ii) buy foreign currency forward. In zone CBD, he has these two choices: (c.i) sell foreign currency forward (c.ii) buy foreign currency spot, and finally, in zone $HOBC$, he can go for (d.i) sell foreign currency forward and (d.ii) sell foreign currency spot. All these can be more clearly stated as follows.

If:

$$\tilde{S} < F \text{ and } \tilde{S} < S\frac{(1+r)}{(1+r^{*})}, \text{ sell foreign currency spot or buy it forward;} \quad (8.12)$$

$$\tilde{S} < F \text{ and } \tilde{S} > S\frac{(1+r)}{(1+r^{*})}, \text{ sell foreign currency spot or buy it forward;} \quad (8.13)$$

$$\tilde{S} > F \text{ and } \tilde{S} > S\frac{(1+r)}{(1+r^{*})}, \text{ sell foreign currency spot or sell it forward;} \quad (8.14)$$

$$\tilde{S} < F \text{ and } \tilde{S}, \text{ sell foreign currency spot or sell it forward;} \quad (8.15)$$

The most pressing question is then: of the two choices in a given zone, which one is the better (superior) one for the investor? To answer this question, one should ascertain the rates of returns of the competing pair of choices in each strategic zone. In zone OAB (where $\tilde{S} < F$ and $\tilde{S} < S(1 + r)/(1 + r^{*})$), the rate of return on selling foreign currency spot is equal to $[\{S(1 + r)/(1 + r^{*})\}/ \tilde{S}]$, and the rate of return on buy foreign currency forward is defined by $[\tilde{S}/F]$. So, it appears then that if:

$$\frac{S\dfrac{1+r}{1+r^{*}}}{\tilde{S}} > \frac{\tilde{S}}{F}, \text{ he should sell foreign currency spot instead of selling it forward;} \quad (8.16)$$

$$\frac{S\dfrac{1+r}{1+r^{*}}}{\tilde{S}} < \frac{\tilde{S}}{F}, \text{ he should buy foreign currency forward instead of selling it spot.} \quad (8.17)$$

From equations 8.16 and 8.17, one can then derive that if:

$$F > \frac{\tilde{S}^{2}}{S\dfrac{1+r}{1+r^{*}}}, \text{ he should sell the foreign currency spot instead of buying it forward;} \quad (8.18)$$

$F < \dfrac{\tilde{S}^2}{S\dfrac{1+r}{1+r^*}}$, he should buy foreign currency forward instead of selling it spot. (8.19)

Obviously, $F = \dfrac{\tilde{S}^2}{S\dfrac{1+r}{1+r^*}}$ is the dividing curve between the above two choices. (8.20)

In Figure 8.3, the curve OBE is the dividing line that represents the condition: $F = \tilde{S}^2/\{S(1+r)/(1+r^*)1+r\}$. So, above curve OBE, the investor should engage only in selling foreign currency spot; below this curve, he should buy foreign currency forward.

Next, consider the rates of return from speculative forward sale and speculative spot purchase of the foreign currency. The rate of return on the speculative forward sale of the foreign currency is defined by $F/\tilde{S}$, and the rate of return on speculative spot purchase is given by $\hat{S}/S\{(1+r)/(1+r^*)\}$. Then if:

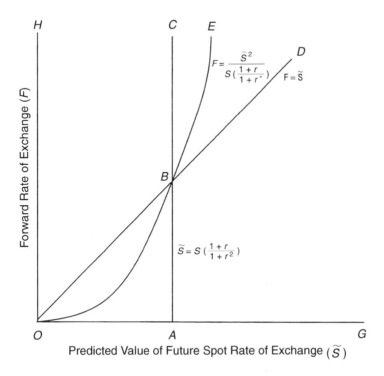

Figure 8.3 Profit menu with single choice under speculation

$$\frac{F}{\tilde{S}} > \frac{\tilde{S}}{S\dfrac{1+r}{1+r^*}} > \text{, he should sell foreign currency forward instead}$$
of buying it spot;   (8.21)

$$\frac{F}{\tilde{S}} < \frac{\tilde{S}}{S\dfrac{1+r}{1+r^*}} \text{, he should buy foreign currency spot instead}$$
of selling it spot;   (8.22)

and if:

$$\frac{F}{\tilde{S}} = \frac{\tilde{S}}{S\dfrac{1+r}{1+r^*}} \text{, he should be indifferent to the above two choices.}$$ (8.23)

It is easily realized that this set of conditions are the same as the one we just derived to determine if the investor should sell foreign currency spot or buy it forward. One may state that if the investor is above the curve *OBE*, then he should sell forward instead of buying the foreign currency spot. Now, it is instructive to check into the zones *HOBC* and *GABD*. In zone *HOBC*, already noted, choices are selling spot and selling forward, and zone *GABD* presents the options of buying spot and buying forward. The rate of return out of selling spot is measured by $[\{S(1+r)/(1+r^*)\}/\tilde{S}$, and the rate of return on selling forward is computed by $F/\tilde{S}$. One can now realize that if:

$$\frac{S\dfrac{1+r}{1+r^*}}{\tilde{S}} > \frac{F}{\tilde{S}},$$

which is equivalent to:

$$S\frac{1+r}{1+r^*} > F \text{, he should sell foreign currency spot instead}$$
of selling it forward;   (8.24)

$$S\frac{1+r}{1+r^*} < F \text{, he should sell foreign currency forward instead}$$
of selling it spot.   (8.25)

Similarly, one can determine that if:

$$S\frac{1+r}{1+r^*} > F \text{, he should buy foreign currency forward instead}$$
of buying it spot;   (8.26)

$$S\frac{1+r}{1+r^*} < F \text{, he should sell foreign currency forward instead}$$
of selling it spot.   (8.27)

Figure 8.4 presents a new set of strategic zones defined by two curves, *OBE* (which represents ($\tilde{S}^2/\{S(1 + r)/(1 + r^*) = F$) and *KBJ* (for which $S(1 + r)/(1 + r^*) = F$). To the left of *OBE* curve and under *KBJ* line, the investor should sell foreign currency spot; to the left of *OBE* curve and above *KBJ* line, the investor should sell foreign currency forward; to the right of *OBE* curve and under *KBJ* line, the investor should buy foreign currency forward, and to the right of *OBE* curve and above *KBJ* line, the investor should buy foreign currency spot.

More clearly, when:

$$F > \frac{\tilde{S}^2}{S\dfrac{1+r}{1+r^*}}, \text{ and } S\frac{1+r}{1+r^*} > F, \text{ and , he should sell foreign currency spot;} \tag{8.28}$$

$$F > \frac{\tilde{S}^2}{S\dfrac{1+r}{1+r^*}}, \text{ and } S\frac{1+r}{1+r^*} < F, \text{ and , he should sell foreign currency forward;} \tag{8.29}$$

$$F < \frac{\tilde{S}^2}{S\dfrac{1+r}{1+r^*}}, \text{ and } S\frac{1+r}{1+r^*} < F, \text{ and , he should buy foreign currency forward;} \tag{8.30}$$

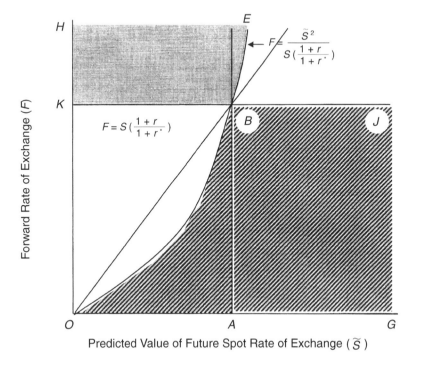

Figure 8.4 Profit zones with single strategy under speculation

$$F < \frac{\tilde{S}^2}{S\frac{1+r}{1+r^*}}, \text{ and } S\frac{1+r}{1+r^*} > F, \text{ and , he should buy foreign}$$
$$\text{currency spot.} \qquad (8.31)$$

FORWARD SPECULATION AND SPOT SPECULATION WITH TRANSACTION COSTS

In this section, we reexamine the conditions for forward and spot speculation with transaction costs. Recently, many works have taken the position of introducing the spread between *ask* and *bid* quotations in-the-spot and forward markets to capture one type of transaction costs, and the difference between the *borrowing* rate and the *lending* rate of interest as the other type of transaction costs in the investment process. Let us rewrite these quotations as follows.

Current spot *ask* rate of exchange (S^a)

Current spot *bid* rate of exchange (S^b)

One-year forward *ask* rate of exchange (F^a)

One-year forward *bid* rate of exchange (F^b)

Predicted spot *ask* rate of exchange one year from now ($\tilde{S}^a$)

Predicted spot *bid* rate of exchange one year from now ($\tilde{S}^b$)

Domestic interest rate of *borrowing* (r_B)

Domestic interest rate of *lending (investing)* (r_L)

Foreign interest rate of *borrowing* (r_B^*)

Foreign interest rate of *lending (investing)* (r_L^*)

Forward Speculation with Transaction Costs

Following the procedures outlined earlier, we can state the rules of rational investment behavior of a speculator as follows. If:

$$F^a < \tilde{S}^b, \text{ buy foreign currency forward, and total profit} = (\tilde{S}^b - F^a) \cdot A_F; \quad (8.32)$$

$$F^b < \tilde{S}^b, \text{ sell foreign currency forward, and total profit} = (\tilde{S}^b - F^b) \cdot A_F. \quad (8.33)$$

Assume, for the sake of simplicity, that S, F, and $\tilde{S}$ are the mid-rates of exchange. That is, S is the mid-rate between S^a and S^b, F is the mid-rate between F^a and F^b, and $\tilde{S}$ the mid-rate between $\tilde{S}^a$ and $\tilde{S}^b$. Under these assumptions then, one can have the following relationships.

$$S^a = S(1+T_S), \ S^b = \frac{S}{1+T_S}$$

$$F^a = F(1+T_f), \ F^b = \frac{F}{1+T_f}$$

$$\tilde{S}^a = \tilde{S}\left(1+T_{\tilde{S}}\right), \ \tilde{S}^b = \frac{\tilde{S}}{1+T_{\tilde{S}}}$$

$$r_B = r(1+\tau), \ r_L = \frac{r}{1+\tau}, \ r_B^* = r^*\left(1+\tau^*\right), \text{ and } r_L^* = \frac{r^*}{1+\tau^*}.$$

Here $T_{S'}$, and T_f are the transaction costs on current spot, forward, and future spot markets. Similarly, τ and τ^* measure the transaction costs associated with interest rates in the domestic and foreign markets, respectively. Now, one can rewrite (8.32) as follows. When:

$$F(1 + T_f)(1 + T_{\tilde{S}}) < \tilde{S}, \text{ buy foreign currency forward.} \tag{8.34}$$

Similarly, (8.33) can be re-expressed as follows:

$$F > \tilde{S}(1 + T_f)(1 + T_{\tilde{S}}), \text{ sell foreign currency forward.} \tag{8.35}$$

Figure 8.5 shows a profitable forward speculation. The horizontal and vertical axis measure predicted future mid-spot rate of exchange ($\tilde{S}$) and mid-forward rate of exchange (F), respectively. The 45E line OA depicts the condition: $F = \tilde{S}$. The line OB represents $F = \tilde{S}(1 + T_f)(1 + T_{\tilde{S}})$, and line OC defines the condition $F = \tilde{S}/(1 + T_f)(1 + T_{\tilde{S}})$. Obviously then, in the area above the line OB in this diagram, $F > \tilde{S}(1 + T_f)(1 + T_{\tilde{S}})$, which means that the speculator should sell foreign currency forward. In area below the line OC where $F < \tilde{S}/(1 + T_f)(1 + T_{\tilde{S}})$, the profit-seeking speculator should buy foreign currency forward. In the cone BOC, there is no scope for profitable arbitrage. A close look at the diagram reveals that the greater the transaction costs, the further out lines OB and OC will be from line OA, which in turn would indicate the smaller scope for profitable forward speculation.

Spot Speculation with Transaction Costs

Again, the same procedures as before yields that the speculator should buy foreign currency spot if:

$$\tilde{S}^b > S^a \frac{1+r_B}{1+r_L^*},$$

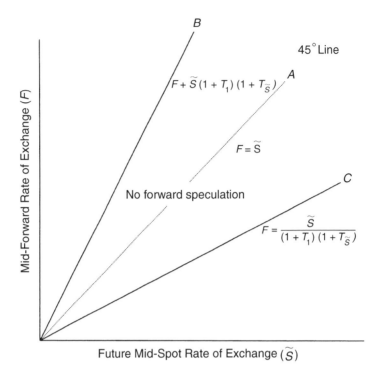

Figure 8.5 Zones of profitable/unprofitable forward speculation

which is equivalent to:

$$\tilde{s} > S \frac{(1+T_S)(1+T_{\tilde{s}})(1+r_B)}{(1+r_L^*)}.$$

(8.36)

The investor should sell foreign currency spot provided the following holds:

$$S^b > \tilde{S}^a,$$

which means:

$$S > \tilde{S}(1 + T_s)(1 + T_{\tilde{s}}).$$

(8.37)

Figure 8.6 portrays the profitable choices of the speculator in-the-spot market. Here, the horizontal and the vertical axis also represent $\tilde{s}$ and F. The perpendicular KL defines $\tilde{s} = S/(1 + T_s)(1 + T_{\tilde{s}})$, and the perpendicular

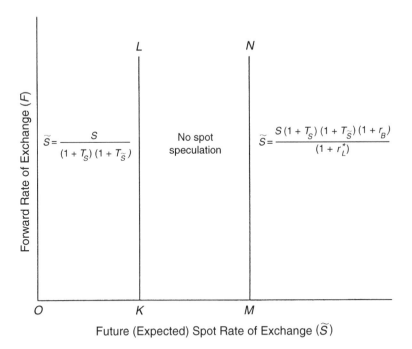

Figure 8.6 Spot speculation

MN represents $\tilde{S} = S(1 + T_s)(1 + T_{\tilde{s}})(1 + r_B)/(1 + r_L^*)$. The area to the left of line KL then represents the condition that $\tilde{S} < S/(1 + T_s)(1 + T_{\tilde{s}})$. So in this area—that is, for any combination of F and $\tilde{S}$ that lies in this area—the speculator should sell the foreign currency spot. It is evident, as it ought to be, that there is no constraint on the forward rate (since it is a spot market strategy alone). The area to the right of the vertical line MN (for which obviously $\tilde{S} > S(1 + T_s)(1 + T_{\tilde{s}})(1 + r_B)/(1 + r_L^*)$) defines the scope for profitable speculation when the investor buys foreign currency spot. The area between lines KL and MN defines the corridor that offers no scope for profitable spot speculation. It should be pointed out that the higher the transaction costs, the wider the corridor, and vice versa. If the foreign lending rate r_L^* is very high, then, *ceteres paribus*, it may tend to exert the effect of narrowing the corridor on nonprofitable spot speculation. One may recall the interest rate relationships we have outlined earlier: $r_B = r(1 + \tau)$, $r_L^* = r^*/(1 + \tau^*)$, make use of these relationships in (8.36), and arrive at:

$$\tilde{S} > S\frac{(1+T_s)(1+T_{\tilde{s}})(1+r)(1+\tau)(1+\tau^*)}{(1+r^*)}. \tag{8.38}$$

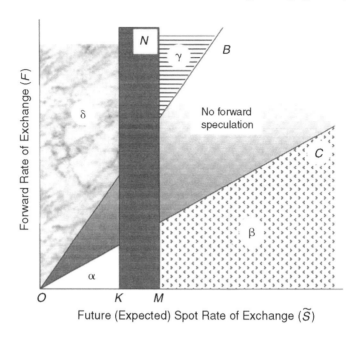

Future (Expected) Spot Rate of Exchange ($\widetilde{S}$)

Figure 8.7 Spot and forward speculation

Forward and Spot Speculation in One Framework

Now, combine Figure 8.5 and Figure 8.6. This shows the graph presented in Figure 8.7. Here cone *BOC* specifies the zone of no forward speculation, and the vertical corridor between lines KL and *MN* demarcates the zone of no spot speculation. The overlapping area obviously defines the scope of nonspeculative activities, both spot and forward. In this diagram, the triangular area (designated here as α) offers the scope for the speculative sell of foreign market and the purchase of it in the forward market. Area β defines the buy forward and sell spot strategy. The area denoted by γ is for buying in the spot market and selling in the forward market, and finally, zone δ prescribes the strategies of sell spot and sell forward. Once again, we provide the following rules of decision for the speculators in the designated zones as follows:

α: sell foreign currency spot, or buy it forward;	(8.39)
β: buy foreign currency spot, or buy it forward;	(8.40)
γ: buy foreign currency spot, or sell it forward;	(8.41)
δ: sell foreign currency spot, or sell it forward.	(8.42)

Once again, one has to choose between the two profitable choices in each area of operation. The exact procedures that we used in the absence of transaction costs will narrow the choice set under different conditions.

COVERED SPECULATION

In this section, we attempt to step out of the zone of unguarded risk by offering some levels of insulation through derivative securities on the currencies under consideration. We specially present some currency options—put and/or call or synthetic combinations thereof—to protect a speculator who has love for risk for better returns but does not wish to sustain a great deal of loss for his lust for money. What can he do under this situation? In this part of the present work, we show a number of possibilities that may sterilize the investor from financial catastrophe resulting from his speculative zeal.

Consider the earlier data and a put option with the following information on it: put option premium (P_p) = \$0.05, its exercise price (X_p) = \$2.35, and its time to expiration matching the maturity of the forward contract. Under this situation, the effective exercise price of the put (X^*_p) is \$2.35 − \$0.05 = \$2.30. In this event, if the speculator expects the future spot rate to be \$3.00, he should buy a pound forward with the purchase of a put. If the future spot rate proves incorrect, he still has the option of getting out with a profit of \$0.15 (= \$ \$2.30 − \$2.15) per pound upon the exercise of the option. As long as the effective exercise price (X^*_p) is greater than or equal to the forward quote, speculative position with forward and put purchase of pound cannot hurt. If the probability of the exercise of the put equals the probability that the investor's expected value of the spot rate will prove true, then speculation is gainful. Technically, $E(\pi) = \{p_1(X^*_p - F) + p_2(\tilde{S} - F)\}A_F$, where π stands for profits, p_1 measures the probability of exercising the option, and p_2 measures the probability of realizing the expected outcome $\tilde{S}^+$. That means, in this illustrative case, $E(\pi) = \{2(\$0.15) + 2(\$0.85)\}1,000,000 = \$500,000$ (the contract size being £1,000,000). If the put is available for \$0.05 with the exercise price of \$2.15 (and hence the effective exercise price of \$2.10), the expected value of the same speculative strategy will be $\{2(\$2.10 - \$2.15) + 2(\$3.00 - \$2.15)\}1,000,000 = \$400,000$. From these illustrations, one may easily arrive at the conclusion that as long as the effective exercise price of the put option is at most the positive difference between the expected future spot rate and the forward rate, speculation is financially worthwhile. Figure 8.8 depicts the kind of speculation the investor should engage in.

So far, we have looked at the expectation that the future spot rate will be above the forward rate. If, however, the expected value on the future spot rate is below the currently quoted forward rate—that is $F = 2.15$ and $\tilde{S}^+ = 2.00$, the investor should enter into a forward sell contract on the British pound. By entering into this sell contract, he will sell pound to get \$2.15 on each pound sold at the end of the contract maturity, then buy each pound for \$2.00, thus making a profit of \$0.15 per pound. Given this scenario, if the expectation is realized, the naked speculative long on forward contract is all that the investor can achieve. However, when he is not so sure that $\tilde{S}^+$

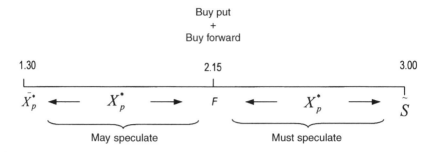

Figure 8.8 Covered speculation with put option

= 2.00, he may (should) hedge his exposure by buying a call option at some appropriate cost. If a call is available at an exercise price of \$2.05 for a premium of, say, \$0.05, his effective exercise price then becomes \$2.10, and his profit upon a possible exercise of the option comes out to be \$2.15 − \$2.10 = \$0.05 per pound. His expected profit is measured by the following:

$$E(\pi) = \{p_1(F - X^*_c) + p_2(F - \tilde{S}^+)\}A_F$$

In this instance, the profit out of a contract of £1,000,000 is then {2(\$2.15 − \$2.10) + 2(\$2.15 − \$2.00)}1,000,000 = \$100,000. It is clear from this case that as long as $X^*_c \# F$, there is no loss in going long on a call. More correctly, as long as $\tilde{S}^+ \leqslant X^*_c \leqslant F$ holds, there is no loss (profits in strict inequality conditions). Figure 8.9 defines the covered profit opportunities and further specifies conditions when one must and when one may profitably speculate with mathematical expectation. In our analysis, we have only considered the possible two outcomes, which may be all right if we are with the European options and the expected value of future spot rate is fixed. However, when American options are introduced in the picture, any outcome from X^*_p to $\tilde{S}^+$ may occur with equal probability. The probability density for this situation is appropriately defined by the uniform distribution:

$$\int_{-\infty}^{\tilde{S}^+} f_s(S)dS, \text{ where } f_s(S) = \frac{1}{\tilde{S}^+ - X^*_c}, \ X^*_c < S < \tilde{S}^+; = 0, \text{ otherwise.}$$

$$= 0 \text{ for } \tilde{S}^+ < X^*_p$$

$$= \frac{Z - X^*_c}{\tilde{S}^+ - X^*_c} \text{ for } X^*_p \# Z \# \tilde{S}^+$$

$$= 1 \text{ for } Z > \tilde{S}^+.$$

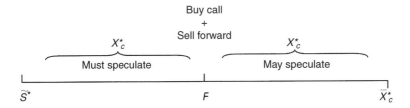

Figure 8.9 Covered speculation with call option

From this probability distribution, the mean $(\Phi_s) = E(S)$, and variance (σ^2) are as follows:

$$\phi_s = \frac{\tilde{S}^+ + X_c^*}{2}, \quad \sigma^2 = \frac{\left(\tilde{S}^+ - X_c^*\right)^2}{12}.$$

Similar results are in order for call options in the American style. These calculations are meaningful only in the event that the investor has either expectation that the value of the future spot rate will be either $\tilde{S}_u > F$ or $\tilde{S}_1 < F$. In reality, however, the investor may be given the prediction on future S within a range such that $\tilde{S}_1 < F < \tilde{S}_u$. In this situation, it appears that he should go long on both a put and a call. Before entering further into this range, we should consider the entire range of possible values on the future spot rate of exchange ($\tilde{S}$) in the interval between 0 and infinity. With effective exercise price of, say, a put option and the expected value of $\tilde{S}$ lying in the closed interval of 0 and 4, the probability density function must be a normal distribution of S, and the moment generating function is defined by the following expression:

$$\int_{X_c^*}^{\infty} \frac{1}{\sigma\sqrt{2\pi}} e^{-0.5\frac{(S-\mu)^2}{\sigma^2}} dS,$$

whence:

$\mu_s = \mu, \sigma_s^2 = \sigma^2$ are given by some *a priori* estimates.

Now we see that the investor is in a position of creating a rich variety of synthetic combinations when the expected value of the future spot rate of exchange is not known. Therefore, we attempt to illustrate a few cocktails with put and call options in this context.

Merton (1973), Garman and Kohlhagen (1983), and Grabbe (1983) have discussed a good deal on options that fit our specific conditions. With a full comprehension of these works and proper utilization of these models, the investor can create a number of straddles, strangles, or delta-neutral ratio spreads to create different U-shaped profit (loss) functions. A *straddle* or a *strangle* is a combination of a call and a put, but in a straddle both the exercise price and the expiration date on put and call are the same; in a strangle, put and call options have the same expiration date but different exercise price. A *spread* is combination of options of different series but of the same class. Figures 8.10, 8.11, 8.12, 8.13, and 8.14 exhibit profit (loss) functions of these three synthetics as follows. At this point, it should be noted that the lower the volatility (σ), the higher the loss, and the higher the volatility, the lower the loss (or greater the profit) for both straddle and delta-neutral ratio spread. A strangle profit is potentially greater with more time remaining and vice versa. If the calculation of the implied volatility exceeds the critical value, it pays to take the covered straddle or delta-neutral ratio spread. Here we present one interesting situation as portrayed by Figure 8.14. The U-shaped curve, *NZM*, here defines the profit levels at different future spot rates of exchange of the foreign currency. The 45° lines *RZ* and *VZ* in this diagram portray the conditions

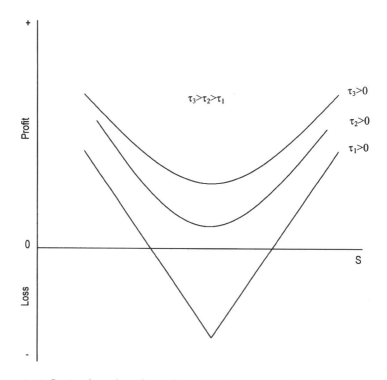

Figure 8.10 Option-based profit profiles at different expiration times.

under which synthetic options should or should not be exercised. In the open interval AB, exploiting the situation as if naked speculation exists is the better choice if OZ is the forward rate; but beyond the range AB, the investor should exercise the options (that is, delta-neutral ratio spread).

MORE ACTIVE SPECULATIVE STRATEGIES

Simple Scenario

In the previous section, we have outlined speculative choices, then narrowed the spectrum further and thus streamlined the operational decision rules for an investor. In this section, we go a step further and show that a more active investor with a more involved strategy set can do better. Remember that in the previous section, to enter into spot speculation, our investor has calculated the dollar cost of one foreign currency one year from that day, and as long as that cost is less (more) than the estimated value of $\tilde{S}$, he should buy (sell) spot contract in order to make a speculative profit. If he thinks that $\tilde{S} = 4.15$, and the current spot rate of exchange $(S) = 2$, $r = 10$ percent, and $r^* = 9.5\%$, he will, as noted earlier, make a profit of $(4.15 - 2.0091324) = 2.1408676$ per pound (or \$214,086,760 on a spot con-

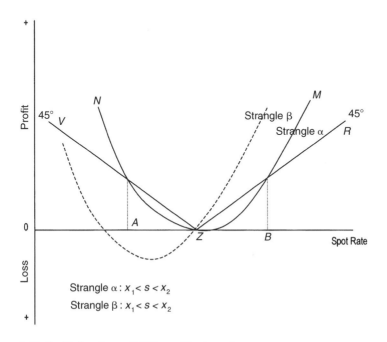

Figure 8.11 Profit (loss) possibilities with strangle

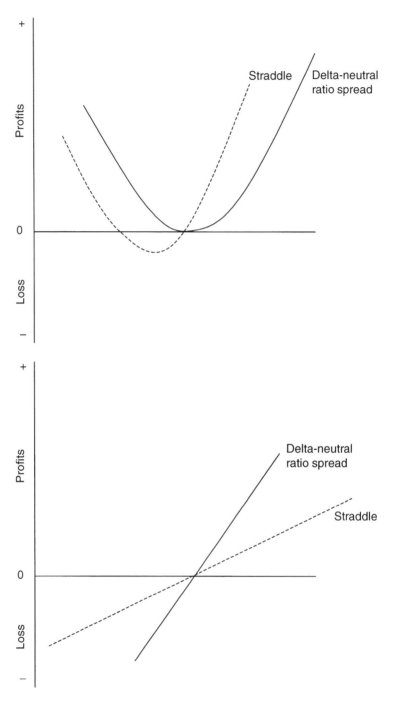

Figure 8.12 Profit (loss) possibilities with straddle and delta-neutral ratio spread

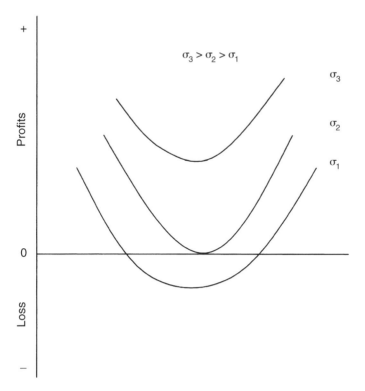

Figure 8.13 Profit (loss) possibilities with different volatilities

tract of £100,000,000). However, with the same set of market data, he can first convert his $2 amount into £1 at the spot market, and put this £1 into deposit in a British bank at 9.95 percent, and thus make his original $2 turn into £1(1 + 0.095) = £1.095 at the end of one year, which can then be sold at the then spot market and get $4.15(1.095) = $4.54425. He must now subtract $2(1 + 0.1) (which is the principal amount plus the accrued interest cost, which he borrowed either from a bank or from himself at 10 percent per annum) from $4.54425 to earn a net profit of $2.34425. On a contract size of A_S = £100,000,000, he now makes a total profit of $234,425,000, which is larger than $214,086,760 that we determined in the second section of this chapter. This excess $20, 338,240 is the additional bonus for being a more active spot speculator in the market. With this modified operational strategy, the investor's profits are measured by $[(1 + r^*)\tilde{s} - S(1 + r)] \cdot A_s$ (as opposed to $[\tilde{s} - S(1 + r)/(1 + r^*)] \cdot A_s$). On a forward speculation, no modification can be made to increase profit levels. So now the structure of decision rules is as follows: When:

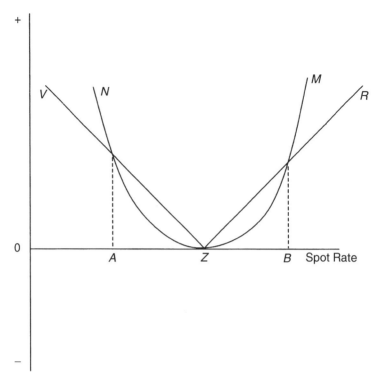

Figure 8.14 Profit possibilities: options *vis-à-vis* forward contracts

α: $\tilde{S} > F$, and $\tilde{S}(1 + r^*) < S(1 + r)$: (i) buy foreign currency forward, and (ii) sell it spot;
β: $\tilde{S} > F$, and $\tilde{S}(1 + r^*) > S(1 + r)$: (i) buy foreign currency forward, and (ii) buy it spot;
γ: $\tilde{S} < F$, and $\tilde{S}(1 + r^*) > S(1 + r)$: (i) sell foreign currency forward, and (ii) buy it spot;
δ: $\tilde{S} < F$, and $\tilde{S}(1 + r^*) < S(1 + r)$: (i) sell foreign currency forward, and (ii) sell it spot.

Although the dual strategies here have emerged in the modified structure with better profit opportunities, the uniquely superior strategic decision rules defined earlier by (a), (b), (c), and (d) still remain unscathed.

Complex Scenario

Consider the investor first converting his dollars into the foreign currency (pound sterling) in spot market, investing the foreign-currency-denominated amount in the foreign country at r^*, next selling the amount at forward rate, and finally subtracting $S(1 + r)$ from that amount. It will give a profit of $(1 + r^*)F - S(1 + r)$ (if it is positive). Let it be defined as ρ_1. That is,

$$\rho_1 = (1 + r^*)F - S(1 + r),$$

the present value of which is $(\rho_{1(0)})$:

$$\rho_{1(0)} = (1/(1 + r))\{(1 + r^*)F - S(1 + r)\}\tilde{S}\beta,$$

where β $\dfrac{(1+r^*)F/S-(1+r)}{1+r}$.

Since this amount is the equity position of the investor at this point, he can make this amount plus the original S dollars to play for another round before the market data changes. Usually, market data stays the same from 20 seconds to several minutes in real life[1], and hence in the time interval within which data remain invariant, the investor with the speed of today's technology can play the arbitrage game a number of times. If that is the picture, then in the second play, he can put his $\$(S + \rho_{1(0)})$ into covered trading and get the following profits after second round of play:

$$\rho_{2(0)} = \left(\frac{1}{1+r}\right)\left(\frac{S+\rho_{1(0)}}{S}\right)\{(1+r^*)F-(1+r)S\}$$
$$\tilde{S}\,\beta(\beta+1)^{2-1},$$

and after nth play:

$$\rho_{n(0)} = \left(\frac{1}{1+r}\right)\left(\frac{S+\rho_{1(0)}+\rho_{2(0)}+\ldots\rho_{(n-1)(0)}}{S}\right)[(1+r^*)F-(1+r)S]$$
$$\tilde{S}\beta(\beta+1)^{n-1}.$$

A point of clarification is needed at this stage rather urgently, otherwise the notion of double (or multiple) counting can cloud our mind.[2] Note that in the second round we plugged in the borrowed amount S dollars (which with the accrued interest on it must be paid again) plus $\rho_{1(0)}$, which is the investor's own fund now, and in the third round he puts in the borrowed amount S dollars plus the profit generated in the first round $(\rho_{1(0)})$ and in the second round $(\rho_{2(0)})$ just the way the original amount of S dollars is being reinvested in every round. So on the nth round, he invests S dollars plus the profit amounts made in the previous rounds (that is, $S + \Sigma_{i=1}^{n-1}$ $\rho_{i(0)}$).This is the basic structure, envisioned in the work of Ghosh (1997a, 1997b), only modified by the fact that the total amount of funds put to work in each covered play consists of the initial fund plus the profits generated in the previous plays.[3]

Remember next that the investor, however, needs the foreign currency (British pound) to be able to sell that currency to buy the home currency (dollar, in this paradigm), and hence he will not sell pound forward on his last iteration; he will sell the pound in the future spot rate of exchange ($\tilde{S}$), and so his profits will be equal to the following measure in the speculative design upon the nth round ρ_n^s:

$$\rho_n^s = \left(\frac{S + \rho_{1(0)} + \rho_{2(0)} + \ldots + \rho_{(n-1)(0)}}{S} \right) \left[(1+r^*)\tilde{S} - (1+r)S \right]$$

$$= \omega + \omega\beta \left[\frac{1 - \gamma^{n-1}}{1 - \gamma} \right],$$

where $\omega \equiv S[(1 + r^*)\tilde{S}/S - (1 + r)$, and $\gamma \equiv \beta + 1$.

For obvious reason, $\rho_{i(0)} = 0$ for $i = 1$.

Next, under the assumed market data set $\tilde{S} = 4.15$, $F = 2.15$, $S = 2.00$, $r = 0.1$, and $r^* = 0.095$, one can compute the speculative profit measures with the mixed bag of strategies involving spot and forward rates as opposed to simple spot speculation (as depicted in the previous sections) as given in Table 8.1.

Table 8.1 hardly needs any further interpretation. Look at the row for the value of $n = 1$ first. If the investor enters into spot speculation, his net profit out of his purchase of £1 now is $2,34425 (given in column 2), and if his initial purchase of the British pound at the spot rate of 2 is £100,000,000, he makes a net profit of $234,425,000 (given in column 3). If the investor can play covered trade with forward contracts under the given market data for one round, then put the profits generated by covered trade in the speculative play. He plays two rounds from which he can make $3.508613829 for his initial purchase of £1 in the spot market and with his purchase of £100,000,000 in the spot market. He can earn a net profit of $250,861,389. Similarly, upon the completion of ten rounds then he can generate the hefty amount of $431,392,916 for an initial spot purchase of British pound with a spot contract size of £100,000,000. Straight spot or forward speculation will provide so little by comparison that an active speculator must not consider simple strategy any more. Remember that the quotes taken for market data are simply for demonstrative purpose, and hence, these extraordinarily large sums of profits may not reflect the reality, although the magnification factors are certainly the main thrust of this work.

A few more remarks should be made at this point. As one knows already that if $(1 + r^*)\tilde{S} - (1 + r)S < 0$, the investor sells foreign currency

Table 8.1
Measures of Arbitrage Profits with Speculation

i	ρ_i^s	$A_s \cdot \rho_i^s$
1	2.34425	$234,425,000
2	3.508613892	250,861,389
3	2.684501934	268,450,193
4	2.872722127	287,272,213
5	3.074139121	307,413,912
6	3.289678194	328,967,819
7	3.520329494	352,032,949
8	3.767152596	376,715,260
9	4.031281364	403,128,136
10	4.313929916	431,392,916

Speculative profits per pound (foreign currency) (ρ_i^s) and total profits per contract size in British pound ($A_s \cdot$) in U.S. dollars (domestic currency) with cumulative iterations where i is the index of cumulative speculative play ($\rho_i^s = 1, 2, 3, \ldots$). Here, spot rate of exchange (S) = 2.00, one-year forward rate of exchange (F) = 2.15, domestic interest rate (r) = 0.1, foreign interest rate (r^*) = 0.095, (expected) future spot rate ($\tilde{S}$) = 4.15, and spot and forward contract size in British pound (A_S) = A_F = $100,000,000.

forward, then the profit measures will be exactly the same because of the reversed strategy in place in symmetric fashion. However, once the transaction costs are factored in, reversal of strategy may not ensure the desired result defined for the trading environment without transaction costs.

Although without substantiation in this chapter, we find that in the presence of transaction costs there are ranges in which neither spot nor forward speculation in isolation will be unprofitable.

CONCLUDING REMARKS

In this chapter we merely attempt to demonstrate that a synthetic structure of currency derivatives in the form of straddle, strangle, and ratio spread can completely, or virtually, eliminate loss and potentially create profit condition under speculative situations. There are numerous combinations—sometimes short positions on options—that can create a better insulation for speculative ventures of an investor. The parabolic profit (loss) functions, the computation of the foci, and the directrices may be the tasks before the investor. Once they are computed and the probability distributions are reasonably captured, speculation is not really a leap into the dark.

This chapter delineates conditions for profitable profit opportunities and specifies speculative strategies with and without cover when anticipated future spot rate of exchange is taken as given. No attempt is made to forecast the future spot rate, but given any expected rate, what the profitable speculative strategies would be is spelled out in a simple environment by making use of current spot and forward rates of exchange and the given interest rates. A more complex trading and speculative designs are also provided in this work when the trader is capable of undertaking iterative arbitrage before the final act of trading with speculation. A numerical illustration of the enormous profit possibilities is computed for each foreign currency and for a given contract size. Additional work involving forward contract on interest rate, as enunciated by Ghosh (1998), or a more stochastic dynamics of interest rates with Brownian motion and Ito's lemma is a possible extension of this chapter.

NOTES

1. Based on the observations of real-time data screen of *Reuters* for months and months in the trading room in CETFI, Marseille, France, and in a currency trading house in Princeton, New Jersey, the authors have been able to make this statement.

2. It may appear that we are making double (or multiple) counting. Note that first, the investor starts with S dollars (borrowed from his bank or from himself) and then converts the amount into British pound and puts the pound amount at the British rate (r^*). He then sells the amount $(1 + r^*)$ at the forward rate—and thus gets the British pound amount converted back in dollars (here that is $\$(1 + r^*)F$). Now he pays off the principal with accrued interest, which is $\$S(1 + r)$, and so his total profit for $\$S$ (here denoted by ρ_1) is equal to $(1 + r^*)F - S(1 + r)$, and its present value ($\rho_{1(0)}$) is:

$$\rho_{1(0)} = \{1/(1+r)\}[(1+r^*)F - S(1+r)]/S\beta, \text{ where } \beta = \frac{(1+r^*)\dfrac{F}{S}-(1+r)}{(1+r)}$$

defined on p. 10 in this current version. This $\rho_{1(0)}$ is the profit made on the first round of arbitrage, and this amount $\rho_{1(0)}$ is put just like the amount S dollars for the second round of arbitrage, and then he makes $\rho_{2(0)}$ by making use of $\$(S + \rho_{1(0)})$. For the third round then he puts the amount $\$(S + \rho_{1(0)} + \rho_{2(0)})$ into play. This process leads to $\rho_{n(0)}$.

One can arguably point out that interest expense on $\rho_{1(0)}$ should also be deducted to account for the opportunity cost of the investor's own funds. Ghosh [11] has indeed referred to that in clear terms.

3. One can introduce the notion of additional leverage, by making use of $(S\sum_{i=1}^{n-1}\rho_{i(0)})(1+\theta)$, where θ is the percentage of funds that investor has under risk-free investment environment. The authors are indebted to Lloyd P. Blenman for pointing out this possible and sharper scenario.

REFERENCES

Auten, J.H. (1961). "Counter-Speculation and the Forward-Exchange Market," *Journal of Political Economy*, 69 (1).

———. (1963). "Forward Exchange and Interest Differentials," *Journal of Finance*, (March).

Baumol, W.J. (1957). "Speculation, Profitability, and Stability," *Review of Economics and Statistics*, 39 (August).

Black, F., and M. Scholes. (1973). "The Pricing of Options and Corporate Liabilities," *Journal of Political Economy*, 1973.

Branson, W.H. (1968). *Financial Capital Flows in the U.S. Balance of Payments*. Amsterdam: North-Hollarnd.

Canterbury, E.R. (1971). "A Theory of Foreign Exchange Speculation under Alternative Systems," *Journal of Political Economy*.

Feldstein, M.S. (1968). "Uncertainty and Forward Exchange Speculation," *Review of Economics and Statistics*, 50 (2).

Friedman, M. (1953). "The Case for Flexible Exchange Rates." In *Essays in Positive Economics*. Chicago: University of Chicago Press.

Garman, M.B., and S.W. Kohlhagen. (1983). "Foreign Currency Option Values," *Journal of International Money and Finance*, 2 (December).

Ghosh, D.K. (1994). "The Interest Rate Parity, Covered Arbitrage and Speculation under Market Imperfection." In D.K. Ghosh and E. Oritz (Eds.), *The Changing Environment of International Financial Markets: Issues and Analysis*. London, England: Macmillan Press.

———. (1997a). "Naked and Covered Speculation in Foreign Exchange Market." In D.K. Ghosh and E. Ortiz (Eds.), *Global Structure of Financial Markets* (pp. 103–143). London: Routledge.

———. (1997b). "Profit Multiplier in Covered Currency Trading with Leverage," *Financial Review*, 32 (1).

———. (1998). "Covered Arbitrage in the Foreign Exchange Market with Forward Forward Contracts in Interest Rates," *Journal of Futures Markets*, 18 (1) February.

Ghosh, D. K, and A.C. Arize. (2003). "Profit Possibilities in Currency Markets: Arbitrage, Hedging, and Speculation," *Financial Review*, 38 (3).

Ghosh, D.K., and A.J. Prakash. (2001). "Strategic Rules on Speculation in the Foreign Exchange Market," *The Journal of Financial Research*, 24 (1).

Grabbe, J.O. (1983). "The Pricing of Call and Put Options on Foreign Exchange," *Journal of International Money and Finance*, 2 (December).

Grubel, H.G. (1966). *Forward Exchange, Speculation, and the International Flow of Capital*. Stanford, CA: Stanford University Press.

Hull, J. (1989). *Options, Futures, and Other Derivative Securities*. Englewood Cliffs, NJ: Prentice-Hall.

Kemp, M.C. (1963). "Speculation, Profitability, and Price Stability," *Review of Economics and Statistics*, 45 (May).

Kenen, P.B. (1965). "Trade, Speculation, and the Forward Exchange Rate." In R.E. Baldwin, et al. (Eds.), *Trade, Growth, and the Balance of Payments, Essays in Honor of Gottfried Haberler*. Amsterdam: North-Hollarnd.

Kindleberger, C.P. (1937). "Speculation and Forward Exchange," *Journal of Political Economy*, 47 (April).

Kohlhagen, S.W. (1979). "The Identification of Destabilizing Foreign Exchange Speculation," *Journal of International Economics*, 9 (3).

Kolb, R.W. (1994). *Options: An Introduction*. Miami: FL: Kolb.

McKinnon, R.I. (1979). *Money in International Exchange*. Oxford, England: Oxford University Press.

Merton, R.C. (1973). "The Theory of Rational Option Pricing," *Bell Journal of Economics and Management Science*, 5 (Spring).

Neihans, J. (1984). *International Monetary Economics*. Baltimore, MD: Johns Hopkins University Press.

Spraos, J. (1959). "Speculation, Arbitrage and Sterling," *Economic Journal*, 69 (1).

Telser, L.G. (1959). "A Theory of Speculation Relating Profitability and Stability," *Review of Economics and Statistics*, 41 (August).

Tsiang, S.C. (1959). "The Theory of Forward Exchange and Effects of Government Intervention on the Forward Exchange Market," *International Monetary Fund Staff Papers*, 7, 75–106.

Wihlborg, C. (1978). *Currency Risks in International Financial Markets*. Princeton Studies in International Finance, No. 44. Princeton, NJ: Princeton University Press.

Williamson, J. (1973). "Another Case of Profitable Destabilizing Speculation," *Journal of International Economics*, 3 (1).

Wilmott, P., J. Dewynne, and S. Howison. (1993). *Option Pricing: Mathematical Models and Computation*. Oxford, England: Oxford Financial Press.

Index

About the Author

EPHRAIM CLARK is Professor of Finance at Middlesex University in London.

DILIP K. GHOSH is KLSE Professor of Finance at Rutgers University.